The Seed of Sally Good'n

THE SEED OF
Sally Good'n

A BLACK FAMILY
OF ARKANSAS
1833-1953

Ruth Polk Patterson

THE UNIVERSITY PRESS OF KENTUCKY

First paperback edition published in 1996
by The University Press of Kentucky

Scholarly publisher for the Commonwealth,
serving Bellarmine College, Berea College, Centre
College of Kentucky, Eastern Kentucky University,
The Filson Club, Georgetown College, Kentucky
Historical Society, Kentucky State University,
Morehead State University, Murray State University,
Northern Kentucky University, Transylvania University,
University of Kentucky, University of Louisville,
and Western Kentucky University.

Editorial and Sales Offices: The University Press of Kentucky
663 South Limestone Street, Lexington, Kentucky 40508-4008

00 99 98 97 96   5 4 3 2 1

Library of Congress Cataloging-in-Publication Data

Patterson, Ruth Polk, 1930-
    The seed of Sally Good'n.
    Bibliography: p.
    Includes index.
    1. Polk. Family. 2. Afro-Americans—Arkansas—Biography.
3. Arkansas—Biography. I. Title.
EL 185.96.P366 1985   976.7'004960730922[B]   85-6117
ISBN 0-8131-1541-8
ISBN 0-8131-0876-4 (alk. paper)

Manufactured in the United States of America

To Papa, who always said, "Somebody ought to write a book about this place"; to Mama, whose dream fulfilled made it possible for me to write it; to Valerie, Henry, Ray, Herbert, and the others who are gone; and to my sons, Tommy, Ken, and Tracey, their children, and the coming generations.

Contents

List of Tables viii

List of Illustrations ix

Preface xi

1. Crooked Marks on the Landscape 1

2. The Wilds 11

3. The First Remove 22

4. Oh, Give Me Land 30

5. Within and Without the Veil 44

6. One Seed Becomes a Singing Tree 58

7. African Survivals and Scottish Airs 89

8. The Last Remove 116

9. For Generations to Come 129

10. Archeology and Artifact 141

Appendix 155

Notes 161

Bibliography 171

Index 175

Tables

1. Slaves Owned by Taylor Polk in 1850   25

2. Members of the Spencer Polk Household, 1880   60

3. Members of the Spencer Polk Household, 1900   61

Illustrations

1. The Spencer Polk homestead   4

2. Map of Montgomery, Howard, and Pike counties,
Arkansas, 1914   24

3. The homestead certificate for Spencer Polk's first
land purchase   32

4. Polk landholdings at Muddy Fork   34

5. Evolution of the Spencer Polk house   38

6. Jimmy Polk's first letter home   80

7. A scaled drawing of the Spencer Polk house site   146

[Other illustrations follow page 88]

Preface

The history of Americans of African descent has been woefully neglected by most writers on Arkansas's past. As a result, few people have an accurate picture of the role played by blacks in the development of the state. At a time when black Americans are searching for identity, and when all Americans are looking for evidence to support the new attitudes of pride and dignity about their ethnic origins, it is important that a broader and more all-inclusive picture of Arkansas history be presented to the general public. The purpose of this work is to provide a more humanistic account of blacks in Arkansas, using the family estate of John Spencer Polk as an example of how blacks were involved in and related to the movement westward, the settling of the frontier, and the development of a way of life in both pre- and post-Civil War Arkansas.

Black men and women were among the earliest settlers to cross the Mississippi from the eastern seaboard in the eighteenth and early nineteenth centuries. Most available references to specific blacks in Arkansas date from the post-Civil War period. According to these sources, blacks living in Arkansas by the 1870s had their origin as slaves or freedmen in other states, mostly Tennessee, South Carolina, Kentucky, Mississippi, and Alabama. Population data show that there were fewer than 2,000 slaves in the territory by 1820. The most significant increase in the state's slave population occurred between 1840 and 1860, when the number of slaves jumped from approximately 20,000 to nearly 112,000. Nevertheless, allusions in early histories and demographic information reveal that blacks helped settle the Arkansas territory in the early nineteenth century, having been brought in as slaves or in other ways attached to the earliest immigrant Arkansas families. It is therefore apparent that a small but significant number of blacks were born in Arkansas before the territory became a state in 1836. It is to this latter group that John Spencer Polk belonged.

Aside from general statements about the extent of slavery and the treatment of slaves in Arkansas, very little has been written about the kind of life led by blacks in the earliest days of the state, and little is known about how blacks adjusted their lives following emancipation. Historical references have shown blacks as being acted upon rather than as actors in the drama of life in pioneer Arkansas. Yet the cultural heritage of Arkansas blacks is rich and diverse, and events on the frontier and beyond affected their lives as much as their presence affected the lives of their masters and of white settlers as a group. In fact, the changes that took place in Arkansas culturally, politically, socially, and economically as the area evolved from a virtual wilderness to a significant agricultural and industrial state can be perceived quite clearly and accurately in the lives of some of its black residents. The presence of blacks in early Arkansas communities had, in turn, a direct influence upon the way the communities developed and progressed. As slaves, their labor contributed to the clearing of land and the establishment of plantations and farms and towns. Following slavery, many blacks were able to acquire land and erect substantial homesteads of their own. Many became leading citizens of their areas. The life of John Spencer Polk, one of the state's early inhabitants of African descent, exemplifies, even in its singularity, the nature of slave life in Arkansas and the manner in which some blacks overcame the ravages of bondage to become self-sustaining, contributing individuals.

The oral history project that produced this manuscript was initiated in 1978 with a grant from the Arkansas Endowment for the Humanities. The project consisted of initial research into the establishment of the homestead, with a detailed description of the log house built by Spencer Polk and the genealogical background of the occupant. The products of the initial project were a fifty-page paper, a slide show of artifacts collected by the author from family members and unearthed during an archeological survey in 1979, and a display of the artifacts at the Old State House Museum in Little Rock in 1980.

The uses of oral history have been well established by contemporary historians and by other writers such as Alex Haley, whose

Roots has helped to define and validate oral history methodology. While some history "purists" continue to raise questions about the reliability of oral history, we must recognize that in many cultures oral tradition is the rule rather than the exception when it comes to preserving the history of the people. Furthermore, personal and individual accounts, reports, anecdotes, and tales handed down from past generations to our older citizens provide important sources of information today that serve as indices to past events in our national history. This is particularly true in the case of Afro-Americans. During the pre-Civil War period, specific records were virtually unknown among the slave population. Events such as birth, deaths, weddings, and the like went unrecorded except in rare instances. Even the census records omitted the names of slaves. Fortunately, however, the oral tradition of their African ancestors was rich among New World slaves, and interest in the past has been kept alive by many present-day blacks. Utilization of this interest and these oral history sources, when carefully applied and substantiated by written records, can open up new vistas of understanding of the American past.

While I have made wide use of oral history sources through interviews and conversations with others, this account of the Spencer Polk family has been drawn also from several other sources, including artifact collection, archeology, genealogy, letters, and orthodox historical methods. I have relied upon personal experiences and recollections only when they were substantiated by other members of the family. I was born in the log house described in this book and spent my first nineteen years living on the farmstead. My father, Chester Alan Arthur Polk, was Spencer Polk's fifth son and the only son to survive his father's death. I first heard the name Taylor Polk from my father's mouth, along with the names of Alf and Cum Polk, all of whom were easily identified from several sources of early Arkansas history.

Whenever possible, I have substantiated oral accounts with documentation from primary sources, but I readily admit that more extensive research would no doubt yield additional supportive material. In fact, as the research has progressed, new information has continued to be discovered, requiring several changes in and additions to my original research findings. For example, the existence of an ell room to the house was well known to me through oral accounts, but there was no evidence of the structure at the time the archeological survey was conducted. Consequently, the survey team did not attempt to probe for the foundation rocks that were easily discovered for the rest of the house. Later, however, a family member produced a picture of the house with the ell room in full view.

This account of the Spencer Polk homestead presents only the most limited details of the life of the Spencer Polk family and their interrelations with each other and the community. There are many more stories that could be written and other branches of the family that are just as interesting. Those stories, however, must hopefully await the time and skills of others.

I am deeply grateful to a number of individuals who helped in various ways in the development of this book. I owe special thanks to Bill Worthen, director of the Arkansas Territorial Restoration, who started me on the project when he suggested that I write a description of my grandfather's house and assured me that many people would be interested in learning about what it was like to live in a nineteenth-century log house. I am indebted also to the sponsoring organization, the Little Rock Branch of the Association for the Study of Afro-American Life and History and to its officers, Dr. Patricia McGraw and Annette Johnson, who assisted in developing the project proposals and organizing the public discussions for the initial project; and to Dr. Anthony Dubé and Jane Browning, past and present directors of the Arkansas Endowment for the Humanities, for their encouragement and support in funding the initial project on the Spencer Polk homestead and for refunding the proposal that enabled me to expand the original manuscript into this book.

I wish to thank Lucy Robinson and the staff of the Old State House Museum for their support of the project idea and for following through with the exhibit, "Spencer Polk: The Man, His Home, His Family." I am grateful also to Dr. Leslie "Skip" Stewart-Abernathy of the Arkansas Archeological Survey at the University of Arkansas at Pine Bluff for his time, energy, and enthusiastic support in conducting the archeological survey of the Spencer Polk house site. I wish to acknowledge the assistance provided by Parker and Lucille Westbrook during the survey and to extend special appreciation to them for advice, encouragement, and assistance throughout the project.

In writing the manuscript, I gained valuable assistance and advice from the following individuals: Dr. Richard Long, director of the Center for African and Afro-American Studies, Atlanta University, Atlanta, Georgia, who first aroused my interest in African cultural survivals when I was a student at Emory and Atlanta University in 1972-1973, and who subsequently gave me advice on the chapter on the Polk family cultural traditions; Dr. LeRoy Williams, professor of history at the University of Arkansas at Little Rock, who served as my research assistant on the initial project and later as a reader of the book manuscript; and Dr. John L. Ferguson, director of the Arkansas History Commission, who advised me throughout the research period and also served as a reader of the final manuscript.

Finally, I owe my deepest gratitude to members of my family and others who allowed me to interview them for this work. Without the help of Pearl Murphy, Willie Bell Maxwell, Adele Mamby, Joe Wheeler Clardy, Eddie Lee Wilson-Johnson, Fay Knott, my brothers Dempsey and Preston Polk, and my sisters Julia Gilbert, Marjorie Bland, and Cindy Howell, this book could not have been written.

The research that produced this work was made possible by a grant from the Arkansas Endowment for the Humanities.

1. Crooked Marks on the Landscape

As one travels north today on Highway 369 from Nashville, the seat of Howard County, Arkansas, the modern blacktop road belies the time when only a narrow wagon path led from Nashville to the community of Muddy Fork, the site of the Spencer Polk homestead. Only three decades ago, as recently as 1953, this was still a little-traveled road that twisted through dense forests of pine, oak, and sweetgum, groped its way from the crossroads where 369 intersects Highway 24, and struggled northward to what early land surveys showed as Township 7 South, Range 27 West of the Fifth Principal Meridian.

It is only a fifteen-minute drive now from Nashville to the place where Highway 369 first crosses the Muddy Fork, a tributary of the Little Missouri River in southwestern Arkansas. This once-huge creek is little more than a trickle now, but the first New World settlers along the stream called it the Muddy Fork of Fallen Creek and named their settlement after it. To get to the township before the blacktop road was constructed, one had to travel slowly around innumerable curves, cross rickety plank and log bridges, and traverse all-too-frequent bogs and mires. The road is better now and the bridges are few. Of those remaining, the bridge that spans the Muddy Fork has for more than a hundred years served as the portal to the Spencer Polk house site.

Only a few short decades ago, the occasional traveler who happened to get off the main roads in Howard County and by chance took Highway 369 northward must surely have been taken by surprise upon crossing the bridge over the Muddy Fork and ascending the gently rising hill that tabled the Spencer Polk house place. If it was spring, the first sight sure to strike the eye was the riot of color that spangled the hill slopes. Here the yellow of daffodils and jonquils covered the earth in profusion and cast a golden glow upward to accent the deep purple of iris and the pristine white of snowball and English dogwood. Later in the spring the daffodils and jonquils would give way to the Chinese red of japonica and wild honeysuckle. In spring and summer, red roses climbed white palings and interjected crimson glory among the pastel offerings of their subordinates.

With such a grand array of accents, the house and outlying buildings and grounds should not have come as a surprise to the passerby. But the entire character of the estate was unique in its every aspect. It was a setting out of character with its time and place in the mid-twentieth century, and had been so throughout its history.

A description of the site as it appeared in an earlier era will illustrate the visual singularity of the dwelling house and its surrounding structures. As a farmstead, the Spencer Polk home reached its height of activity and prosperity around the turn of the century, between 1890 and 1910. Pictures, tax records, and oral accounts from family members provide information upon which the following description is based. The author also used her personal memory of the structures as they appeared during her own childhood, making note of certain basic changes that occurred over the years. With the exception of general decline, however, few changes in the homestead took place until after the late 1940s, when its very rapid dissolution began.

Facing the west, with a slight angle to the northwest, the Spencer Polk home was a forty-foot-long log edifice set some twenty yards back from the road. The roof was covered with weather-grayed, hand-hewn shingles, and a break in the roof line from east to west indicated a deliberate division in the architectural arrangement of the building. The north section of the roof, or approximately twenty-seven feet, was at least twelve inches higher than the south section, and its slant and break suggested the gabled roof often seen in Arkansas's earliest log cabins.[1] The lower roof of the south section ran for approximately six feet and intersected the north/south slopes of an ell roof, the shingles and structure of which suggested the hip roof lines of a later architectural period.

At the north and south ends of the house, huge chimneys made of hand-chiseled rock plastered with yellow clay rose from the earth, climbed the outer walls, and towered several feet into the air. A third chimney reaching only to the rooftop could be seen on the eastern side of the south wall, and still a fourth chimney, tall and narrow, rose from the center of the roof to carry away smoke from the kitchen stove. A zinc lightning rod, twisted and gray-green, traversed the length of the roof from north to south and dropped off to a grounded position in a chimney corner.

On the outside walls of the house, huge hand-hewn oak logs at each end contrasted with board-and-batten walls on the ell room and the western facade of the north room. A wide hall, or dogtrot, further divided the house into two distinct parts, with the south wing extending to form the ell that jutted out toward the setting sun. A wide porch ran along the length of the main log-pen room, intersected the open hall, and continued on to form a second hall, or breezeway, between the main south room and the ell room. Heavy oak planks placed upon upright logs of graduated heights formed the steps that led from the porch to the front yard.

In the front yard, a well with pulley and rope suspended from a wide beam sat under a shingled shed that complemented the architecture of the house. A long-necked hollow gourd dipper hung from a nail on one of the posts. A smokehouse constructed of logs that matched the upper section of the house stood near the northeast corner of the dwelling house.

The house was surrounded by trees with an understory of flowers and shrubs. In the front yard, a giant catalpa, with its yearly cycle of fragrant white blossoms, horned black caterpillars, and long brown beans, guarded the front gate. To the north of the gate, a box elder and an elm stood approximately ten feet apart. South of the catalpa, a rugged silver poplar with a dog's leg bend about half way up its height stood surrounded by smaller poplars, and a large cottonwood stood directly behind the main south chimney. A plum tree, a pear tree, and a grove of persimmon trees paced the south slopes of the yard.

Closer to the house, between the well and the porch, a plump chinaberry tree offered deep lavender blossoms in the spring and musky yellow fruit in the fall. Still closer to the house, a gnarled white mulberry stood, pierced here and there by rusting spikes on which a variety of small tools and horseshoes hung. Along the fence that bordered the north end of the yard, another white mulberry

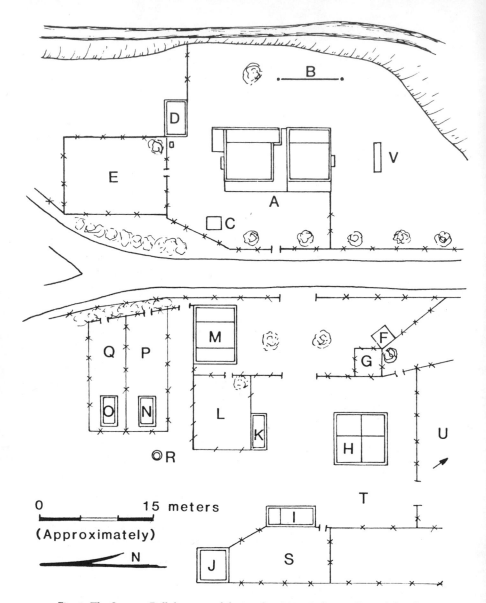

Fig. 1. The Spencer Polk homestead during the 1930s. A, house; B, wash benches; C, well; D, smokehouse; E, garden; F, woodshed; G, hog pen; H, stables; I, corncrib; J, barn/car shed; K, chicken coops; L, garden; M, barn; N and O, cowsheds; P and Q, cowpens; R, well; S, corral; T, horse lot; U, to mint patch and sorghum mill; V, beehives. Drawing by the Arkansas Archeological Survey, University of Arkansas at Fayetteville.

stood near the smokehouse. Behind the house, still more white mulberries shaded the wash benches and wash pots. A red mulberry farther down the hillside offered purple drupes as a summer treat for blackbirds and young folk.

Across the road from the house, more mulberry trees, two black walnuts, and two "hope" trees gave shade for livestock and protection for parked wagons. A bois d'arc tree idled in the fence corner, its shade too scant for comfort and its wrinkled, chartreuse fruit rejected by blackbirds and youth alike. The most impressive trees, however, were the huge cedars that tunneled the road as it passed the house and continued north. Not more than two hundred yards north of the house the road formed a Y, with one branch going eastward to Nathan and the other traveling westward to Dierks and New Hope. The cedars, twelve on each side of the road, standing about ten feet apart, began in front of the house just beyond the elm tree and shaded the lane all the way to the "forks of the road." They had been planted by the occupant soon after the house was built.[2]

Surrounding the house was a fence that went through several stages in the evolution of the homestead. Originally, tall white pickets ran from the south limits of the hillside, along the front yard, and beyond the yard to the north end of an adjacent garden plot. A gate directly in front of the house led across a culvert-covered ditch to the road, while another, wider gate between the first two cedars provided entrance to the garden for the mules and plows. The other three sides of the garden were fenced with tall wire, but there was no permanent fence around the back of the house, where the yard dropped sharply down a bluff to a small stream, or "branch." A tangle of weeds, native bamboo or switch cane, and vines grew beneath chinaberry trees, bois d'arcs, mulberries, and giant elms to form a miniature jungle from the top of the bluff to the banks of the stream.

Along the fence that separated the garden from the yard, except where the narrow gate was fashioned in the center, red, yellow, and white climbing roses obscured the rusting wire; and along the back of the garden, hop vines intertwined with the wire fence to form a thick roll of brown or green, depending on the season. Between the garden and the bluff, plum thickets grew, yielding both red and

yellow varieties of summer fruit. In the center of the garden, a con-
spicuous mound of earth gave evidence of an ancient turnip kiln.
Between the garden gate and the smokehouse a huge dinner bell
hung on its mountings between two oak posts. In the back yard near
the wash benches, an ash hopper stood under the mulberry trees next
to the huge black pots, where the toil and trouble of soap-making
was a seasonal event. Two rain barrels sat under the eaves to collect water for the multipurpose pots and zinc wash tubs, which served
for clothes washing, soap-making, hog killing, and summer bathing.
In the south section of the yard, near the snowball bush and the
English dogwoods, stood the apiary, several neat white beehives that
contrasted sharply with the rugged texture of the house. Outside the
front fence, just beyond the well, a large grindstone and a vise for
sharpening and making farm tools were appropriately mounted.
Nearby squatted a heavy iron blacksmith's anvil. Beside the culvert
that covered the ditch in front of the house, a zinc mailbox with
a red flag rested on top of a square post.

The outlying buildings and fields suggest a great deal about the
history of the homestead. Directly across the road from the house
was a rather wide expanse that led to the fenced horse lot. In the
south part of this area was a woodshed, a wood pile, and a pigsty.
To the north and outside the fence was a barn with a hayloft; an
extended roof on each side provided a wagon shed on the side next
to the road and a buggy shed on the other side. On a straight line
from the front of the house, and behind the fence, stood the corncrib. Set high on its foundation stones to discourage rats, the crib
was constructed of hand-hewn logs with a shingled roof, portray-
ing an exact replica of the north section of the house and suggesting
that the crib and smokehouse were built at the same time as the
original cabin.[3] At a later period a lean-to was added on the north
side of the crib to serve as a second wagon shed and a repository
for farm implements and horse gear.

Four adjoining stables, two for mules and two for horses, were
located near the crib. Above the mule stables was a fodder loft.
Behind the crib was a small corral for breaking horses, and behind
this was another structure built after 1900 to serve as a car shed;
this building also had a loft for hay and fodder. Inside the livestock
yard that surrounded these buildings were several troughs, some
made of planks and others made from hollowed logs, for feeding

the animals; one served as a salt lick. There were also troughs mounted inside each of the four stables.

North of the horse lot was a truck patch which served as a second garden after the 1920s. Between the second garden and the livestock yard stood chicken coops and nests, turkey roosts, shelters for guineas, ducks, and geese, and pigeon cotes. Still farther north were the cowpens and stalls and sheepfolds, all of which were originally constructed entirely of logs. Beyond the northwest corner of the garden was a second well for watering the livestock and to serve a second group of tubs and pots to handle extended family washings.

Beyond the outlying buildings and livestock shelters, pastureland stretched westward to a wooded area where a grove of pear trees and an old well with a pile of rocks gaping from its mouth suggested a former homestead long gone. To the south of the livestock yard, a wide gate led to more pastureland and a fruit orchard. As the terrain sloped toward the Muddy Fork, a wet, marshy area yielded patches of mint and calamus used for cooking and home remedies. Beyond the mint and calamus, groves of hazelnuts grew along a small stream that ran from the northwest and emptied into the Big Muddy. Along this stream was located the original sorghum mill. On a fall day billows of smoke would rise from the stick and daub furnace, and small children would climb mountains of green "pummings" (pomace) as black and white neighbors gathered to make the new crop of sorghum molasses.

The farmlands lay on the hills northeast of the Y in the road, across the branch behind the house on another hill, and across the Muddy Fork in the rich bottomlands to the southeast. On the hills to the northeast were cotton fields, bean and pea patches, and a vineyard, which as late as the 1930s still yielded a scanty crop of Concords. A peach orchard was located directly east of the house beyond a patch of sagebrush. Across the creek in the bottomland were cornfields, watermelon and cantaloupe patches, fields of sweet and Irish potatoes, and more cotton. Between the house and the creek, sorghum grew on both sides of the road. Around and among all of these were dense proliferations of jimson weed, stinging nettles, cockleburs, sticktights, beggar's lice, and bramble briars. There were also hull gulls, blackberries, mayapples, goldenrod, sweet williams, maypops, and touch-me-nots.

On a typical day—as the author recalls from her childhood in the 1930s and 1940s—the farmstead was a bustle of activity. In the early hours before dawn, the occupants of the old log house would be aroused from sleep by the crowing of several roosters. Spencer's son Arthur, by this time the only man in the family, was always the first to arise. If the weather was chilly he would make the fires in the two fireplaces. Then he would fill up all the buckets with water from the well in the front yard. Next, he would hang an iron kettle of water over the fire in the fireplace and proceed to fire up the cookstoves in the two kitchens. With the house set in motion, Arthur would cross the road to the barns and stables to feed the livestock.

As soon as the house was warm, the women, Arthur's wife and sisters, would arise to begin their daily chores. The cows had to be fed and milked first. The fresh milk would be brought in and strained, first through a sieve and then through a square of thin muslin, and placed in stoneware churns to clabber. With the milk taken care of, the preparations for breakfast would begin. The women would take turns going to the smokehouse to carve meat from the slabs of pork in the storage bins. Soon the indescribable aromas of frying salt bacon and wood smoke lured the children from their pallets and beds to gather around the basins in their respective kitchens to wash their hands and faces.

By the time the sun rose high enough over the eastern hill to shine through the kitchen windows, breakfast would be over and Arthur and his sister Frances would begin harnessing the horses and mules and hitching them up to the wagon, which was loaded with plows, hoes, rakes, seeds, and other equipment needed for the day's work. With the horses pulling the wagon and the mules following behind, the two adults would head down the lane and across the creek to the southeastern farmlands. Later in the morning the older children would be prodded off to the fields to carry water and to plant seeds, chop weeds, pick cotton, strip cane, or pull fodder—depending on the time of year.

During the day, the other women and smaller children worked in the gardens, tended the cows, slopped the hogs, and managed the flocks of fowls, which were everywhere. The cackling surprise of hens laying eggs could be heard in a continuous chorus from every direction. Sometimes a flock of chickens would boldly enter the hallway or an open kitchen door to forage for bits of food dropped on the floor by the children. Then the women would go into a flurry of shooing, scattering the intruders with flailing brooms, and the chickens would hurry back across the road to join the turkeys, geese, ducks, and guineas, whose gobbling, honking, quacking, and rattling, along with the clucking of the chickens, the mooing of cows, and the squealing of pigs, kept the entire farmstead alive all day long.

At noontime, Arthur, Frances, and the older children would come home for dinner, which consisted usually of boiled greens, peas, or beans seasoned with salt pork, boiled potatoes, cornbread, and buttermilk. In better days, during Spencer's lifetime, the family would have enjoyed a side of beef or a leg of lamb for dinner, but by 1930 the only meat the family had was occasional wild game or chicken and dumplings on Sunday.

After dinner Arthur would sit on the porch and read the paper in warm weather. Sometimes he would be joined by a white neighbor, usually Old Man Henry Reed, an elderly bachelor who always visited the Polk home around dinnertime and sat at the table and ate with the family. Sometimes Arthur would be summoned by his father-in-law, Bud Bullock, to come out and sit under a mulberry tree near the woodpile to talk. There was never any hurry to return to the field after dinner, but sooner or later Arthur, Frances, and as many of the children as could be rounded up, would return across the creek to get in a few hours' work before night.

In the evening the workers returned from the fields. The mules would be unharnessed and led back to the creek to drink, with the smaller children riding their backs. After the horses and mules had been watered and fed, the cows would be driven from the pasture where they had grazed all day, and be milked again. The eggs would be gathered from the many nests attached to the sides of the barns and stables or hidden away in the haylofts, and the chickens and other fowls would be fed and cooped or seen safely to their roosts.

As the dusk grayed into darkness, Arthur and the older boys would congregate at the woodpile between the house and barns to chop wood for the night and the next morning. The girls and smaller boys would form brigades to carry the wood to the house, some loading the wood upon the outstretched arms of others, who would troop to the kitchens to unload the stove wood in the boxes in the corner or to the front porch to stack the fireplace logs and pine kindling.

At night the kerosene lamps would be lit in the two main rooms of the house and in the kitchens, and the family members would settle down for supper. In winter, when the evening meal of milk, bread, sorghum syrup, butter, and fried meat was over, they would sit around the fireplace hearth and crack walnuts and hickory nuts, roast sweet potatoes and peanuts in the ashes, tell stories, read school books, and recite poetry. In summer they would sit on the front porch until the house was cool enough to go inside to bed. In many ways their life was the same as that of previous generations raised on the old homestead.

The house site and farmlands constituted less than half of the acreage owned by the Spencer Polk family. Spencer and his sons did not own the land because they were farmers; rather, they farmed because they owned the land. Spencer Polk was caught between cultures on the fringes of history. He was somewhere between the New South axiom of "intelligence, character, and wealth"[4] (which meant ownership of land) and the overextension of the seldom-kept promise of "forty acres and a mule." Between 1867 and 1900, Spencer acquired over 500 acres of land, an unusually large amount for a former slave. The way he acquired his land, the way he and his family lived, and his relationship with the other residents of Muddy Fork Township can be better understood if we look at Polk's genealogical background to determine the total milieu out of which emerged this unique and at the same time exemplary Arkansan.

2. The Wilds

Spencer Polk was born in 1833. His tombstone, still standing in the cemetery at Muddy Fork, attests to the dates of his birth and death. From historical records, both oral and written, we learn that he was born in Montgomery County near the county seat, Mt. Ida. Just how he happened to be born there and the facts of his lineage are intriguing. To delineate the history of his parentage and early life, it is necessary to look at the "farthest back" person in his life, as Alex Haley has suggested.[1]

The road is long from County Donegal in Ireland, via the West Coast of Africa, to Caddo Cove in the valley of the Ouachita in southwestern Arkansas. The road is long, and the winding turns in between are no more characteristic of the global distance than are the twists and turns of human fate over time and space among the people who converged on that wilderness settlement in the early 1800s. One leg of the journey as it relates to Spencer Polk began in the 1600s when one Robert Polk of County Donegal, Ireland, set out to seek his fortune in America.[2] This early Scottish-Irish immigrant settled on the eastern shores of Maryland. His descendants scattered over the new colonies from Cumberland County, Pennsylvania, to Mecklenberg County, North Carolina, where in 1780 Taylor Polk was born. Taylor was the son of Captain John Polk, the son of William (1), the son of William (2), who was the son of the immigrant Robert Polk from County Donegal. Taylor was thus in the fourth generation of Polks born in America.

Taylor Polk left North Carolina soon after his marriage to Jency Walker in 1798 and moved to Davidson County, Tennessee, near Nashville. It was here that a son, also named Taylor, was born in 1800. In 1808 the family moved from Tennessee to what would even-

tually become Arkansas.[3] Since the territory had opened to settlement only five years earlier, after the Louisiana Purchase in 1803,
the Polk family were among Arkansas's earliest white settlers. The
Polks called their home "The Wilds," and their neighbors were few
and far between. By 1810 there were only 1,062 settlers in the whole
territory.[4] It was at "The Wilds" that Spencer Polk would eventually be born.

The exact spot of "The Wilds" was difficult to pinpoint at first.
Early records indicate that the Polks settled "on the road from Hot
Springs, not far from Caddo Cove."[5] One of the earliest references
to the younger Taylor Polk is in the Sheriff's Census of 1823 &
1829,[6] where he is listed as residing in Clark County. The Census
of 1840 shows Taylor, along with his brothers Benjamin, James,
William, and Cumberland, living in Hot Spring County.[7] At first
it appeared that the Polks had moved around several times between
1808 and 1850, because their names are recorded in three different
counties. Research revealed, however, that only the county names
changed and the family homestead remained where it was originally established.

County maps show Caddo Cove and other nearby places on the
Caddo River (a tributary of the Ouachita) as being located in Clark
County. The Caddo area was situated in the portion of Clark County
designated as Hot Spring County in 1829. Finally, Caddo Cove was
at the center of what became Montgomery County when it was
carved out of Hot Spring County in 1842.[8] An 1858 map of Arkansas shows Caddo Cove to be a short distance west of Mt. Ida on
the road from Amity to Panther.[9] The site today lies southwest of
Norman.

Certain place names that have existed down to the present time
are associated with the Polk family. For example, deed records show
that on August 25, 1840, Taylor Polk paid $400.00 to William Peyton
for the Sulphur Springs "between Caddo Cove and Washita Cove."
The transaction noted that Peyton had bought the Sulphur Springs
from Polk's brother Benjamin in April of that same year.[10]

Further evidence of the location of Spencer Polk's birthplace is
revealed in the record of a marriage between one of Taylor's sons,
Anderson, and Eliza Epperson in 1848. Anderson is listed as being
from Caddo Township and his bride as being from Gap Township,
both in Montgomery County.[11] Additionally, in a specific reference

to the Polks of the area, Lacy McColloch, in an article on the life of Alfred Clay Hale, wrote: "In time, William Hale found a more desirable location to rear his family. He sold his place and bought what was known as the Taylor Polk place, located on the South Fork of Polk Creek in the same country. . . . Polk Creek ran nearby at the rear of the property, and there was a wonderful peaceful view up the valley."[12] According to McColloch, the Hales moved into the Polk cabin at the turn of the century and lived there for about fifteen years. Place names in the article include Black Springs, Womble (now Norman), and Caddo Gap.

Finally, in January 1981 the author received a letter from Mack A. Guinn of Mt. Ida, Arkansas. Having read a newspaper account of the research project on the Taylor Polk slave family, Mr. Guinn wrote: "I think I own the farm you are looking for. I am 70 years old, Tho I'll be glad to show you over the place."[13] A trip to Mt. Ida and a visit with Mr. Guinn corroborated the evidence on the location of the Taylor Polk homestead. A copy of the abstract which Guinn received when he purchased the land shows that 43.10 acres, "more or less," were acquired by a homestead patent filed by Taylor Polk in 1849. Apparently, it was necessary to acquire the patent in order to sell the land, because the Polks (Taylor and his wife Prudence) quitclaimed the land to Joseph Willis Embry for $400 on April 8, 1850, the year the Polks left Montgomery County. Mr. Guinn confirmed that the land he bought included the original Taylor Polk log house site described by McColloch.[14]

A visit to the site where Spencer Polk was born was enlightening. Although the original Taylor Polk house has been replaced by a neat, modern white frame structure trimmed with red, all other details of the site are starkly reminiscent of the Muddy Fork lands on which Taylor, and later Spencer, constructed the new homestead. Like Muddy Fork, the first Polk site is far removed from any vestiges of civilization. To reach it one must travel to Norman, past the Werger Quartz Crystal mines, past the city limits, take Highway 27 south and 8 east, leave the blacktop for a dirt road, and travel several miles into an area of dense forest that leads into the Polk Creek bottoms. The house site is on a hill in the angle formed by the intersection of a small stream with Polk Creek. To the southeast, in front of the house site, the gentle slopes of Fodder Stack Mountain rise up in surprise from the skyline of thick pine treetops.

The most striking feature of the site is the pair of cedars, one on each side of the entrance. Perhaps in earlier days they enjoyed adjacent companions, but today, grisled and mangy, they seem the ancient ancestors of the huge trees that once shaded the lane in front of the Spencer Polk homestead.

The Polks remained at "The Wilds" in central Montgomery County from the time of their arrival in Arkansas in 1808 until they all moved to Muddy Fork Township in 1850. It was in the valley of the Ouachita, then, that Spencer Polk was born and grew to manhood. It was an idyllic setting that has changed very little over the years. In a newspaper article of 1884, Caddo Cove is described as "this valley, beautiful as Sonora . . . [with the] finest scenery on earth . . . walled apart from the world by mountains, with their projected cliffs of blue limestone and the coolest water dripping and gushing."[15]

When the Polks first arrived in Arkansas, they owned no slaves.[16] The absence of slaves on the Polk plantation may have been due to the controversial nature of the slave question in the Arkansas Territory during the early years of settlement. As late as 1810 there were only 136 slaves in the combined areas of the Hopefield and St. Francis settlements and the Arkansas Post, the most populous areas of the territory later designated as Arkansas. In 1819, when the Arkansas Territory was established by President James Monroe, a heated debate arose as to whether slaves would be allowed in the new lands. The proslavery faction was headed by Henry Clay of Kentucky, who argued that " 'the lot of slaves would be improved if they were spread out' (the diffusion theory)." Clay also maintained that in Arkansas "the land was so bad that only slaves could cultivate it anyway."[17]

The antislavery faction, headed by John W. Taylor of New York, contended that "farmers from non-slaveholding states could emigrate to Arkansas and cultivate southern crops of cotton and tobacco without trying to compete with slave labor."[18] Perhaps that is what the Polks intended to do when they moved into the territory without slaves in 1808. By 1820, however, one year after the territory was opened to settlement without any restrictions on slavery, there were 70 slaves in Clark County out of a total population of 1,040. The leading slavery county at that time was Lawrence County, with 490 slaves in a total population of 5,602.[19] Soon after 1820 the first slave was brought to "The Wilds."

It was at "The Wilds," set in a wilderness of dense forests, mountainous cliffs, and clear streams, that the younger Taylor Polk grew to manhood. Like his father Taylor, who "stood six-foot-three in his stocking feet,"[20] young Taylor was a big man, and he apparently began to participate in territorial politics at an early age. The *Territorial Papers of the United States* for 1821 includes a petition signed by Taylor Polk and others, asking the president to reconsider a treaty with the Choctaw Nation giving them lands already "proved by settlers." The petition was sent from the Arkansas Post and asked for repeal of "the Treaty lately concluded between Commissioners Plenipotentiary on the part of the United States and the chiefs of the Choctaw Nation."[21]

By 1830, young Polk's political interests had gained him the position of magistrate, or justice of the peace, of Hot Spring County.[22] Residents of the area around Mt. Ida still recall that their parents and grandparents often told legends about Taylor Polk. They said he was a big man in their day, meaning not only his physical stature but also his position in the community and the territory. He is said to have held a leading political office in his day.[23] As the historian Orville Taylor points out, the justice of the peace "occupied a key position in the legal control of slavery, since higher judicial officials were few and likely to be far away."[24] Thus, by the time he was twenty-one, Taylor Polk was helping to establish the laws that governed the territory.

From all indications, it was during the years between 1820 and 1830 that the Arkansas branch of the esteemed Polk family of America (they would later boast a president, James Knox Polk, and a renowned Methodist bishop, Leonidas Polk) made their West African connection. The elder Taylor Polk was nearing the end of his journey (he died in 1824), and the younger Taylor had taken over the reins of the family. Sometime during the 1820s young Taylor made a trip to the "Indian Country," as it was called. Perhaps he went to trade with the Indians or to reconnoiter their status in the territory, considering the 1821 petition he signed. Whatever his purpose, his most obvious transaction during the trip was the purchase from the Cherokees of a young African slave girl named Sally.[25]

The Choctaws and Cherokees were being dispersed from their lands to the south, and between 1817 and 1828 they settled on tracts of land in Arkansas as designated by government treaties. The Jackson-Hinds Treaty of 1820 gave the Choctaws a reservation west of a line extending from Point Remove Creek to Fulton on the Red River.[26] This treaty would have forced the Polks and other settlers to move from southwestern Arkansas. The treaty was never enforced, however, and few Choctaw ever settled in the state. The Cherokee Nation West, on the other hand, occupied a reservation in Arkansas from 1817 until 1828, on lands extending from Fort Smith southward to the mouth of Point Remove Creek near Morrilton. Some Cherokee settled south of the Arkansas River in what is now Yell County. The "Indian Country," therefore, was located just north of the area where the Polks lived.[27] Furthermore, the Cherokees brought with them into Arkansas their own African slaves.[28] Sally belonged to the Cherokees, and for some reason— whether fate, ambition, or some undefined need—Taylor Polk bought her. She was his first slave. The tax assessment records of Hot Spring County for 1830 show Polk owning only one slave, a female, between the ages of sixteen and forty-five.[29]

All that is known of Sally comes from accounts handed down orally by the descendants of other slaves who knew her and by her own children, one of whom, John Spencer Polk, is the subject of this book. According to Spencer Polk, who passed the story on to his children, Taylor Polk "went into the Indian Territory and bought Sally," probably as early as 1821, about the same time he signed the petition against the Indian presence in Arkansas.[30] Polk was undoubtedly a man of unusual disposition, for, although he was apparently happily married to his first wife, Prudence Anderson, whom he had wed in 1821,[31] the slave girl Sally caught his eye, it is said, and he bought her for his concubine. Those who remember their grandparents talking about Sally say she was Polk's "servant" or "housekeeper" or "maid."[32] Legally, she was his slave.

Sally was a very beautiful "brown-skinned" girl, according to those who saw her and told their children about her. Taylor Polk may have kept her in or near Fort Smith at first, entrusted to the care of a friend, or he may have left her with the Cherokees. Oral sources insist that Sally was left in Fort Smith, which Polk frequented

in the interest of his political activities. No evidence of these trips
has been found, but the oral reports insist that whenever Polk went
to Fort Smith to trade or conduct business, he had his trysts with
Sally. As a result of these encounters, Sally's first child, a son named
Peter, was born in 1827. Sally later produced two more sons by
Polk—Frank, probably born in 1829, and John Spencer, born in
1833. During this period Taylor Polk was rearing a family by his
first wife; his first legitimate child, Eleanor, was born in 1823.[33]
Sometime before 1833 Polk brought Sally to Caddo Township, to
"The Wilds," and built her a cabin next to his own. It was here that
the youngest son, Spencer, was no doubt born. Sally occupied her
little cabin and continued to serve Polk, in spite of the vehement
disapproval of Polk's legitimate spouse.[34]

In 1836, Polk decided to go into the slave business in earnest. Tax
records show that between 1830 and 1835 he owned only one adult
slave, but that in 1836 he owned eleven.[35] Up to that time, none of
the other Polk families—Taylor's brothers, four of whom lived in
Arkansas—owned any slaves. In fact, only six other families in Hot
Spring County owned slaves at the time.[36] But these six families
represented a significant percentage of the small population in the
area. Hot Spring County (and later Montgomery County) was
among those with the lowest slave population in Arkansas. Moreover, Taylor Polk's eleven slaves represented an especially large holding in a state where the average number of slaves per family was
only four.[37] Although the number of slaves per family was small,
the percentage of slaveholding families in Arkansas was significantly
large. Orville Taylor reports that "42.5 percent of the state's white
population was directly involved in the institution of slavery, either
by ownership or by being a member of a slaveholding family."[38]

Between 1835 and 1838, the slave Sally gave birth to her fourth
child, a girl named Eliza. It is said that Sally's three sons looked just
like "the Old Man," as Taylor Polk was known by his descendants.
The three sons were definitely mulattoes; all had fairly straight hair,
the characteristic high-bridged, enormous nose, and very fair com-
plexions, and one had blue eyes. But Eliza was "dark." Not only
was her skin dark, but soon after her birth her hair began to take
on too much of the natural African curl and had not grown as long
as "white" hair should.[39]

Apparently out of a combination of jealousy and ignorance, Taylor Polk sold Sally shortly after Eliza's birth. Sally's descendants say that she was sold "down the river to New Orleans." Polk, according to oral reports, believed that his concubine had proved unfaithful, taken up with a slave man, and conceived Eliza. Spencer remembered that he was only four years old at the time. Mrs. Pearl Murphy, Spencer's oldest living descendant, wrote of her great-grandmother in a 1978 letter:

> She was named Sally, a part Negro and Choctaw Indian girl. In those days Federal Court was held at Ft. Smith (probably once a year) and prominent citizens were called there to serve on the jury, and Taylor Polk was one that would be called. So on one of the times he was there, he picked up this girl and brought her back as a slave. If she had any family name except Sally no one ever knew.
>
> She became the mother of three sons, Peter, Frank, and John Spencer and later a girl named Eliza. The girl was black and after her birth the mother was sold. My grandfather was only four years old when she was sold away from them. The children were kindly treated and they never suffered for care and really never felt like slaves. I think, however, the fact that their mother was sold away from them at a tender age testifys to the harshness of the slave system in the U.S.[40]

Later, in a personal interview, Mrs. Murphy insisted that Sally was part Cherokee, not Choctaw, and other family members confirmed the Cherokee lineage.

Though apparently deeply affected by the loss of their mother, Spencer and his brothers seldom discussed their maternal lineage. Spencer told his own children only that Taylor Polk "went into the Indian Country" and bought Sally, and that when Eliza was born he sold her away because of suspected infidelity. The act of selling a mother away from her children no doubt caused little concern among the slaveholding class in Arkansas. According to Orville Taylor, "Since there was no legal requirement of keeping husbands, wives, and children together, there were many instances of separation."[41] While the information on Sally is scant, the details of how Taylor Polk acquired her and how he got rid of her are strongly etched in the oral history handed down by all the descendants of Spencer Polk.

Much of the information that does exist about Sally was passed on by the descendants of another slave family, the slaves of Blount Bullock, another early Arkansas settler. The Bullock families, both black and white, intermarried with the Polks and lived in close proximity to them in both Montgomery and Howard counties.[42] It was from the Bullock slaves and their descendants that Sally's status with Taylor Polk was most clearly delineated.[43] Blount Bullock's slaves passed the story on to their children, who told it to later generations of the Polk family. The Bullocks were the first to reveal that Taylor Polk kept Sally in a little cabin next to his own, and that Sally's children were sired by her master. The Bullock descendants also described in detail how Sally and the child Eliza looked. The following transcript from an interview with Mrs. Willie Bell Bullock Maxwell is revealing:

QUESTION: Did you ever hear anything about Taylor Polk's connection with Spencer Polk's mother Sally?

MAXWELL: Taylor Polk raised a bunch of kids by her, didn't he?

QUESTION: That's what I've always heard.

MAXWELL: Yeah. This Sally was a slave, and this Taylor Polk, he raised a bunch of kids by her. And this Sally—Aunt Puss you know, that was Uncle Spencer's half sister. She was dark. She was black, and she had short hair. Kinky hair. 'Cause I've seen her when I was very small.

QUESTION: You saw her?

MAXWELL: Yes.

QUESTION: She was Spencer's sister?

MAXWELL: Half sister.

QUESTION: And that was Sally's—

MAXWELL: Sally's daughter.

QUESTION: How many others did Sally have?

MAXWELL: Mmm—I just don't know. Anyway when Taylor—When Aunt Puss was born, that's when Taylor run Sally off.

QUESTION: Who told you that? Is that what you've always heard?

MAXWELL: Always heard. Because when the black one
was born—. Let's see now. Did he run her off or did he run
the black one off?
QUESTION: What was his connection with Sally? Was Sal-
ly his slave?
MAXWELL: Yeah. Sally was his slave.
QUESTION: Did he have any other slaves?
MAXWELL: No, I don't know of any more. Anyway, Sal-
ly had a house. He had a house out there Sally lived in and
every year she'd bring a child by him.
QUESTION: Spencer Polk was one of those children?
MAXWELL: Yes. Spencer Polk was one of them and Peter
Polk was one of them—and so after that, after Aunt Puss was
born, he got rid of Sally.
QUESTION: Did you ever hear anything about what Sally
looked like?
MAXWELL: Sally was a big bright woman. That's how Uncle Spencer and 'em get they—. Sally was a bright woman [fair
skinned].
QUESTION: You say she was big?
MAXWELL: Yeah. Somebody said she was a big bright
woman, and by Old Man Taylor Polk being white and Sally
was a big yellow Negro woman, well, there wasn't but one
black one in the bunch, and she taken wa-a-y back.[44]

The descendants of Spencer Polk said that Sally was a beautiful
brown-skinned Indian girl with very little African blood. But the
Polks had never willingly admitted any African heritage, and for
this reason the Bullocks' description of her was probably a more accurate one. If Sally had any Cherokee strain, it was probably slight,
or, put another way, her African lineage was no doubt very strong.
The child Eliza's dark skin and the "short, kinky" hair everyone said
she had attest to a strong African genetic strain. And while the black
Polks accepted the story of Sally's infidelity, it was not necessarily
true. Sally had served Polk faithfully for more than a decade and
must have known something of the man's tyrannical disposition and
the consequences if she practiced deception with him. Moreover, it
is entirely possible that Sally could produce a child by Polk whose
features were more black than white. But in those days on the Arkan-

sas frontier, the fact of genetic dominance would hardly have been known or accepted. The selling of Sally probably occurred in 1838, for in that year the valuation of Taylor Polk's slaves decreased by two hundred dollars and the number of slaves reported on tax records dropped from eleven to ten.[45]

When Sally was sold away, her four children remained on the plantation with their master-father. From accounts by family members, Polk's first wife was a kind woman who took over the care of the baby Eliza, and Taylor Polk kept the young boys close under his own protection. Sally's offspring apparently lived in close proximity to Polk's other slaves in the quarters. But at the same time it is clear that the three boys received special attention from the Polk family. They carried the Polk name and developed an intimate relationship with Taylor's legitimate children. Apparently Taylor Polk established a sort of unspoken admission of his parentage of Sally's children. Orville Taylor contends that there is "irrefutable proof in the birth of children known to have been fathered by white men. It is impossible to ascertain the frequency of such births. Sometimes, because of legal ramifications, white men admitted fathering slave children. More often there was no such admittance."[46] Taylor Polk, legal ramifications notwithstanding, was one of those white men who admitted, albeit in uncertain terms, his parentage of three of Sally's children, and Spencer, being the youngest and only four years old when he was separated from his mother, was singled out for a favored place in Taylor Polk's plantation-life structure.

Spencer Polk, like many other blacks of his day, was a product of both southern planter aristocracy and the human bondage of chattel slavery. He became a living example of what W.E.B. Du Bois called a "twoness of consciousness," a man melded into an existence both within and without the "veil" of racial separation in America.[47]

3. The First Remove

By the time Spencer Polk reached adolescence, the Taylor Polk family was fully settled in the Ouachita Valley community around Norman. The village was small and the Polks were among the most prosperous settlers. Caddo Township became a part of the newly formed Montgomery County in 1842 and Taylor Polk by then had a well-established plantation system in this charming but isolated setting. He was paying taxes on forty acres of land[1] and no doubt cultivated much more. A close examination of tax records shows that the amount of land a settler owned, occupied, and farmed was often much more than the number of acres on which taxes were collected and recorded for a given year. According to residents of Mt. Ida, Taylor Polk not only owned a large and prosperous homestead but also owned and operated a racetrack at one time. Mack Guinn, who now owns the site, pointed out the area along the banks of Polk Creek where Polk is said to have had his racetrack.[2] He owned nine slaves of more than ten years of age, and several children who were growing up along with Spencer Polk, the son of Sally the slave girl lately sold away.

Spencer later was fond of remembering his half-brothers, the legitimate sons of Taylor Polk, one of whom was the same age as Spencer. Henry Clay Polk was born of Prudence Polk in 1833. Fireside stories handed down by Spencer's children often centered around the experiences Spencer had with his master-father's children; the names Alf and Cum, and two who were called by the nicknames "Buige" and "Tecumseh," were often spoken. Alfred Sapington Polk and Cumberland Polk confirmed by census and genealogical records, were constant companions of the young slave.

Between 1830 and 1849, Taylor Polk became one of the most

prominent citizens of southwestern Arkansas. By the 1840s, Montgomery County had a population of 276 persons identified as free and white, and 51 persons identified as slaves. The county had 61 town lots, 4,508 acres of settled land, two sawmills, one distillery, two pleasure carriages, 549 horses and mares, 15 mules, 1,627 neat cattle (just plain old cows), and one tanyard. Of the 51 slaves, Taylor Polk owned up to 11, while the other slaveowners had from one to four slaves each. Polk also owned twelve horses, two mules, and thirty neat cattle.[3]

Sometime around 1849 to 1850, Taylor Polk decided to leave "The Wilds."[4] On his reasons for moving we can only conjecture. Perhaps the area was becoming too populous; perhaps it was an effort to acquire more or better farmland. Whatever the reason, the family—Taylor, his brothers, his grown sons, their children, and the slaves—left the "wilds" of Montgomery County for the "woolies." They chose to settle in an area even more isolated and unpopulated than the valley of the Ouachita—along a tributary of the Little Missouri River known then as Fallen Creek, in Pike County.[5] The creek had two branches which came together a few miles east of the new Polk homestead. The lower branch of Fallen Creek was referred to as the "muddy fork," and apparently the township derived its name from this allusion. The name Fallen Creek or Falling Creek appears on maps as late as 1900, but after that it is replaced by Muddy Fork. Falling Creek was one of the place names handed down by Spencer Polk to his descendants, and was an important lead in identifying the movement of the Polk family.

Spencer Polk was not yet twenty years old when the Polks removed. The slave census of 1850 identifies Taylor Polk as living in Muddy Fork Township and corroborates important information about Spencer Polk's genealogy. Taylor Polk at that time owned twelve slaves between the ages of three and thirty-five, as shown in Table 1. The list of slaves, identified by age, sex, and color but not by name, would be insignificant except for the fact that "color" is designated as "B" for black and "Mu" for mulatto. The three male slaves designated as mulattoes have ages that correspond with the known ages of two of Sally's sons by Polk. Sally's oldest son, Peter, born in 1827 according to his grave marker, would have been twenty-three in 1850, and Spencer, the youngest son, born in 1833 according to his headstone, would have been seventeen. The twenty-one-

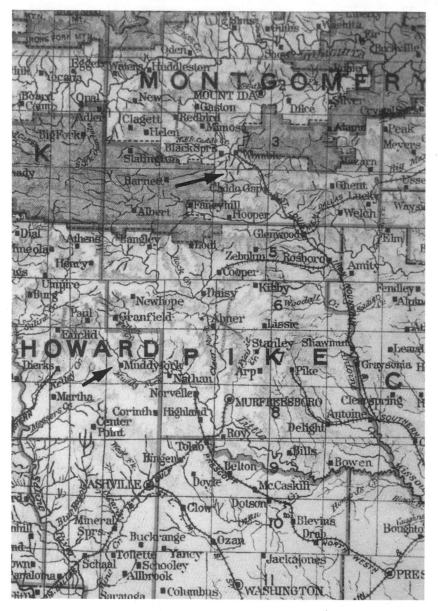

Fig. 2. Map of Montgomery, Howard, and Pike counties, Arkansas, 1914. Arrows point to Muddy Fork in Howard County and the site of the first Taylor Polk homestead in Montgomery County. U.S. Department of the Interior, General Land Office, 1914. Courtesy of the University of Arkansas at Little Rock Archives.

Table 1. Slaves Owned by Taylor Polk in 1850

Age	Sex	Color
35	M	B
30	M	B
23	M	Mu
21	M	Mu
17	M	Mu
9	M	B
6	M	B
35	F	B
13	F	B
12	F	B
5	F	B
3	F	B

Source: U.S. Bureau of the Census, *1850 Slave Schedules of Arkansas*, on microfilm at Arkansas History Commission, Little Rock.

year-old male mulatto slave is no doubt Frank, Sally's second son, of whom no dates of birth and death have been found. The thirteen-year-old black female could very well be the girl Eliza, whose birth took place prior to 1838.

Spencer Polk told his children about the family's move to the Muddy Fork community and his early life there. With eight slaves over ten years old to work the rich farmland along the Muddy Fork, Taylor Polk established himself as the leader in the township. Records show that in 1850, before he left Montgomery County, he was the highest bidder on a sawmill and gristmill.[6] Apparently he transferred these assets to Muddy Fork, for he soon became one of the wealthiest farmers in the area. In the 1852 tax records he is found paying tax on forty acres of land valued at $500; his nine slaves over ten years old were valued at $3,900; and his livestock was valued at $1,231.[7] By 1853 he had acquired 200 acres of land in the township. Two years later in 1855, he had 400 acres, and in 1856, 600 acres. By 1856 he also listed one sawmill among his holdings. By 1860, Polk had more than 800 acres of land in four different townships in Pike County.[8] More significantly, he owned land in and built his log house on Section 29, Range 27 West, a plot of land adjacent to the site on which Spencer Polk later established his own homestead.

It was at Muddy Fork, between 1850 and Emancipation in 1863, that Spencer Polk reached manhood. His early days at "The Wilds" had apparently been carefully molded and shaped by his master's family. From what Spencer said himself, he spent a great deal of his youth in the company of his master and Taylor Polk's legitimate sons, the two youngest of whom were near Spencer's own age. According to Spencer, Polk's sons treated the young mulatto like a "brother." To say that Taylor treated him like a son would not be entirely accurate. Spencer obviously knew that Taylor was his father, but he also knew he was both illegitimate and a slave. While Taylor Polk singled out Spencer for special treatment, Spencer lived the life of a slave, and Polk never freed any of Sally's offspring, if for no other reason than that free blacks were not welcome in the territory.[9]

In fact, Arkansas reflected a negative attitude toward free blacks from the earliest days of settlement. There were few free blacks in the state—only 59 in 1820 and 608 by 1850. In 1843 the Arkansas legislature passed a law prohibiting further entrance of free blacks into the state.[10] Addressing the question again in 1859, the legislators adopted a law barring free blacks from living in the state after January 1, 1860. The Arkansas General Assembly repealed the law in 1861, however, and its effects were shortlived, if it was effective at all.[11] Spencer and his brothers lived almost like free blacks, according to oral reports, which suggests that they may have been as "free" as any blacks who enjoyed the legal status of free, in a state where the attitudes and the laws created conflict.

As a child, Spencer acquired the rudiments of learning. Oral reports indicate that Taylor sent Sally's sons to school with his own children, which attests to the special treatment Spencer and his brothers received from the Polk family. Most slaveholding states had strict laws against teaching slaves to read and write. Orville Taylor asserts that there "are few known instances of educated Arkansas slaves." And while Arkansas had no laws against teaching slaves, "withholding education was merely accepted as a normal practice in the system of slavery." The records show clearly that Arkansas slaveholders were not interested in providing an education for their slaves because, like slave masters in other states, they believed that education made slaves "troublesome."[12]

From his own account to his children, Spencer was put in charge of keeping up the operations of the plantation and transacting plantation business, such as selling the crops and buying supplies. It was he, sometimes accompanied by his white half-brothers, who went into the county seat (first Murfreesboro and then Center Point) to get the mail and make purchases for the farm. Spencer was also a blacksmith and a carpenter, and he practiced these crafts on the plantation and in the community in the years before Emancipation.

Spencer Polk's relationship with his master's family was unique. He was not a "house slave" in the general sense of the term. He went on hunts with his half-brothers, served the plantation as a blacksmith, and worked in the fields with other slaves. He even "hired out" on occasion. He told his children, for example, of an incident in which he hired out, along with other slaves, to a neighboring farmer. One night Spencer and his comrades decided to go to a "breakdown" (an adaptation of traditional African dancing) in the slave quarters of still another plantation. On their return in the early morning hours, their substitute master ordered them all to remove their shirts for a lashing. Spencer refused, got on his horse (he had one of his own), and returned to the Polk farm. The neighboring farmer followed hot on Spencer's heels, but when he arrived to report the rash conduct of the young slave, Taylor Polk informed the man that Spencer was not to be whipped. When the astonished farmer asked how they controlled Spencer without whipping, the alleged reply from Taylor was, "Oh, we don't bother Spence. We let him do just about whatever he wants to do, and we don't let nobody whip him."[13]

While Spencer was responsible for overseeing the operations of the plantation, he was not an "overseer" of the other slaves, though he associated closely with other slaves on Polk's plantation and in the community. He was a highly intelligent, highly skilled man in many ways—ways which he learned from both his master and his fellow slaves. He not only shod horses and cut nails, but he also knew carpentry and tool-making. He practiced bark and cane weaving, masonry, and cultivation in the African tradition, and he passed these skills on to his own sons.[14]

In addition to the labor he contributed to the plantation, Spencer exemplified the loyal, trustworthy servant. He often told about the time when there was a tragedy in the family and a young step-daughter of Taylor's had to be fetched from Caddo Gap. The girl's family trusted no one but Spencer to make the trip and accompany her back to Muddy Fork, an overnight journey by horseback.[15]

Spencer was a gentle man, the complete opposite of Taylor's legitimate sons, who were widely known frontier toughs armed with six-guns. As a young man, Spencer was tall and big, with a shock of thick, jet-black hair that started out straight and then took on the characteristic African curl, causing it to stand away from his head like a fan. As an 1865 tintype shows, his full beard seemed even blacker than his hair. With a long, high-bridged nose and a wide mouth, he would have had a fearful aspect had it not been for his eyes. He had the eyes of an artist—wide-set, dark, alive, and smiling.[16]

In contrast to Spencer, Taylor's other sons were desperate men who rode the frontier trails carrying not only six-guns but also long rifles strapped to their saddles. They were a law unto themselves, but they loved and protected Spencer. The story is often told about a time when Spencer went into town and certain whites who resented the presence of an "educated" black attempted to attack the youthful slave. It was in the general store that the fracas began, and quicker than wind the word reached the brothers Polk, who were awaiting Spencer in a nearby saloon. By the time the altercation got to the "Nigger-stay-in-your-place" stage, the would-be molesters found themselves looking down the barrels of the Polk brothers' six-shooters. With a clear warning never to lay a hand on Spencer, the brothers escorted their protege out of the store and galloped away to the Muddy Fork.[17]

In the decade preceding the Civil War, Taylor Polk was one of the most prosperous men in Pike County. He owned both land and slaves and was able to provide his family with the best that pioneer Arkansas had to offer in the way of creature comforts. This fact is reflected in the lives of his slaves, particularly in the life of Spencer Polk and the homestead he established between 1860 and 1870.

When the Polks moved to Muddy Fork Township in Pike County around 1850, Spencer was only seventeen years old, and his young adulthood came during the years immediately preceding the Civil

War. Very few details of that life can be ascertained except through oral reports handed down by family members, but a great deal of information exists about the white Polks. It is evident from records that by the time the Civil War agitation began, Taylor Polk's sons had reached adulthood and had begun to drift away. One son, Anderson, went to Texas and took Spencer's brother Frank with him. Two sons, Henry Clay and Cumberland (known as Cum), joined the Confederate forces and fought with the Arkansas Militia. Henry Clay became a first lieutenant and Cum experienced hair-raising exploits with Company I, Nineteenth Arkansas Infantry.[18] It was Sally's sons Peter and Spencer, therefore, who remained with the "Old Man" through the war years, sustaining their master in his old age, and he in turn supported them in their "leap from slavery to freedom."

If one can excuse the selling of Sally—and anyone with human sensibilities must surely find that hard to do—then one could say that Taylor Polk was a "kind master." His slave-sons revered him, seemingly accepting the explanation of their mother's infidelity. For such an offense some men beat their women and some even kill them. Taylor Polk, as an owner of human flesh, simply sold his unfaithful concubine. The act was as cruel and final as death. Nevertheless, Polk's slaves in general had in him the embodiment of paternalism. Spencer is said to have often contrasted Polk's kindness with the meanness of his second wife, who chided Taylor about indulging the slaves and put a padlock on the smokehouse door so the servants could not help themselves to meat as often as they had done before her arrival.[19]

Because of his close association with the Taylor Polk family, and because of the influence of both familial and paternal relationships with the white Polks, Spencer as an adult developed a life-style that in almost every respect emulated that of his master. Materially, in fact, Spencer outdid the "Old Man" in surrounding his family with an aura of southern "cornbread" aristocracy that surpassed that of most whites who lived in the Muddy Fork community. Between 1865 and 1900, Spencer Polk created in planned isolation a world that was as nearly like that of his former master as he could possibly make it.

4. Oh, Give Me Land

It was sometime during the 1860s that Spencer Polk acquired land and erected his own homestead. Documentary evidence, combined with oral history, makes it possible to determine the origin of the house and farm, although exact dates are not available for construction of the house. Oral reports on the origin of the first log house are conflicting. Some of his descendants maintain that Spencer told them the house was built by slaves, though he may have meant former slaves, or freedmen. One relative insists that the house was built in the 1870s.[1] There is, however, strong circumstantial evidence that it was built before 1870, perhaps even before the end of the Civil War.

One piece of evidence that supports an 1860s date is the fact that Spencer was married and rearing children by 1860. Spencer's first marriage probably occurred in the late 1850s. Although no written records of the marriage are to be found, oral reports attest to a marriage to a "Turrentine woman" from adjoining Sevier County in Polk's young adulthood.[2] This woman was no doubt a slave of the Turrentines, one of the most prominent of Sevier County families. One son, Douglass, was born of that marriage. The census record of 1880 shows Douglass, the eldest son of Spencer, as being twenty years old; this would indicate a birth date of 1860. The house may have been acquired at the time of this first marriage.

Spencer's second marriage, like his first, is unrecorded, but oral evidence and census data suggest that the marriage took place in 1867, perhaps following the death of his first wife.[3] Spencer's second wife, Ellen Murphy, a mulatto like Spencer, was chosen by Taylor as a suitable bride for his protege, according to one source. Another source indicates that Ellen was a half-sister to Spencer's first wife, and that both wives came from the Crabtree plantation in Sevier County.[4] Oral sources also say that at about the same time that Taylor arranged the marriage between Ellen and Spencer, he also arranged for his slave-son to acquire land and build a house.

The Pike County Courthouse burned in the 1920s, and most of the records were destroyed, but some information is extant. The first reference to Spencer Polk in the existing records of Pike County appears in 1867. The record of taxes for that year shows immediately under the name Taylor Polk the names of Peter, J.S. (John Spencer), Joel, and Thomas Polk. Beside the names of all four is the designation "col'd" for "colored." These were the only "colored" men paying poll taxes in the county in 1867. The record also shows that Spencer and Peter owned horses and mules but no land.[5] It is quite possible, however, that both Peter and Spencer were farming land that they later acquired legally.

Extant records also show that Spencer Polk homesteaded a 160-acre tract of land in 1869. This included 40 acres in the southwest quarter of Section 28 and 120 acres in the northwest quarter of Section 33, Range 27 West, Township 7 South. The patent was issued in 1875, but tax books show that it was applied for on August 13, 1869.[6] The certificate registering the patent was entered at the Land Office at Camden, Arkansas, and issued to John S. Polk under the Homestead Act of 1862, which provided that 160 acres be distributed to settlers after a five-year residency. The certificate is signed by Ulysses S. Grant, President of the United States.[7]

In acquiring his large acreage, which eventually amounted to as much as 560 acres, Spencer Polk was the exception rather than the rule. Landownership of more than forty acres was rare for blacks in Arkansas in this period. In the first place, Arkansas's black code forbade ownership of land by freedmen. Landownership would mean that blacks could become self-sufficient; without land they would have to work for wages that whites were not obliged to pay. Thus, a new form of slavery could be instituted.[8]

During the late 1860s, the Freedmen's Bureau was put in charge of distributing abandoned lands to loyal refugees and freedmen. In Arkansas there were 106,140 acres of such land available to former slaves. Because of difficulties in assigning the abandoned lands throughout the South, Congress approved an act providing for the dispersal of public lands. Known as the Southern Homestead Act

The United States of America,

TO ALL TO WHOM THESE PRESENTS SHALL COME, GREETING:

Homestead Certificate No. 537,

Application 1611, **Whereas,** there has been deposited in the **General Land Office** of the United States, a CERTIFICATE of the Register of the Land Office at *Camden Arkansas.* , whereby it appears that pursuant to the Act of Congress approved 20th May, 1862, "To secure Homesteads to actual settlers on the public domain," and the acts supplemental thereto, the claim of *John S. Polk.*

has been established and duly consummated in conformity to law for the *south east quarter of the south west quarter of Section twenty-eight, the south east quarter of the north west quarter, and the west half of the north west quarter of Section thirty-three, in Township seven south, of Range twenty-seven west, in the district of lands subject to sale at Camden Arkansas, containing one hundred and sixty acres,*

according to the Official Plat of the Survey of the said Land returned to the **General Land Office** by the SURVEYOR GENERAL.

Now know ye, That there is therefore granted by the UNITED STATES unto the said *John S. Polk,* the tract of Land above described: **To Have and to Hold** the said tract of Land, with the appurtenances thereof, unto the said *John S. Polk,* and to his heirs and assigns forever.

In Testimony whereof, I, *Ulysses S. Grant,* PRESIDENT OF THE UNITED STATES OF AMERICA, have caused these letters to be made Patent, and the **Seal of the General Land Office** to be hereunto affixed.

Given under my hand, at the CITY OF WASHINGTON, the *first* day of *July,* , in the year of Our Lord one thousand eight hundred and *seventy five* , and of the Independence of the United States the *ninety-ninth,*

By the President: *U. S. Grant*

By , Sec'y.

, Recorder of the General Land Office.

Fig. 3. The homestead certificate for Spencer Polk's first land purchase, dated 1875 though applied for in 1869. Copy from the U.S. Land Office, Maryland.

of 1866, it provided for setting aside millions of acres of land for exclusive settlement by freedmen and loyal whites in five southern states: Alabama, Arkansas, Florida, Louisiana, and Mississippi. The bill was to be in effect until January 1, 1867.[9]

Although many former slaves were anxious to homestead land in Arkansas under the Southern Homestead Act, very few were able to do so. By 1866 most former slaves had hired themselves out to employers in order to survive. Having bound themselves to work for wages, they could not meet the requirement of improving the land, which would have necessitated months of hard labor. Another requirement the freedmen could not meet was the five-dollar registration fee, along with the charges for the land, which ranged from $.50 to $1.25 an acre. In some cases blacks had been able to lease land for farming and had already planted crops when the act became effective. In addition to the foregoing problems, the prevailing racial attitudes of southern whites served as a major barrier to acquiring lands under the act. White officials simply refused to tell blacks where the lands were located. Finally, one of the most serious problems facing the newly freed slaves was that they did not have the necessary tools for clearing and farming the land, nor money with which to buy seeds and other supplies for planting crops.[10]

In spite of the difficulties, a few blacks in the state were able to acquire lands, mostly in eastern Arkansas, around Pine Bluff and near Fort Smith. In all, of the 10,807 homestead entries completed in Arkansas under the Southern Homestead Act, only 6 percent, or about 250, were completed by blacks. By 1880, only 25 percent of black farmers throughout the South owned their own land. In the south-central region of Arkansas, the average acreage owned was around forty-eight acres.[11] Spencer Polk's acquisition of land under the earlier Homestead Act, that of 1862, may be attributed to his close association with the white Polk family, who no doubt helped him acquire the homestead patent for his first 160 acres.

Tax records also show that in 1881 Spencer bought a 160-acre tract in Sections 28 and 33, adjoining the land he had homesteaded on the east and north. The new tract was purchased for $1,400 from George Epperson, but the deed was transacted between Spencer and Sarah Epperson, George Epperson's wife.[12] Sarah was a daughter of Taylor Polk and a half-sister of Spencer. Interestingly, Sarah's brother Anderson was married to George Epperson's sister Eliza. Part

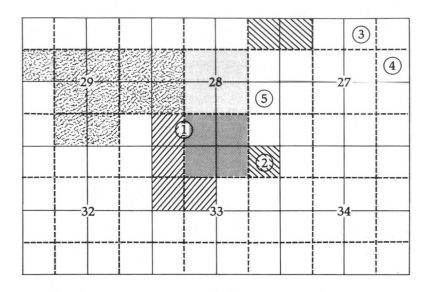

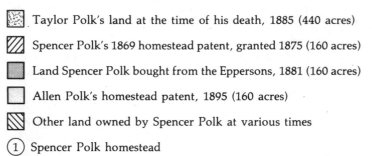 Taylor Polk's land at the time of his death, 1885 (440 acres)

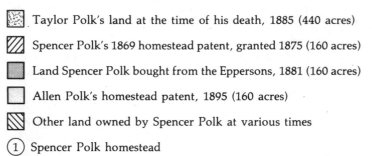 Spencer Polk's 1869 homestead patent, granted 1875 (160 acres)

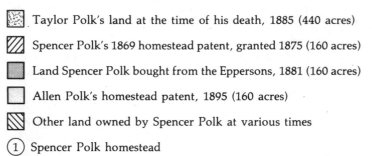 Land Spencer Polk bought from the Eppersons, 1881 (160 acres)

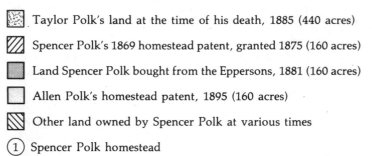 Allen Polk's homestead patent, 1895 (160 acres)

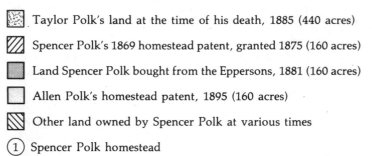 Other land owned by Spencer Polk at various times

① Spencer Polk homestead

② Land lost to Bud Bullock

③ Polk Meeting House (church and school)

④ Cemetery

⑤ "Negro" church and site of brush arbor school, later of schoolhouse

Fig. 4. Polk landholdings at Muddy Fork.

of the 160-acre tract had been acquired by a Thompson Epperson (probably George T. Epperson) in 1855. This was a 40-acre parcel, and records show that Spencer was paying taxes on this land as early as 1875. Since the house site stood partly on this land and partly on land Spencer had homesteaded earlier, it seems probably that the house had been constructed by this time. The fact that the house site was chosen without regard to survey lines is unusual.

A logical assumption is that at some juncture, possibly between 1860 and 1869, and certainly by 1875, Taylor Polk assisted Spencer in choosing a tract of land on which to build a house. It was land that was in close proximity to the Taylor Polk plantation and part of it had been homesteaded by the family of Taylor's son-in-law and daughter-in-law. Spencer homesteaded the unclaimed portion and, through agreement with the families and perhaps on installments, bought the section homesteaded by the Eppersons. It is clear from both tax records and oral accounts that Spencer was occupying the land and had established his homestead long before 1881, when he acquired the deed to the Epperson property.

By 1881 Spencer's family had grown considerably. In addition to a son by his first marriage, Spencer had five children by his second wife, according to the 1880 census.[13] He also had another son, Allen, born in 1860 outside the legal bonds of marriage. Interestingly, Spencer had exercised some choices of his own in dealing with women during his young manhood. Having been brought up as an "almost white man," it was in keeping with plantation tradition of the time that he took as a wife a woman of genetic bearing similar to his own. Both his wives were mulattoes like himself. But, like the "Old Man," Spencer was not immune to the attractions of darker beauties. During the same year that his first legitimate son, Douglass, was born, Spencer sired a son by a "common black slave woman," according to oral reports.[14] And, as his master-father had done by him, Spencer took his dark illegitimate son, Allen, into his household and brought him up along with his and Ellen's children. Allen Polk is listed in the 1880 census along with Spencer's other six children, all of whom are identified as mulattoes. Beside Allen's name is a neatly inked "B" for black.[15]

Considering that Spencer Polk started out as an ex-slave with a one-room log cabin and that he paid taxes on only 40 acres for several years, the growth of his farmstead was phenomenal. By 1889 he owned 320 acres, making his one of the largest farmsteads in the Muddy Fork community.[16] By 1900 he owned over 500 acres. This included, in addition to the 320 acres, a 160-acre tract homesteaded by his son Allen in 1895 which reverted to Spencer when Allen died shortly after that.[17] Spencer had also purchased 40-acre tracts in Sections 27 and 33. These land acquisitions made him one of the most prosperous farmers in the newly formed Howard County. By 1900 he also had ten children, and his household included in addition a nephew and the nephew's wife and children.

Personal property tax records for 1889 also reveal the following property: three horses, twenty neat cattle, three mules or asses, twenty-eight sheep, twenty-six hogs, and one carriage "or wagon of whatever kind."[18] Most individuals in the township in 1889 owned only one horse, five to six cattle, and eight to ten hogs. Few owned sheep or mules, and still fewer owned as many as Polk did. The community was small, with only 568 persons counted in the 1880 census. Of these, only 61 were black. Only one other family owned more land and property than Spencer Polk in the Muddy Fork community in 1889, and that was the Epperson family, which had inherited the land owned by Spencer's former master, Taylor Polk, who died in 1885.[19]

Through industry, ingenuity, and hard work, Spencer Polk was able to start out with a modicum of assistance and to succeed on his own as a freedman. Although he surely received support from his former master during the immediate post-Civil War period, after Taylor Polk died Spencer was on his own. Taylor Polk's relatives apparently did little to assist their "darker brother" after the "Old Man's" demise. In fact, as executor of the older Polk's estate, George Epperson sold all of his father-in-law's farming implements at public auction and took control of the rest of Taylor's assets. It is clear that Epperson did not award Spencer any of his master-father's legacy. Ironically, among the assets sold at auction was a set of blacksmith tools, no doubt the very ones that Spencer had used as a slave on the Polk plantation. The day the auction was held, the first item to go was a set of blacksmith tools, sold to Spencer Polk for fifteen dollars.[20]

Spencer probably bought the tools more out of sentiment than need. He practiced blacksmithing on his farm and passed some of the skills on to his sons, but he did not practice the trade for a living. It was strongly emphasized by those who knew him that "Spencer Polk never shod anybody's horses but his own."[21] He made his living as a subsistence farmer, albeit on a grand scale. He often kept hired laborers living on the place when the homestead was at its peak of productivity.[22] Once he got his start in a one-room log cabin and a plot of ground, he was on his way to becoming a rather prosperous man.

Although it has not been possible to arrive at the exact date when Spencer's house was built, it is highly probable that he had established a home by 1869. That was the year of the homestead entry on the first 160 acres he is known to have acquired. It is also the year of birth of his first child by his second wife, Ellen. Spencer was now thirty-six years old, had two nine-year-old sons, owned livestock, and was paying his poll tax. It is very likely that he had his own house. And although the date of its structure has not been established, it is clear that the Spencer Polk house represented one of the earliest examples of mid-nineteenth-century log-style dwellings in the area.

Utilizing his master's sawmill, his own skills as a carpenter and smith, and the labor of other blacks in the community, Spencer Polk erected his original log cabin on a hill overlooking the Muddy Fork on a site that had once been the gathering place of prehistoric man.[23] He ultimately fashioned his house after the original Taylor Polk homestead at "The Wilds." McColloch describes the latter as follows: "The house was a large double log structure. The two log-pen rooms were sixteen feet square with a ten-foot breezeway between them. The plate logs that tied the two rooms together were a little more than forty-two feet long. The loft provided additional sleeping space used by the boys."[24] The Spencer Polk dwelling was a close replication, except that it developed over time into a much larger structure, and the two main rooms separated by a breezeway were not built at the same time.

The house evolved in several stages. Originally, Spencer Polk erected a one-room log cabin approximately eighteen by twenty-seven feet. The foundation logs, set on slabs of limestone, were hewn from virgin pine and oak. The walls of the cabin were made of huge logs, some measuring as much as eighteen inches across. At the north end of the cabin was a fireplace with chimney made of fossil-

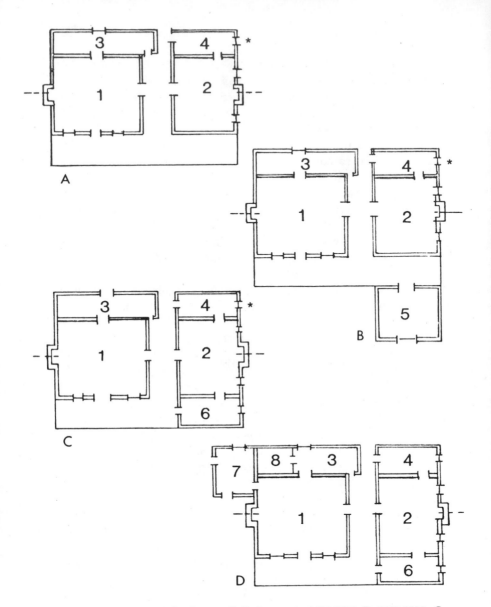

Fig. 5. Evolution of the Spencer Polk house. A, 1880-1905; B, 1905-1920; C, 1920-1935; D, 1935-1950. All dates approximate. 1, log living room; 2, log bedroom; 3, kitchen; 4, bedroom; 5, added bedroom; 6, bedroom/enclosed porch; 7, added kitchen; 8, kitchen/bedroom. *An original fireplace was replaced by a window before the 1930s. Drawing by the Arkansas Archeological Survey, University of Arkansas at Fayetteville.

encrusted limestone rocks, many of which had been hand-chiseled to form neat blocks. The stones were mortared with yellow clay mixed with grass. Inside the cabin, the fireplace jambs were smoothed over with white clay. The original hearth was no doubt clay, too, but at some later period a cement hearth with a sprinkling of smooth stones was laid in a more modern fashion.[25] A crude plank slab mantel crowned the fireplace opening.

The ceiling of the original cabin was covered with oak planks approximately twelve inches wide and supported by three-by-six beams. Above the ceiling was a loft used for sleeping quarters in the early days of the house and for storage later on. In the final years, a collection of wine bottles, broken chairs, ancient wooden and gourd bowls, and a scythe and cradle were kept there. To enter the loft, one ascended short narrow planks nailed on two beams, ladder-fashion, near the left side of the fireplace, which led to a square trapdoor in the ceiling. On the south exterior wall of the cabin, footholds were cut into the logs to provide access from the outside. These footholds led to a window in the center of the loft wall. A second window was located above the trapdoor in the north wall of the loft.

Originally, there were two doors in the cabin. The main entrance was a heavy oak door with latch and string in the west wall. There were two double windows, one on each side of the door. Two more windows, half the size of the front windows, were located in the north wall, one on each side of the fireplace. The second door was cut in the south wall.

One can only speculate as to the kind of furnishings that complemented the original cabin. Cooking was certainly done in the fireplace. The metal rods and hooks and the huge covered iron pots and skillets were still being used for fireplace cooking as late as the 1930s. The master bed took up most of the room in the cabin. It was a rope bed, entirely hand-made. The side boards were joined to the head and foot boards with wooden pegs, and large sisal ropes crisscrossed and looped through the posts for additional support. The four-poster was hewn of solid oak. Spencer told his children that the bed posts were carved by slaves. The massive posts were artistically beveled and curved, the wood unstained and natural. Later this bed would be moved to the south wing of the house.

Between 1870 and 1910, Spencer added a second log-pen room, a kitchen, and an ell off the west side of the second log-pen room.

The breezeway extended to form a porch for the kitchen, and a smaller, lean-to room was joined to the south room across from the kitchen on the east side. The ell room was constructed of board and batten and gave a modern look to the older log house. The late Walter Westbrook, a prominent white resident of Nashville, Arkansas, for many years, was once Spencer Polk's neighbor, and he recalled when the ell room was added to the house:

> QUESTION: Well, you know, I grew up in the house, and it seemed awfully big at that time, when I was a child.
> WESTBROOK: It was a good big house—several rooms—hall—dogtrot, they call it. Porch—front porch. It's hard for me to remember just how it was located. . . . Seems like he built a new room out in the front one time—an extension on the south end out towards the gate.
> QUESTION: Yeah. Originally it must have been a one-room log house, don't you think?
> WESTBROOK: No, it was a two-room log house with a hall between. Then he built this room on the south end of it that stuck out west, and when you went in, you went in on the end of that porch there, and walked down the porch into the hallway. It's hard for me to remember just how it was.
> QUESTION: Do you remember when the addition was put on the house?
> WESTBROOK: Oh, it was a-way back there in the early 'teens; . . . —back there before 1912.
> QUESTION: Before 1912?
> WESTBROOK: Yeah. Back there somewhere about that. I went by there when I was just about seven years old. That would be in '96. Later on, I went by several times after that, and they had that new addition on it.[26]

The house was at its acme around 1900, with five rooms and a loft to serve Spencer's extended family of ten children, nieces, nephews, and grandchildren.[27]

The house was furnished with a collection of articles that reflected the old and the new, the hand-made and the factory-produced, the primitive and the modern. Most of the furnishings remained in the house from the time they were acquired until the place was abandoned in the 1950s. Some of the articles were then carried away by Polk's heirs, while others were left in the house to be carted away by vandals or to rot among the pile of logs and debris when the house collapsed.

A description of the furnishings as the author remembers them from the 1930s and 1940s will perhaps illustrate the kinds of material attributes with which Spencer Polk surrounded his family. The original main room served as a sitting room and a bedroom. The four-poster rope bed had been moved to the south room by the 1930s, and a green iron bedstead had taken its place in the southwest corner. The bed was covered with goose down mattresses and hand-made quilts. In another back corner of the room was a clothes safe, or chifforobe. A large trunk, a Singer sewing machine, and a collection of cane-bottomed chairs made up the other furnishings. Next to the northernmost window on the west wall was a medicine cabinet, and in the opposite corner a tall, huge grandfather clock with a swinging gold pendulum ticked away the time. In front of the fireplace, an antique rocking chair held center stage.

Across the hall, or dogtrot, the central south room contained most of the relics from the past. The four-poster bed had been moved there sometime in the 1920s. It too was piled high with mountainous feather mattresses. A larger chifforobe and shelves for linen occupied the east wall, and a spinning wheel stood in the left corner of the fireplace. Erected above the fireplace was a delicately fashioned mantel, whitewashed and shining. In the right-hand corner was a bookshelf with double glass doors, referred to as the "library." A second grandfather clock stood next to the chifforobe, and a second Singer sewing machine was located in front of the linen shelves. A modern-looking rocker and a pair of cane-bottomed chairs completed the furnishings.

Between 1920 and 1930 the ell room disappeared, and no one living is willing or able to tell exactly when or how. The east bedroom, much smaller than the other rooms, contained a small cot for sleeping, but the rest of the room was piled high with a collection of artifacts from the past: a violin, a small trunk, bark baskets, stoneware jars, a shoe last, levels, chisels, scales, bellows, quilting frames, augers, and countless other items, both in and out of use.

The kitchen which was added to the east side of the original log cabin ran along the entire length of the room and extended to the south about six feet. It was furnished with a large Ben Franklin stove, two cupboards, and a long, handmade table. Several captain's chairs sat around the table. A variety of cooking and dining utensils were in use, including stone jars, churns, china, pottery jars and jugs, wooden bowls, wrought iron skillets and kettles, and tin and zinc water pails and tubs. Outside the kitchen at the end of the hall, a shelf held a stoneware water pitcher and basin for washing up.

In the wide hall separating the two main sections of the house were various pieces of furniture at different times. There were chairs, a swing, a "hall tree," and a wide, tall chest referred to as the "bureau." This "bureau" was piled high with a variety of articles for everyday use.

Spencer Polk died in 1919, and the character of the house changed significantly during the following years. Spencer was survived by only one son, Arthur, and by four daughters who occupied the house with their brother. When Arthur married Mattie Ann Bullock, the daughter of a neighboring farmer, in 1921, arrangements had to be made to accommodate the rapidly increasing family. The old African saying that "what women don't want to share is not the man but the kitchen" was exemplified in the Polk family home. At first the women shared the huge kitchen, but tensions mounted as time passed, and a new kitchen had to be constructed for Arthur's wife. With the help of a white neighbor, Arthur built the kitchen himself. The second kitchen was furnished with a small stove, a long hand-made table with matching benches on each side, a pie safe in one corner, a wood box in another, and storage shelves along the west wall. There were two small windows on the east side, and a larger window with swinging closures and a shelf that projected to the outside was built on the north wall. The projecting shelf was used for family ablutions. It contained wash pans and water buckets.

The smokehouse stood approximately fifteen feet from the northeast corner of the second kitchen. Inside the smokehouse were wooden bins along the west wall for salted meat. Shelves lined the east wall. There were huge barrels for flour and meal, and a chopping block stood in the center of the hard-packed dirt floor. On the shelves and sitting around on the floor were stone jars, buckets, jugs, fruit jars, and other containers for soap, sorghum molasses, cracklings, lard, tallow, and home brew. Low rafters had hooks and nails for hanging meat as it cured. The smokehouse door had an iron latch.

With construction of the second kitchen, the house expanded to six rooms. From the time it was built to the time of its demise, the Spencer Polk residence put its "wooden arms" around four generations of the black Polk family. Between 1869 and 1890, Spencer raised ten children in the house. Two of his daughters had one child each, and after 1920, his surviving son had ten children, all born in the old log house. Two great-grandsons were born in the house also. In addition to his heirs who occupied the house, the 1880 census shows that Spencer had other relatives living with him, including a nephew and the nephew's wife and a twelve-year-old unidentified mulatto hired girl.[28] These data support the oral accounts that Spencer Polk often had hired hands to do much of the work on his farm, and that sometimes these workers, white as well as black, lived in the house with the family.

Like many other houses built during the Victorian era, Spencer's home was a multiple-family dwelling. With its loft, wide halls, and separate wings, the house was meant to be lived in by many people. And like the human souls who passed their lives within its shelter, the house grew and enlarged from its humble beginnings, stood for a while in splendid form, began to fall away after its allotted "three score and ten years," and finally succumbed to the ravages of time.

5. Within and Without the Veil

Spencer Polk represents both the unique and the exemplary in the annals of Arkansas history. His uniqueness is illuminated by several characteristics, including his genealogical background, his physical traits, his personal character, and his accomplishments as a member of a developing community in early Arkansas. At the same time, Spencer Polk can stand as a model for many Americans who have been just ordinary men and women struggling to establish a home, to make a decent living, and to raise a family by working hard and using the natural resources of the land. His background, though different from others in some specific details, illustrates the kind of background out of which many Arkansans have come. Slavery, racially mixed parentage, and survival in the isolated backwoods of the South are elements in the heritage of many other people, both in Arkansas and in the nation. Furthermore, the life-style that Spencer Polk created for his family reflects the way a large number of people have lived, white as well as black.

At the turn of the century, the community of Muddy Fork was a busy little village of fewer than a hundred families. In order to arrive at the total makeup of the township, one must examine the censuses for both 1900 and 1910 because the latter is incomplete. According to the 1900 Census, there were seventy-six families living at Muddy Fork, ten black and sixty-six white. The black heads of household listed are Thomas Benson, Dock Bullock, Edward Bullock, William Bullock, Emily Counts, Martha Flowers, Samuel Griffin, Spencer Polk, Jacob Taylor, and Anderson Willis.[1] The 1910 Census lists a total of seventy-four heads of household but only three black families, those of Dock Bullock, Harrison Bullock, and Spencer Polk.[2] The census omitted several black families in 1910, including those of John and William Bullock. These families did not move away from Muddy Fork until after 1920.[3]

The 1910 Census identifies Spencer Polk as head of household number 9 in the listing for Muddy Fork Township. He is the only head of household named Polk shown as living in the community at the time. His brother Peter and all of the white Polks had long since moved away, Peter to Center Point and the white Polks to other states. Spencer is further identified as a farmer, and the members of his household include his wife Ellen, four daughters, three sons, and two granddaughters. Polk and all of his family members are designated as mulattoes, and Spencer's age is given as seventy-six.

By the turn of the century, the Spencer Polk estate was recognized as the half-way point between the communities to the north and west—New Hope, Dierks, Caddo Gap, Nathan, and Murfreesboro—and the county seats, first Center Point and later Nashville.[4] Among the homes of the few families, black or white, in Muddy Fork, the Spencer Polk place was one of the grandest in scale if not the most elegant in texture. Spencer had developed a self-contained farmstead, with many conveniences of rural living. Travelers from far and near on their way to and from Center Point and Nashville often stopped to spend the night, to rest, to get a drink of water, or simply to pass the time of day with Spencer Polk. Needless to say, most of these travelers were white.

Those few living persons who remember the man and his farmstead have only the fondest memories mixed with awe. They speak of the cordial hospitality that he always extended to friends and strangers alike. He was highly respected by his white neighbors and coolly admired by his black neighbors. Spencer liked to boast that he lived like "white folk." When visitors came, he "rolled out" the best accommodations that could be obtained at the time, short of an established inn. As one relative put it, "Spencer Polk laid that honor on whites that he learned as a slave, and they in turn honored and respected him, mainly because they knew who he was."[5] Some of the whites in the community still refer to him as "Uncle Spencer," not only as an appellation denoting that he was a respectable, acceptable "colored" man, but also because he was truly the uncle of some of them (the descendants of Taylor Polk's legitimate children).

More importantly, Spencer's keen intelligence and warm humani-
tarianism attracted people. His kind generosity was spoken of far
and wide, and people returned again and again to his fireside.

Considering the sheer isolation of the place from the main roads
of commerce and communications, Spencer Polk's estate was a
marvel. He owned only the latest and best in farm equipment, including elaborate hayrakes, harrows, cultivators, planters, plows,
and wagons. The family traveled in a stylish black buggy on special
occasions and a chaiselike two-wheeled vehicle called a hack for
short, informal trips. In the 1920s the family was among the first
and few residents to purchase a motor driven vehicle, a Model-T
Ford truck.[6]

The Polks farmed several hundred acres in cotton, corn, and other
crops. Wine, home brew, and whiskey were made from home-grown
grapes, hops, and corn. The family raised sheep for wool and geese
for down. In addition, there was an abundance of other livestock
and poultry, including horses and mules, cows, hogs, turkeys, ducks,
chickens, guineas, and pigeons. For many years the south yard was
alive in the spring with the hum of bees from the dozen or more
bee gums sitting among the flowers and shrubs in the back yard.
A conversation with a relative revealed that Spencer Polk believed
in having only the best when it came to supplying his family with
their needs. Spencer's nephew Taylor Wilson, a man now in his
eighties who resides near Lockesburg, recalled that when he was
about ten years old, his parents visited Muddy Fork. On the day
they arrived, Spencer was in a rage because the night before wolves
had attacked and killed a prize boar which Spencer had just acquired
through a mail-order firm.[7]

A taped interview with the late Walter Westbrook revealed much
information about Spencer Polk as head of his household and good
neighbor:

QUESTION: I am still trying to get some information on my
grandfather Spencer Polk, and I thought you might remember
some things you could tell me about him—what sort of man
he was, and that sort of thing.

WESTBROOK: Well, I don't know a whole lot other than
what I told you the other day. It's just—where he came from

or his fore-fathers or anything. I don't know anything about that. He never did tell me anything.

QUESTION: I'm going to write an article about the house and the furnishings in the house and the kind of work Spencer did. Were you ever in the house?

WESTBROOK: Oh, numerous times. Visited there several times.

QUESTION: Oh, you did?

WESTBROOK: Ate dinner there several times. Umm hmm. Dined in the dining room—. My dad bought a store in Nathan, and I was working there in the store, you know. I was eighteen years old, and Uncle Spence would come down there and I'd talk with him. And that's how I knew so much about him as I do. We put a huckster wagon on the road and just buying chickens and eggs. Didn't have a peddling wagon.

QUESTION: What kind of wagon?

WESTBROOK: Huckster. And we'd just take—money and buy chickens and eggs all over the country. And feller running that wagon for us was named Tom Paine. And David, he couldn't go. I'd go instead. And I'd get up there about Uncle Spencer's about 'leven, twelve o'clock, and he never let me leave without eatin' dinner.

QUESTION: Is that right?

WESTBROOK: Ate dinner there several times.

QUESTION: He was getting on up in age by that time.

WESTBROOK: Well, yeah, I imagine so. I wouldn't know how old. Maybe sixty, sixty-five. He had grown children. Children older than I was. I was just eighteen, twenty. You take Arthur, you know. He was, shoot, he was a lots older than I was. And I think he [Spencer] had some girls—three or four girls—much older than I was. They'd be around the dining table waiting on the table and I was eating by myself. I'd try to get 'em to sit down and eat with me, but they wouldn't do it. They'd wait on me, and I'd sit there and eat by myself. And when I got through, they'd all sit down and eat, and I'd sit over in the corner. And they wouldn't eat, and I'd say, "come on and let's all eat." Now, they wouldn't do it. Uncle Spence was peculiar that way. He said it wasn't nothin' to him,

but it was what other folks would think about it. That was
the way he was. He didn't want to tread on anybody's rights.
He wouldn't do anything that'd cause anybody to have something to talk about. Very nice old man, and I loved to talk
with him. He'd come to the store in the spring of the year when
everybody was out to work. We'd sit on the porch and talk
about the Civil War and first one thing and then another.

QUESTION: He was a grown man at the time of the Civil
War.

WESTBROOK: You know I don't remember everything
when I was a kid. He took a liking to me some way or another.
If he wanted anything, he'd send down there and tell me to
send it to him. He never would tell anybody else. He'd tell Arthur or whoever was gettin' it to tell me to send it, and I'd send
it to him.

QUESTION: That was in your father's store?

WESTBROOK: Yeah. Well, he always came around and pay
for it. A good customer. But he didn't come too often. When
he did come, he bought a large amount of stuff. He wouldn't
come often. . . . When I first went by that house it was '97.
Dad and I went to Center Point with a load of wool. Old Man
John Reese had a wool mill over there, and I went by his house.
The road ran east and west. There was a lane of cedars—

QUESTION: You remember the cedars?

WESTBROOK: Oh, yes. I remember when we had the store
down there I had to go to Dierks on business—was riding
horseback. Went over there one day on horseback. I stopped
by there and was talking to him. It hurt me a little bit to ride
a horse, and he had me put my horse to his buggy and let me
go in the buggy.

QUESTION: He did?

WESTBROOK: Yeah. That'd be about 1915 when he let me
use the buggy. He was a good liver, hard worker. He tried to
have meat, homemade meal, corn—he didn' buy any of that.
Uncle Spence had plenty. . . .

QUESTION: You were telling me before when I was here
that Spencer Polk was a big man?

WESTBROOK: Oh, yeah. He was tall and straight. He

wasn't no hump shouldered man. Straight up—big square shoulders. Oh, I imagine he weighed two-hundred pounds, maybe more. Full breasted man. You ever see Bert Toland?

QUESTION: I remember hearing the name—.

WESTBROOK: Well, he was just a perfect picture of Dr. Toland, far as form and makeup.

QUESTION: I remember hearing the name of Dr. Toland.

WESTBROOK: Well, they favored a lot. Of course, Uncle Spence was a good deal darker. But Uncle Spence was far from being black! But he and Dr. Toland could pass for twins as far as makeup and size and everything. Big, full breasted men, two hundred pounds. Just exactly alike.[8]

Although he was fast approaching ninety years of age when this interview was held in 1978, Mr. Westbrook remembered a great deal about Spencer Polk, who was often called 'Spence,' and it is clear that what Westbrook reported is accurate. He seemed reluctant to talk about the female members of Spencer's household, but he talked freely about the male members, Spencer's sons Arthur, Jimmie, and Charley, who will be discussed along with other family members in the next chapter.

Another source, Mrs. Willie Bell Maxwell, substantiated Westbrook's description of Spencer Polk with her own vivid details:

QUESTION: Were you born at Muddy Fork?

MAXWELL: I was born at Muddy Fork.

QUESTION: Did you ever know Spencer Polk?

MAXWELL: Oh, yes! I went over to Old Man Spencer Polk's a-many and many a time and seen him sittin' up there on the porch.

QUESTION: What did he look like?

MAXWELL: He was a great big old red man. He had white moustache, his eyes was red like. His eyes always was red. Un hunh! And he had real good hair and he was a very kind old man. He be walkin' with his stick. I can see him now![9]

Spencer Polk raised his family in the southern planter tradition. Although his sons worked in the fields alongside the hired help that he often used, Spencer insisted that his daughters portray the image of the Southern Belle. They dressed in the latest fashions and often attended square dances and parties with the white neighbors, according to oral sources. Spencer also saw to it that all of his children received an education. At one time or another they all attended school, either at the Academy, as it was called when blacks and whites attended together in the 1800s, or at the "arbor" school established on Spencer's farm after 1900.[10] One daughter, Emma, was sent to Philander Smith College in Little Rock for a short time, and she taught in the school at Muddy Fork in the late 1880s. According to the 1880 Census, five of Spencer's seven children were enrolled in school, and the 1910 Census reveals that all of Spencer's household could read and write, with the exception of Spencer himself, who could read and handle figures but could not write, as far as the census shows. Relatives, however, insist that Spencer could also write.[11]

Mrs. Maxwell insists that Spencer himself once taught school. It is possible that he did so at one time, perhaps in the years after the Civil War. After all, he was one of the few individuals at Muddy Fork who could read. Even his white master, Taylor Polk, was unable to read or write, according to the 1880 Census.[12]

Spencer Polk, like many other blacks at the turn of the century, tried to establish a life-style as far removed from his slave ancestry as possible. His day-to-day associations were mostly with whites, although he held an important position in the community as a black man. The *Nashville News* referred to him as "one of the finest colored men in this part of the country" in an article written in 1910.[13] He attracted the attention of an earlier newspaper, the *Howard County Advocate*, in 1883 when it reported that "Spencer Polk and his Sister-in-Law, Mrs. Clemens and her daughter called to see the Advocate April 25. They were shown how the press was worked when the paper was printed, and they enjoyed themselves quite pleasantly. Mr. Polk and his brother are warm friends."[14] Spencer's sister-in-law was his wife Ellen's sister Julia, who married George Clemens and later moved to Little Rock. Spencer's brother mentioned in the article was Peter Polk, who subsequently lived in Center Point.

Mrs. Willie Bell Maxwell, the daughter of Harrison (Bud) Bullock, a long-time neighbor of the Polks, sums up the attitude of Spencer's family toward blacks in the following manner:

QUESTION: Did they [the Polks] have a good relationship with other black people in the community?

MAXWELL: Right. To a certain extent. They was really—they would turn accommodations to 'em. Umm hum. I know Aunt Ellen, she came over there in the snow [to deliver Mrs. Maxwell's sister Alice].

QUESTION: But they considered themselves sort of—

MAXWELL: Oh, yeah! They would do things, but still yet, they was just like white folks used to be. They would help out colored, but still yet, they thought they was, you know—

QUESTION: They thought they were better?

MAXWELL: They thought they were better!

QUESTION: They didn't consider themselves white, though?

MAXWELL: Oh, yes! They considered themselves white.

QUESTION: The other whites in the community didn't consider them white, did they?

MAXWELL: Well, to a certain extent. They'd come over there and eat with them.

QUESTION: Well, they did that when I was growing up.

MAXWELL: They'd come over there, and they'd fix big dinners for 'em, and they'd stay all afternoon with 'em.

QUESTION: So they just went across both—

MAXWELL: They communicated both across—each race, you see. They were nice—they were nice to colored people—very nice to 'em.

QUESTION: But they were sort of in between—

MAXWELL: They had so far to go with colored. There was a certain extent, like I said, and then they'd go to pulling back, you see.[15]

From all indications, Spencer accepted his "Negroness" as an unfortunate badge that he and his offspring had to bear. It is alleged that because he considered himself more white than black, he did not allow his children to mingle freely with other dark-skinned blacks. In fact, he frowned upon intermarriage of his children with blacks, and forbade black men to call upon his daughters. This attitude was not unlike that of others of the so-called "mulatto class," who believed at the turn of the century that the survival of the race depended upon "whitening out" the group through intermarriage with only light-complexioned mates. This phenomenon prevails in the folk history and literature of Afro-Americans and accounts for the establishment of castes like the Blue Vein societies, which the writer Charles Chesnutt describes in his short story "The Wife of His Youth."[16] Leon Litwack argues that skin color determined the "Negro's place in the social order," and that color valuation associating a lighter skin with a superior type was accepted among both blacks and whites.[17]

An accurate assessment of America's preoccupation with skin color—or epidermicism, as it has been termed by one Afro-American scholar—must include an explanation of the so-called "mulatto" phenomenon. The complexity of the phenomenon requires much more objective research than has been done in the past. Most scholars who have written about mulattoes have viewed those born of black and white parentage mainly from the perspective of their relationship to other Americans of African descent. This narrow view does not reveal the whole picture. African-Americans born of one white and one black parent came to be viewed as making up a special group or class only because of the attitudes, perceptions, and behaviors of white people toward them, and these so-called "mulattoes" existed as a group only in a misinformed ideology. Blacks themselves have not used the term "mulatto" widely. In fact, most blacks of white/black parentage are rightly offended by the term.

The so-called mulatto was an invention of whites, who conjured up the term out of the social-Darwinistic mythology of race that permeated American thought in the mid-nineteenth century.[18] The term "mulatto" is derived from the Spanish word for mule. Whites believed that black and white people were of an altogether different species and could not, therefore, intermix by nature. The "unnatural" coupling of black and white human beings, it was thought, could only result in an offspring that was biologically incomplete; and, like the mule offspring of a mare and a donkey, the hybrid offspring of a black/white admixture could not reproduce. To paraphrase W.E.B. Du Bois, the white man created a "tertium quid" and called it a mulatto.[19]

At the same time, however, the mythology held that because mulattoes had "white blood" they were genetically superior to their "pure black" relations in intelligence and moral character. The myth was perpetuated through the folklore and scientific literature. It affected the attitudes and behavior of most whites and, to a lesser degree, of blacks themselves. It was these attitudes and behaviors that created a mulatto class that was identified on the slave census by 1850 and on the national censuses of 1880 through 1910.[20]

Scholars who have attempted to analyze the mulatto phenomenon have sent out mixed messages. For example, both Litwack and more recently Eugene Genovese have argued that there were certain advantages for the mulatto class. Genovese, however, contends that class distinctions between mulattoes and other blacks developed only after Emancipation, that during slavery mulattoes were treated on the whole just like any other "niggers."[21] This was certainly not the case with Spencer Polk, and neither was it the case with many other slaves of white parentage, according to oral accounts of numerous blacks today who had slave grandparents or great-grandparents of mixed ancestry. Genovese contends that there were very few exceptions to the standard of treatment among the slaves, and argues that "those mulattoes who received special treatment usually were kin to their white folk."[22] Of course, all mulattoes were "kin" to white folk. Unless the master sold them away or freed them and sent them north out of deference to the sensibilities of his white womenfolk or to educate them, these mulatto "shadow families" remained on the plantation and in close proximity to the white men who fathered them.

In his analysis of the mulatto phenomenon, Joel Williamson refers to blacks born of one black and one white parent as "new people," another distinction and perception that is popular among white scholars but unacceptable to most blacks. But Williamson makes more valid and accurate points than do most scholars. He argues that mulattoes were tied to their white neighbors by "bonds of kinship and *culture.*" Williamson's research revealed that numerous slave owners produced a "shadow family," or children born of a black mother who was kept in close proximity to the master's ligitimate family and produced offspring almost one-to-one with the white mistress, a situation mirrored in the family produced by Taylor Polk and his slave Sally. Williamson's argument is exactly opposite Genovese's. Prior to the Civil War, according to Williamson, there was an alliance between whites and their mulatto offspring. After the war the whites began to see miscegenation as the "big sin because whites saw their offspring as a reminder of that sin and their losing the war."[23] It was only after the death of Taylor Polk and the migration of the white Polks from the Muddy Fork community that the Spencer Polk family began to feel the effects of white antagonism, a condition that had little to do with the "big sin" of miscegenation that produced the Polk family, but rather a result of the rise of anti-black feelings and Jim Crowism, which "reached a crescendo in the South around 1907."[24]

Williamson's most important point is that mulattoes were tied to their white families by bonds of culture. It was not so much the biological heritage that made Spencer Polk unique; it was his cultural heritage. There were numerous mulatto families in the lower South and on the frontier, particularly in the states of Kentucky, Missouri, Arkansas, and Texas.[25] Not all of them acquired a standard of living comparable to that of the Spencer Polk family, but some did. Genovese was probably correct when he asserted that slaves who were the product of paternalistic white families "had greater access to education and skills and provided a natural leadership among the blacks during and after the war."[26] But this analysis could be applied to both so-called mulattoes and non-mulattoes. Occasionally a slave of no white admixture was singled out for special treatment by his master or former master for various reasons. It was the close proximity to the culture and access to the resources of whites that account for any socioeconomic difference between the "mulatto class" and their "black" former comrades-in-bonds.

The main difference between blacks who had one white parent and those who did not was that a lighter skin color and/or recognized support from a distinguished white family often opened doors to the white world that were otherwise closed to most former slaves. Blacks who were beneficiaries of entrance to the white world used their legacy in different ways. Some, such as Frederick Douglass and Walter White, become outspoken advocates for freedom, civil rights, and equality. Others, particularly around the turn of the century, withdrew by passing for white or creating little worlds of their own, such as the "blue vein" societies. The majority have experienced no noticeable exceptions in their lives as black Americans. A few, including Spencer Polk, have tried to transcend race by the coalescence of their double conscience into a life of service and cooperation among their white and black kinsmen. In this respect, Spencer Polk was more an individual than a member of a class called "mulatto."

The leadership role that Spencer Polk played in the Muddy Fork community is evident from oral reports that indicate that he was an early school director at Muddy Fork as well as a teacher in the first school established there. It is said that both black and white leaders of the community met at the Polk Meeting House, the structure established by Taylor Polk as a church, school academy, and town meeting house. Spencer Polk was a Mason; the black and white Masons met together in the early days, and Spencer was highly visible at those sessions. Family members recall allegations that Spencer Polk rode with the vigilantes at Muddy Fork after the Civil War and helped to keep law and order in the vicinity. He told his children that he was the only "colored" man to sit on a jury in Howard County. That was during the 1880s; presumably he was called to sit as a juror on the Circuit Court at Nashville, the county seat.

Although no written sources have been found to support the oral accounts of black and white intimacies at Muddy Fork during the period from 1867 through 1900, close relationships between the races did exist in many instances in the South as a carryover from slavery. C. Vann Woodward argues that "there are a number of indications that segregation and ostracism were not so harsh and rigid in the early years as they became later." In fact, in some areas whites and blacks mingled in bars, saloons, and restaurants and used the same assembly halls and parks for gatherings, meetings, picnics, and ball games. Whites and blacks attended schools together to some degree, especially in rural areas, a practice that began with the establishment of Freedmen's Bureau schools, which made no distinctions of race and were free to all who desired an education.[27]

At the same time that practices promoting equality and integration of black and white life were in evidence, there came a tidal wave of racism that swept away all of the good intentions and reasonable social mores of those whites who were not opposed to contact between the races. Between 1873 and 1898, those who opposed such contact used their influence to repeal existing laws that protected the rights of blacks and passed new laws that upheld separation and exploitation. In addition, by establishing an ideology of social-Darwinism, so-called scholars in the field of biology, anthropology, sociology, and history flooded the plains of human thought with "the doctrine that the Anglo-Saxon race was superior to all other races."[28] The world of black and white soon became completely separated as though a darkened veil had suddenly lowered between them.

Spencer Polk lived, as it were, on neither side of the veil, but was somehow caught up in its folds, which permitted him, or rather forced upon him, conditional access to both worlds. Yet, although he existed in a world between his black and his white neighbors at Muddy Fork, he gained the respect of all. He was keenly interested in the political climate of his times. One source, Walter Westbrook, recalls seeing Spencer sitting on the porch of the Westbrook store at Nathan reading the newspaper.[29] Westbrook insisted that Polk was a Democrat, and he may very well have espoused that party for a time, but the surviving family members were staunch Abraham Lincoln Republicans who never once voted Democratic until John F. Kennedy ran for the presidency in 1960. Even though Spencer Polk thought of himself as more white than black, he expressed the hope that some day blacks and whites would no longer live under the burden of separation of the races.

After *Plessy* vs. *Ferguson* in 1896, which made separation of the races the law of the land, the precariousness of Polk's position as a black man intruding upon that white world became clearly evident by the personal tragedies of two of his sons. But in spite of the tightening restraints of separation and racism that reached even the remoteness of Muddy Fork after 1900, Spencer Polk remained optimistic and unembittered. His house retained its status as an oasis of Old South gentility in the ever widening desert of Jim Crowism. Even after Spencer's death in 1919 and after other black families had left Muddy Fork, the Spencer Polk house remained the place where travelers stopped to pass the time of day with Spencer's surviving son Arthur, who carried on the open-door, good-neighbor tradition of his father. Sometimes at night a rider would stop to sleep by the fire until morning. Often certain ones would come by and sit down to dine with the family. Or they would just stop by to get a drink of cool water from the huge well, or to rest in the shade of the mulberry tree.

Spencer Polk's death in 1919 was probably caused by the effects of diabetes. The family said he developed gangrene in the big toe of one foot and died from the infection. He was eighty-three years old and had been in poor health for several years. His wife Ellen had died two years before. One can only imagine the effects of Spencer's death on his children, grandchildren, and great-grandchildren, who had revered him as the patriarch of the family and the stabilizing force between the family and the rest of the community.

When he was dying, oral reports say, he gathered all of the family around his bed and instructed them to remain together and hold onto the land. Mrs. Maxwell recalled that relatives from distant places returned to Muddy Fork for his funeral, which was attended also by several white neighbors. After his death, Spencer's name became a kind of legend in Howard County. Everybody knew his name, and family members had only to say that they were Spencer Polk's descendants to get a friendly smile, a warm greeting, an opened door, or a kind favor.

6. One Seed Becomes a Singing Tree

The main themes of family legends handed down by the descendants of Spencer Polk centered around the Taylor Polk family and Spencer himself. The overriding ethos in the black Polk family was pride in the family bloodline that reached back, through Spencer, to Taylor Polk, a white man. The knowledge that Spencer's lineage placed him in one of America's leading white pioneer families was the substance that kept the legend alive. The Polk family, after all, had given the country a president, and that was something. To carry the name of Polk itself was considered an honor beyond all other honors that could be bestowed on black folk. For example, one descendant, writing about the oral history project that produced this work, pleaded with the author not to exploit the family heritage by "pulling the name Polk down into any black history."[1]

The awareness of their lineage was the seam that both held the black Polk family together and tore them asunder. The pride with which Spencer and his offspring wore the mantle of "high brow" ancestry was the substance on which they nurtured themselves through good times and lean. Their moral fiber was both strengthened and weakened by the Polk family influence. The name Polk was at once whispered solemnly over the cookstove and flung out in despair to the winds in the cornfield.

Every adage or piece of morality handed down by Spencer's sons and daughters always began with, "Now, Pa always said . . . ," meaning Spencer, of course. The tales sometimes included evasive but distinct references to "Old Man Taylor Polk." Very little information about other family members was given. Slavery was not generally a part of the legends, and their grandmother Sally was not. If one asked about either, the answers came with apologies and frustrated mumblings. Occasionally, caught up in the emotions of remembering, a family member would blurt out a long-kept secret about some event that had seemingly just come to mind.

Having inherited a legacy of slavery and a lineage of both African and European genetic material, Spencer Polk's children were heirs to a sociopsychological environment that was created more or less for them, not by them. And its influence derived not so much from their recognizably mixed ancestry as, more importantly, from the cultural heritage that determined their way of life.

Spencer Polk, like Taylor Polk before him, was the image of the family patriarch. He was revered and respected by every member as the head of the Polk household. At the same time, Spencer's wife Ellen and each of their ten children were independently unique personalities, even though their lives orbited around the central figure of Spencer.

In 1880 there were eleven members of Spencer Polk's household, as listed in Table 2. They included Spencer's and Ellen's six children, Spencer's nephew Franklin and his wife Jane, and a twelve-year-old hired girl. The family members are identified as both black and mulatto, which reflects the tendency of the nineteenth-century social-Darwinists to place human beings on a scale of gradation that not only separated the so-called racial groups,[2] but also made distinctions within the African-American family.

By 1900, Spencer and Ellen had four additional children and two grandchildren, as shown in Table 3. The two oldest sons, Douglass and Allen, had both left home, but with the additional children the Polk family was still large, with twelve members living in the household, representing three generations of the Polk clan. A glimpse at the lives of Ellen Polk and the second generation Polk children sheds a great deal of light on how the Polks interacted with each other within the family, how they interacted with their neighbors, and how their lives affected and were affected by the entire Muddy Fork community.

Ellen (1842-1917)

Ellen Polk (nee Murphy) was born in Kentucky in 1842. The census records give the date of her birth, and her tombstone at Muddy Fork

Table 2. Members of the Spencer Polk Household, 1880

Name	Race	Age	Relation/Occupation	Place of Birth
POLK, Spencer	Mu	48	/Farming	Arkansas
Ellen	Mu	35	Wife/Housekeeping	Kentucky
Douglass	Mu	20	Son/Attending school	Arkansas
Allen	B	20	Son/Attending school	Arkansas
Emma	Mu	10	Daughter/Attending school	Arkansas
Charley [Charlie]	Mu	7	Son/Attending school	Arkansas
Alice	Mu	5	Daughter	Arkansas
Benjamin	Mu	2	Son	Arkansas
Franklin	B	24	Nephew/Laborer	Arkansas
Jane	Mu	24	Wife of Franklin	Arkansas
Jane	Mu	12	Laborer	Arkansas

Source: U.S. Bureau of the Census, *Population Schedules for 1880*, seen on microfilm at the Arkansas History Commission, Little Rock.

bears also the date of her death. Ellen was a slave, and her family was no doubt brought into Arkansas by their owner, one Dick Murphy, who occupied a plantation in Sevier County near Lockesburg. Ellen's father was named Gideon Murphy, and her mother was Lyla.[3] Unlike most slaves and freedmen, the family continued to carry the name of their master after Emancipation. The family members were of mixed parentage, no doubt the offspring of Dick Murphy himself.

Ellen had three brothers, Reuben, Henry, and Daniel, and three sisters, Julia, Lively, and Arbella. Descendants of the family still live in Sevier County. Mrs. Daisy Cabean, the daughter of Lively Murphy Turrentine, lives in Lockesburg, and Taylor Wilson, the son of Arbella Murphy Wilson, lives on a farm near Lockesburg.

Ellen and Spencer were married in 1867, according to census data, and she became the mother of eight of Spencer's ten children (all but Douglass and Allen). In oral reports and photographs, Ellen is pictured as a rather slender woman with long black hair that hung below her hips. She is alleged to have had some Cherokee Indian lineage.

Along with her husband, Spencer, Ellen enjoyed a prominent position in the community. As midwife, she delivered many of the

Table 3. Members of the Spencer Polk Household, 1900

Name	Date of Birth	Marital Status	Age
POLK, John S.	June 1832	Married	67
Ellen	1842	Married	55
Emma	Sept. 1869	Single	33
Charles H.	Oct. 1872	Single	28
Alice	Jan. 1875	Single	25
Benjamin F.	Mar. 1878	Single	19
Mary Frances	Feb. 1881	Single	17
Chester A. A.	Mar. 1883	Single	14
Anna M.	May 1886	Single	14
James G. B.	Mar. 1889	Single	11
Hazel P.	Dec. 1895	Granddaughter	4
Lillian P.	Dec. 1896	Granddaughter	3

Source: U.S. Bureau of the Census, *Population Schedules of 1900,* seen on microfilm at the Arkansas History Commission, Little Rock.

neighbors' children, black as well as white. Mrs. Maxwell gave the following account of Ellen:

QUESTION: What kind of woman was Ellen Polk?

MAXWELL: Ellen Polk was a tall, light complected lady with long black hair. She used to come over to our house and she was the midwife to several of us.

QUESTION: She delivered some of you?

MAXWELL: Oh, yes! She delivered several of us. I believe the last time she came—that was Alice—or was it Georgia? I remember she and Alice came over there when Alice was born.[4]

The first Alice mentioned was Ellen's second daughter, born in 1875; the second Alice, the one Ellen delivered, was Mrs. Maxwell's sister, born in 1911. Mrs. Maxwell went on to point out that Ellen Polk was a very accommodating woman who always gave a willing hand to her neighbors. She was adept at many skills, including quiltmaking, sewing, and weaving homespun on the family loom.

In her last years, Ellen suffered poor health and took to her bed much of the time. The family nursed her and fussed over her, but when she got a splinter stuck in her hand at age seventy-five, she died from the infection, or "blood poisoning," the family said. Her youngest daughter, Annie, used to lament that "Ma just up and died from a splinter in her hand," as if no such insignificant thing as a splinter should have caused the death of an important person like her mother. Emma, the eldest daughter, became the female head of the household, which apparently continued to be run in the tradition that her mother had established.

The family placed a tall tombstone at Ellen's grave, and the inscription on it expresses their sentiment and love:

ELLEN
Wife of
SPENCER
POLK

Born
May 12, 1842
Died
Feb. 11, 1917

'Twas hard to
part with thee
But Thy will
O Lord be done

When Ellen died, her husband Spencer, five of her eight children, and two granddaughters were still occupying the house. Three of her four sons had preceded her in death.

Douglass (ca. 1860-1920)

Douglass was Spencer's oldest child. His name appears before Allen's on the census record, although no month of birth is given for either. Douglass was born before Emancipation, and the double s on his name suggests that the subject Spencer had in mind was Frederick Douglass, the black abolitionist, and not Stephen A. Douglas, the white orator and slavery compromiser. That he named his son for Frederick Douglass indicates the duality of Spencer's consciousness.

Several of his other sons were named for prominent whites, but naming his first-born after the great black antislavery orator probably reflected Spencer's dream of freedom from slavery.

Douglass Polk married Josephine Gibson in 1881.[5] They had two children, Essie Lela and Willie Douglass. The couple apparently left Muddy Fork in the late 1880s or early 1890s. They moved first to Butte, Montana, and later settled in or around Dallas, Texas. Douglass died in Belton, Texas, and his family migrated to Los Angeles, California, during the first decades of the twentieth century.[6] Douglass's daughter Essie returned to visit the family at Muddy Fork for the first time in 1942.

Allen (ca. 1860-?)

Allen Polk was always spoken of with sibling fondness by his half-brothers and half-sisters. Born out of wedlock to a slave woman on the Taylor Polk plantation in 1860, Allen is listed as a member of the Spencer Polk household on the 1880 census, but not on the 1900 census. Oral accounts indicate that he moved to Hot Springs in the 1890s, where he died a short time later. He never married, and consequently left no heirs. Before he left Muddy Fork he received a patent for 160 acres of land, dated July 1895. When Allen died, this land became a part of the Spencer Polk estate.[7]

Emma Jane (1869-1943)

Spencer's first child by Ellen Murphy was a daughter, Emma Jane, born in September of 1869. She was tall and straight as an arrow shaft, with straight black hair and piercing black eyes. A bout with infantile paralysis (polio) during her childhood left one of her legs slightly shorter than the other, and she walked with a decided limp. She always walked very fast, and the limp caused her to move in a kind of hop across the floor. When she stood still, however, she was as straight as a pin.

Emma was no doubt the apple of Spencer's eye, for he sent her off to school at Philander Smith College in Little Rock. A search through the records by the present registrar at Philander Smith did not yield any information to substantiate Emma's attendance there, but several oral sources insist that Emma did enroll there for a short while in the 1880s. At any rate, when Emma returned to Muddy Fork and began to teach school there, Spencer added the ell room to the house for her own private use. The room contained her "library" and served as a parlor for entertaining "white" company.[8]

Emma apparently enjoyed the privilege of white society at Muddy Fork. It is a part of the family legend that she and her sister Alice attended the parties and dances held in white homes, and that much entertainment of whites went on under Spencer's roof as well, particularly during the 1880s and 1890s. A familiar anecdote passed on by the Bullock family illustrates their attitudes toward the Polks. The story is that the Bullock men, William ("Bill"), Dock, and John, used to go over and hide in the chimney corner and listen to the conversations and party chatter that went on between Spencer's daughters and their white visitors. When the Bullock men tried to court Emma and Alice, they were coldly rebuffed, not only by the women but also by Spencer.[9]

In 1896, Emma gave birth to a daughter, Spencer and Ellen's second grandchild. Emma and her daughter remained in the household until around 1907, when Emma went to the Indian Territory in Oklahoma, where she married one J.R. Blackwell, according to Howard County marriage records.[10] She apparently did not remain with Blackwell very long, for on March 14, 1910, Ellen's brother Jimmy wrote to their sister Anna Mae ("Annie") from Atoka, Oklahoma: "Say tell Emma that Mr. Blackwell is pretty sick, he is not dangerous but he is in a pretty bad shape. The doctor said he has pneumonia but I don't think he has. I think he has just got a bad case of La grippe, but Emma certainly ought to wait on him. He is very weak. I don't think he would weigh over 100 lbs. He is looking awful bad."[11]

Emma must have returned to Muddy Fork shortly after her marriage, but it is not clear whether she had separated from Blackwell or was just visiting. From all indications, Emma, her daughter, and other family members continued to have ties with Blackwell, and it is possible that Emma went back to him for a while. She often spoke of having lived in Ft. Towsen, Oklahoma, and her daughter married an Indian man there in 1917.[12] But from around 1920 until her death in 1943, Emma never left Muddy Fork for any great length of time. In the 1930s she took her daughter, who had also returned to Muddy Fork shortly after her own marriage, and her daughter's son, and went to Portland, Oregon, where they "passed" for a while, but they soon returned to Muddy Fork.[13]

Emma's dream was to have the old log house at Muddy Fork all to herself, and after her brother Arthur's marriage in 1921 she constantly nagged him to take his dark-skinned wife and children and go elsewhere. At one point she demanded that her share of her father's land be separated from the rest. This was done, and she hired a white neighbor to erect a little log cabin for her a few yards north of the fork in the road, just above the original house. But she never occupied the cabin. Embittered by the presence of her brother's family under the same roof, she seldom smiled and never laughed. She seldom emerged from the south wing of the house, which she occupied with her daughter and grandson. She did not allow her brother's wife or children to venture beyond the entrance to the hall unless she invited one of them to do an errand for her, or unless her brother sent one of them to carry a message to her or her sister Frances, who lived in another small room on the south wing.

On occasions, the prominent white women in the community visited Emma, and so did her sisters and their families living away from Muddy Fork. When she died in 1943, she was laid out on a pine plank atop the four poster rope bed, and it was her brother's wife's family who sat up with the body all night until the doctor came and pronounced her dead. She is buried in the cemetery at Muddy Fork near the graves of Spencer and Ellen.

Charles H. (Charlie) (1872-ca.1900)

Charlie Polk was Spencer's oldest son by Ellen. Born in 1872, Charlie apparently began having neurological or mental disorders ("went crazy") sometime during his early adulthood. The story goes that his ailment was precipitated by a blow on the head by unnamed parties—according to some accounts, a white man or men. When he began to have what the family called "fits," he was kept locked up in the small room on the east side of the main south room. On occasions he would be brought out of the room and allowed fresh air. At those times he was tied up to the mulberry tree in the front yard.

Walter Westbrook recalled seeing Charlie tied to the tree and gave
the following details:

WESTBROOK: They had a boy named Jim. Did you know
that?
QUESTION: That got killed? Yes.
WESTBROOK: They had another boy that went wild or
crazy or use any term you want to.
QUESTION: Do you remember when Jimmy got killed?
WESTBROOK: [Ignoring the question about Jimmy and
continuing to speak about Charlie] Yeah. And this boy, now
they tied him out in the front yard to an oak tree with a swing
line where he couldn't get to the tree or fence or nothin'. He
was tied to the end of a rope just like you tie a dog. But the
boy lost his mind or something or other. He didn't live but
a year or two and died. They told you about him I guess.
QUESTION: Yes. That was my father's brother Charlie.
WESTBROOK: I've seen him tied out there to the oak tree
in the front yard with a limb swinging out. They tied him out
to the end of the limb . . . he was desperate, dangerous. They
were afraid of him. They had a special little room for him.[14]

The tree Charlie was tied to was a mulberry tree, but with that
exception Mr. Westbrook's details are the same as those passed along
in the family. The family, however, whispered that Charlie died from
the blow he received when he tried to crash a "white folks' party"
where his sisters were do-se-do-ing with the neighbors. He was sent
to the state mental hospital at Benton, where he was first refused
admittance because he was "colored," but later on, with the help
of those same neighbors who had hit him on the head, he was admitted to the hospital, where he died a short time later.

Mrs. Julia Polk Gilbert, the oldest daughter of Spencer's son Arthur, reported that she was given the details privately one day in
the cornfield by Charlie's sister Frances. Her version of the story says
that Charlie got half drunk one night and decided that if his sisters
could attend the party given by the neighbors, then he should be
allowed to attend, too. Certain white men, angered by his presence,
put him out, and an ensuing struggle resulted in Charlie's being hit

on the head with a stick of wood. He never regained his senses, and an autopsy performed on him when he died revealed a large growth on his brain as a result of the blow.[15]

Alice (1875-1953)

Spencer and Ellen's third child was Alice, born in 1875. Alice is remembered as a tall, slender woman with soft, grayish brown hair and warm blue eyes. Her hair was rather curly, not straight like her sister Emma's, but she nevertheless looked very "white." She produced Spencer and Ellen's first grandchild, a daughter born in 1895, just one year prior to the birth of Emma's daughter.

Somehow Alice managed to leave Muddy Fork between 1910 and 1920. She lived in Hot Springs and Nashville, where she worked as a domestic in prominent white households. During her later years she lived with her daughter's family in Austin, Texas. She visited the old place occasionally and seemed less bitter than her sister Emma. She would sit on the porch and talk with her brother and his family, and, unlike Emma, would visit in the room occupied by Arthur's wife and children. Alice died in Austin, Texas, in 1953.

Benjamin Franklin (Ben) (1878-1916)

Named for Taylor Polk's son Benjamin, who was named for Taylor's brother Benjamin, who was no doubt named for the gentleman from Philadelphia, Spencer Polk's son was called Ben, and he was a big, rugged, dark complexioned man with curly black hair. He was deeply loved by his brothers and sisters, for those who outlived him spoke of him often with reminiscent fondness. Before his death in 1916 from a bout with rheumatic fever, he was the backbone of labor on the Spencer Polk farm. He never married. His tombstone at Muddy Fork is exactly like that of his mother and father and stands next to theirs among the pine trees and honeysuckle vines in the cemetery.

Mary Frances (1881-1952)

Perhaps the most tragic figure of all of Spencer's children was Frances. Born in 1881, she was the third daughter and fourth child of Spencer and Ellen Polk. It is said that she was a very beautiful woman in her youth, but she fell in love with a "Negro" man named Tom Benson, and Spencer forbade the match. Benson's name appears in the 1900 census of Muddy Fork residents. Frances vowed that she would never look at another man, and she did not. Instead, she devoted her life to the care of her sisters and her brother Arthur. Small and brown, she worked like a man, ploughing the fields and gathering in the crops. She owned herds of cattle and hogs and droves of turkeys, guineas, and chickens. She tended the garden and chopped wood to keep the south end of the house warm in winter for the sake of her loved ones. She milked the cows, cooked, and put the food on the table for Emma and her family. Accompanying her brother Arthur to the fields each day, she worked with a passion that was punitive. Sometimes the tragedy of her lot caught up with her, and she would lament her fate, saying she was the "nigger," the slave, to her sisters and their offspring.

She loved her brother Arthur deeply, and truly sacrificed her own comfort and ease for his. When times were hard during the Depression years, she always prepared enough food in the big kitchen to stretch out the scant nourishment available in Arthur's end of the house.

She was more tolerant of her brother's children than was her sister Emma, but when Arthur married in 1921, Frances vowed never to speak to his dark-skinned wife, Mattie Bullock. The two women would hold "conversations," however, sending their messages and retorts by way of the children. "Now, you tell your mother . . . ," Frances would say, and her sister-in-law would respond in like fashion. The two women would also borrow snuff and other small items from each other, but they never spoke to each other outright.

Frances was one of the last to leave Muddy Fork. A mole on her face became malignant during the 1940s, and when the disease had destroyed half her face, she was taken to live with her sister Annie at Columbus, Arkansas. She died there in 1952, and her body was taken back to Muddy Fork for burial.

Chester A.A. (Arthur) (1883-1964)

Born in 1883 and named after the Scotch-Irish president Chester Alan Arthur, who gained prominence as a fighter for the rights of slaves and free blacks,[16] Spencer's eighth child and fifth son was called simply Arthur. Tall and straight like his father, Arthur was in contrast a very thin and frail man with jet black hair and hazel eyes. He attended school through the eighth grade and was regarded by his children as the smartest man that ever lived. His sister Annie said he should have been a college professor or a lawyer. It is evident from family tradition, oral reports, and other data, however, that Arthur spent more of his early days working on his father's farm than attending school. After 1900, it was he who made the trip to the county seat at Nashville twice a year to pay the taxes on the land and buy supplies for the farm. Original tax receipts on the land for 1909 and 1912 bear Arthur's signature.

That he walked in his father's shadow is also evident. Arthur apparently learned the blacksmith's art and carpentry from his father, among many other things. He shod his own horses and mules, made square nails, wove cane-bottomed chairs, hewed ax handles, split rails and shingles, and kept his farm tools sharpened on the stone wheel and vise that stood in front of the house. He raised a variety of crops, including cotton, corn, sorghum cane, potatoes, and watermelons. In addition, he knew how to gather herbs and barks for medicine, and on occasion he would gather ingredients and make a churn of spirit beverage. (For a description of this and other family activities, see Chapter 6.)

The Polks were one of the few families in the neighborhood who owned a sorghum mill. Arthur and his sister Frances made the sorghum syrup for most of the white families in the community. In the fall the sorghum mill became a community gathering place, where neighbors from far and near came around to watch the golden syrup form in the long pan. The real treat came when the first batch was ready, and Arthur permitted everybody to take a bucket lid and collect the fresh molasses to sop with the fingers or a peeled cane stalk.

Arthur was the only one of Spencer's sons, except for Douglass, who grew to manhood, married, and had children. Arthur's position as the only male living in the house was therefore unique. The story was told time and again that when Spencer was on his deathbed in 1919, he made Arthur promise to remain on the place and care for his sisters, all four of whom were still living in the house without husbands at the time. Arthur kept his promise, and the homestead remained as Spencer left it until 1921, when Arthur decided to marry.

Arthur chose for his bride Mattie Ann Bullock, the daughter of Peter Harrison "Bud" Bullock. Bud was the son of Leander Bullock, called "Mint," who was the slave of Blount Bullock. Mint, it is said, came straight from Africa, and the Polks referred to his son Bud as "that old African." The Bullocks, then, were never held in very high esteem by the Polks. For one thing, they were too dark in skin color to suit the sensibilities of the fair-skinned Polks. For another reason, Bud Bullock became the Polks' staunch enemy when he confiscated forty acres of land from the Polk estate around 1900. The records show that before 1909, Spencer owned 200 acres in Section 33, and Bud Bullock owned only forty acres in an adjacent tract. In 1909, the record shows that Polk's holdings had declined to only 80 acres in section 33, and Bullock's holdings had increased to 80 acres in that section.[17] It is said that from time to time when Spencer's land would go up for sale for delinquent taxes, everybody respected Spencer's rights and would not venture to buy the land, giving him a chance to recover it in the fall when the cotton was sold. Bullock, however, felt no such compunction to be neighborly, and when he saw a chance to acquire more land, he took it. The Polks never forgave him for his breach of friendship.

In spite of the enmity between the two families, Arthur began to be attentive to Mattie Ann Bullock when she was only twelve and he twenty-seven.[18] A bundle of love letters from Mattie was found among Arthur's possessions when he died in 1964. The letters were neatly packaged in a red leather case and tied with a faded blue string. The letters, twenty in all, were dated from August 28, 1918, through July 11, 1920.[19] They are signed almost always "Your loving friend, Mattie A. Bullock." Mattie was twenty in 1918.

The first letter in the series explains why the courtship was such a long, complicated one and why the two did not marry until she was twenty-three and he thirty-eight.

> Muddy Fork, Ark.
> Aug. 28, 1918
> Mr. Arthur Polk Dear loving friend. . . . I have been thinking over what we was talking about. I am willing to arrange for us to be alone. But you know my folks would not like it if they knew it and I do not know of any way to do it. . . . I have made up my mind for us to marry this fall. I know your

folks would not like it. If we could go somewhere else it would be better but you won't never talk of that very much.

from your loveing friend
Mattie A. Bullock

The second letter in the series indicates that Arthur had responded to her letter in writing.

Muddy Fork, Ark.
Oct. 5, 1918

Mr. Arthur Polk Dear loving friend I read your letter with much pleasure. Of course I expected your asking to beg pardon. And of course I was very surprised of what you done. And I know how come you to do it and know you did not mean any harm. I am not angry with you at all. I sure hate to hear of you being so dishearted. I wish I could help you but I do not expect I can. You ask me would I expect a present from you. I sure will.

In December of 1918 Mattie wrote again: "I have been thinking over your letter. . . . The way everything is now I can't hardly see no way for us to marry unless we do go away. I would not mind to do that very much. I want you to tell me just what your folks say about it. You wont never tell me a word they say. I think it is time for us to marry or hush talking about it one way or another." Clearly, between the August letter and the December letter, things had developed fairly rapidly in the courtship. In an undated letter that was probably written in the fall of 1918, she wrote: "Dear sweetheart, no one saw you attall. They haven't anyone said anything about you. . . . I love you dearer than I ever have loved you. I do not think it is any harme for us to love each other the way we are loving now but we must stop at this. I enjoy your loveing the two times we met all right. But we must stop at kissing." The letter was unsigned and folded into a tight wad. It is evident that Arthur pursued his bride-to-be passionately, for she stalled off any intimate relationship for some time. She begged him to understand her position and explained that she hated to refuse intimacy, but she had no choice because of the objections of both their families, which precluded any chance of marriage. He claimed his heart was broken, and plied her with gifts. Mattie later told her children that it was Arthur who bought her her first pair of shoes. And near the end of the courtship, he bought the trunk for her trousseau. The trunk was one of the main items of furniture in the north room. In an undated fragment of letter, Mattie wrote to Arthur: "Darling, if you can let me have the money to buy the trunk, I will buy it. You can bring the money over to the cotton patch tomorrow morning."

By January of 1919, Arthur had apparently approached Bud Bullock about marriage to his eldest daughter and had seemingly been rebuffed. Mattie wrote on January 14, 1919: "Dear loving friend, I received your letter and am somewhat surprised. I am sorry indeed that Papa talked to you like he did today. Dear one, I don't know what to do. . . . But I will tell you the truth. Papa was not talking about you. Of course I know it hurt you for him to talk that way to you. . . . I would like to talk with you about what Papa was talking to you about, for I know you would not tell anyone what I say." Whatever Bullock was talking about, it was enough to cause Arthur to tell Mattie that he would not visit her again. She ended the letter by saying that if Arthur would just meet her somewhere on Saturday, she would do anything to please him.

On February 10, 1919, Mattie wrote that she would accept Arthur's proposal of marriage, but that they must not say a word to anyone about it. She went on to inform him:

> I have talked with Mother about it and she do not like it and I know none of the others will either. So I cannot tell you what time we will get married. . . . It is like you said. We have not talked over our business. We need to talk and have some understanding about what we are going to do. We have as much right to talk as anybody else. Excuse bad writing. I do not feel well atall today.
>
> Your loving friend
Mattie A. Bullock
>
> P.S. I will never smoke tobacco again.

The romance continued throughout the summer of 1919. Arthur continued to press her for intimacy and/or marriage, and she demurred on both counts, evidently waiting until he gave some indication that he would take her away from Muddy Fork. By the summer of 1920, the last dated letter contains these lines: "I told you I would marry you and I mean to prove to you that I love you. Of course I cannot if you go back on what you said. Now Doll Baby, you write and tell me just what you are going to do. If we don't get marryed by Xmas I am going away. I don't think I will ever see you again."

The letters were all hand delivered by Mattie's younger brothers. In a short note to Arthur on one occasion, she warned him: "Do not give Hubert another letter to give to me. He gave it to Dee, and I didn't get it until yesterday. Dee had opened it." The Bullock family was large, and Mattie had three brothers besides Hubert and Dee, who no doubt served as letter carriers for her and her paramour.

The courtship continued through the fall of 1921. Mattie often mentioned in her letters that there was another man interested in her, Arthur's cousin Clay Murphy, Ellen Polk's nephew. Murphy was nearer Mattie's own age, and in later years often confessed his own attraction for Mattie. He always added, however, that she was the only woman his cousin Arthur ever looked at.

Finally, in the fall of 1921, Mattie became pregnant, and on a gray Monday morning, November 21, the couple traveled by buggy to Center Point, where they were joined in wedlock at the Methodist church, with a Reverend Storey performing the ceremony. When asked about the Bullock family's reaction to the turn of events, Mattie's sister, Mrs. Willie Bell Maxwell, replied, "Well, Ma was upset, but Papa didn't say anything much. You know, he always liked Arthur."[20]

The reaction of Arthur's sisters to his marriage was predictable. They never cared for their brother's wife and did not bother to conceal the fact. Arthur accepted his sisters' intolerance with patience. When he married his long-time sweetheart and took her to live in the north room of the house, his four dependent sisters were living in the south wing. In addition, one of his two nieces spent most of her time there along with her small son, who was born in 1917. Arthur was devoted to all of his family, serving as chief provider, protector, peacekeeper among the women, and the role model of morality, industriousness, character, and love for this truly extended family.

Exactly seven months after he and Mattie were married, their first child, a son named William Henry, was born. Nine other children followed in rapid succession, and although Arthur was the chief laborer on the farm, he took on a major share of the responsibility in the care of the children. He assisted his mother-in-law, Viney Bullock, and the doctor, when there was one, in the delivery of all of his ten children, carrying hot water from the kitchen stove to the big room in the small wrought iron kettle that is one of the heirlooms still owned by a family member. As the children grew up, he would gather them around the fireplace at night and wash their feet in a small "foot tub" before sending them to bed in their straw mattresses on the floor in the back of the room.

If there was anything Arthur loved more than his family, it was the land his father Spencer had left in his care. He and his household often went without food in order to take the little money from the cotton crop to pay the taxes on the 480 acres that made up the estate by 1920. He often took the children on long walks through the woods and over the hills, pointing out landmarkers, house places, and old grave sites. He taught them the names of all the trees and how to distinguish between the kinds of berries and wild fruits and nuts that were good to eat. He would make the children sit still and listen in solemn respect to the sounds of the whip-poor-will, bob white, and mourning dove. He tended every stalk of corn and cotton plant as if it was a living soul. His crops never yielded as much as they should have because he would not allow the rows to be thinned out properly. He could not bear to see the young, healthy plants cut down to wither in the sun.

Arthur left Muddy Fork only twice before he left for the last time. Around 1908 he went to Little Rock and stayed a short while with his uncle and aunt, George and Julia Clemens, who lived on Center Street. Then, in 1937, he moved his family to Center Point and tried to make it there for a short while. He gave up on the project, however, and after a few short months moved them all back to Muddy Fork. After he and Mattie moved to Nashville in 1952, he continued to return to the scene of his youth every chance he got. Whenever family members visited him in Nashville, a special trip to Muddy Fork was a routine event. Arthur would walk up and down the lane in front of the house, stand and talk about what used to be there, and poke around in the decaying remains of what had been the home. When his wife died in 1962, he asked the children to take him to Muddy Fork immediately after the funeral. He stood in front of the house site and remarked that this would be his last visit there. Two years later, in October 1964, Arthur Polk died. He is buried beside his wife in Sunset Gardens Cemetery at Nashville.

Anna Mae (Annie) (1886-1968)

Spencer's fourth and youngest daughter, Annie, was born in 1886. Like her sister Frances, Annie was small and short. Her complexion was fair, however, and her black hair was more curly than straight. Annie remained in the household until she was thirty-six years old. In 1922 she married Floyd Johnson of Washington, Arkansas. Johnson was a widower, also thirty-six years old, and he had a small son Glenn by his first marriage. Annie bore one child by Johnson, but the child died at birth. Annie moved to Columbus, Arkansas, where she lived with her husband and stepson until Johnson's death in 1963. After Johnson's death she went to Austin, Texas, to live with her niece.

During the years she lived at Columbus, Annie visited the home at Muddy Fork often. Johnson was a rather prosperous cattle farmer, and he always had an automobile in which to travel, so Annie was able to return to the old home place regularly. She always came bearing gifts of foodstuffs for her brother and his family. The main feature of her summer visits was a lemonade ritual in which all of the family participated, and it was one of the few occasions when Emma and her offspring interacted informally with Arthur's wife and children. On the way to Muddy Fork, Annie and Johnson would stop at the ice house in Nashville and buy a large block of ice. They would also bring sugar and lemons, and upon their arrival a huge churn of lemonade would be prepared, much to the delight of young and old alike, for ice-cold lemonade was a rare treat. The churn would be set up on the front porch, and Annie would invite everybody to come around and partake of the cooling summer drink.

Annie was a compassionate woman. She could afford to be, of course, since she was far removed from the everyday struggles of the overly large extended family. But she always tried to help Arthur's family as much as she could. She helped Arthur pay the yearly taxes, and she provided both food and clothing for his children.

As the children grew up, Annie took at least a half-dozen of them, one at a time, to live with her during the summer months. She would take the children to her farm at Columbus and "fatten them up" on ham and eggs, milk and butter, chicken and turkey, which she and her husband produced in abundance. She was always making cakes, cookies, and pies during the time when she had the children in her care.

Annie was the only one of the Polk family who would talk extensively about slavery. She had a passion for politics and history and would talk incessantly to anyone who would listen—about Abraham Lincoln, Frederick Douglass, and Marcus Garvey, whom she called a devil for wanting to take the "colored" people back to Africa. She read Zane Grey novels, which came out as serials in the local paper, and she would go into a "tizzy" over how the Indians massacred the good white people traveling west. When she visited Muddy Fork, she and her brother Arthur always discussed current political events and compared what was going on with what went on when Bryan ran for president or when Grover Cleveland had the country in tow. They would talk long hours about the immediate ancestors, the Polks and the Murphys, rattling off names that reached all the way back into Tennessee and Kentucky.

When her husband died in 1963 and she was preparing to go to Texas with her niece, Annie stood on Arthur's porch in Nashville and wept, while he stood tight-lipped, hands hanging loose. It was as if they knew this was the last link breaking. They never again saw each other alive. Annie returned to Arkansas to attend Arthur's funeral in 1964. She stood over his grave crying, "Oh, he was so smart. Pa never should have kept him at Muddy Fork. . . . he had the most beautiful voice when he recited poetry."

In November 1966 Annie wrote to the author from Austin, Texas. Her letter reveals at once her love of family, people, and politics, and her keen sense of history, a characteristic she shared with Arthur. Her letter bore three different dates, the first, November 10:

I would have loved to went to Cousin Hardy and Evelena's funerals, but as usual it wasn't convenient for me to go. Some people dont care to go anywhere, but I do. What do you think about the election? Wasn't you glad Winthrop Rockefeller beat

Jim Johnson and is the Governor of Arkansas. So glad Nelson Rockefeller was elected. I got a letter from Cousin Mattie [Sanders] in Nashville and she said she would rather vote for a democrat, but she couldn't support Jim Johnson. I wish there could be some way to put Axhandle [Lester] Maddox in his place. . . . I don't like [Stokely Carmichael] and his talk. It is sort of treasonable to talk about black power. He ought not to try to divide white and black people any more than they already are. . . .

Friday, Nov. 11th
Armistice Day in 1915 [sic]. I remember it so well. Arthur your Papa got his second call card to the army that day. It [armistice] was all that saved him from going to France. . . .

Sat. Nov. 12th
Glenn sent me a telegram and I understood that he is elected Associate Judge of the Circuit Court. I think he will make a good judge. . . . What do you think about President Johnson and the war? It must be impossible to win a victory there, but how to get out, to turn it loose? Are you getting your Gospel Advocate? I hope you are and that you like it. I am doing fine with my Bible Correspondence Course. Make 100 every time. I am staying up fairly well by paying out 12 dollars a month for medicine.[21]

She ended the long, detailed letter with, "Much love to you all, Your Aunt Annie." She was eighty years old when she wrote, and two years later, in 1968, she died. She is buried in Austin, Texas.[22]

James G.B. (Jimmy) (1889-1910)

The darling of Spencer's family, the youngest child, was a son called Jimmy. It has not been discovered what the initials "G.B." in his name stood for. Two letters he received in 1908 were addressed to James K. Polk. The census record of 1910, however, lists James G.B., and it is assumed that that was his official name and that he was not named for President Polk, even though the census takers were not always correct in what they set down, nor were black Americans always completely candid in what they reported to strange whites who came around seeking personal information.

Handsome and dashing and very proud of his white ancestry, Jimmy Polk was to be no seedy ploughboy. Born in 1889, this youngest son of Spencer and Ellen was a very brilliant young man, and the family wanted him to be a scholar. His sister Emma wrote to him from Oklahoma in 1907, "Well, Jim, if you have got off to school, study hard and try your best to make up for all the time you lost. You have the ability, and you can catch up if you will try. I would like to see you with your new suit on."[23] Jimmy never "got off" to school, however. He attended the school at Muddy Fork intermittently and was considered an outstanding student. The family wanted him to go to Philander Smith College in Little Rock and be a great man. But Jimmy liked fiddling and girls and parties and dancing. He also liked adventure and traveling and hunting and guns.

James Polk's short but intriguing history can be traced from a series of letters and other documents found in a small trunk which belonged to him. The letters were written between September 1907 and May 10, 1910. Among them were both letters he wrote and letters he received from family members and friends. During this four-year period, Jimmy received correspondence from four young women: Florence Ferguson and Lee Nora Wesson of Center Point, Oshie Berryman of "the Gap" (Caddo Gap), and Ophelia Walton of Bingen. The bulk of the letters are from Miss Walton, and the earliest examples are postmarked Reine and Nashville, Arkansas. Later, in 1908, Miss Walton apparently enrolled at Philander Smith College, for most of the letters after 1908 are from the capital city.

Jimmy's fondness for girls and theirs for him are evident from the contents of these letters. Miss Walton wrote long, ardent letters, and although she often questioned his loyalty to her, she continued to write to him up to March 1910, when Jimmy left Muddy Fork for the last time. By then Miss Walton had completed her courses at Philander Smith and had returned to southwestern Arkansas. Her 1910 letters are postmarked Highland, Arkansas.

The letters Jimmy received from Ophelia Walton shed a great deal of light on his personality and provide insight into the kind of person he was. From Philander Smith College in 1908, she admonished him, "Have you stopped being bad yet? I think I am getting better, I'm trying and I hope you will do so too, for I don't like bad and lazy people, for I am not."[24] For Ophelia, being good, as opposed to being bad, meant going to preaching and picnics and, above all, making something of oneself by going to school. These are the activities she talked about at length in her letters. Jimmy, however, refused to go to school for any great length of time, but liked to travel instead. In the same letter, Ophelia mentioned Jimmy's having made a trip to Dallas, Texas, and elsewhere. "I was glad to hear of your having a nice time on your vacation days. Why didn't you stay? I think I would like very much to see Dallas. Why didn't you come through Little Rock when you went out yonder? How do you like out there?"[25]

She often chided him about not taking the opportunity to go to school. In most of her letters she asked him about his school attendance. On December 1, 1908, she wrote from Little Rock, "James, if you don't go to school after Xmas, I think I shall stop corresponding with you for sure this time because I don't believe you want to be anything extra." And on April 10, 1909, she wrote again, "I told you if you didn't go to school I was going to stop writing you, didn't I? And I meant it, for you know I don't joke much. You could have made better grades than I did and I am just going on if I am low, for the longer I stay out of school, the less I'll know, and you too."

It appears, however, that Jimmy was a restless young man who liked to travel rather than sit in a classroom. It also appears that the opportunity to travel was much greater for Jimmy Polk than one would have thought possible for blacks living in such an isolated area in the early 1900s. Miss Walton's allusions to "out yonder" and "out there" no doubt had reference to Jimmy's trip to Oklahoma in 1908, when he went to live with his sister Emma's husband, J.R. Blackwell.

Miss Walton's letters also indicate that she was truly swept off her feet by this restless young man. Although she threatened many times to break off the relationship, she never did, and she continued to write to him often up to a few months before his death. He sent her gifts and greeting cards, and he even proposed marriage. She was inclined to accept his offer but reminded him that engagements by mail were "unlucky."

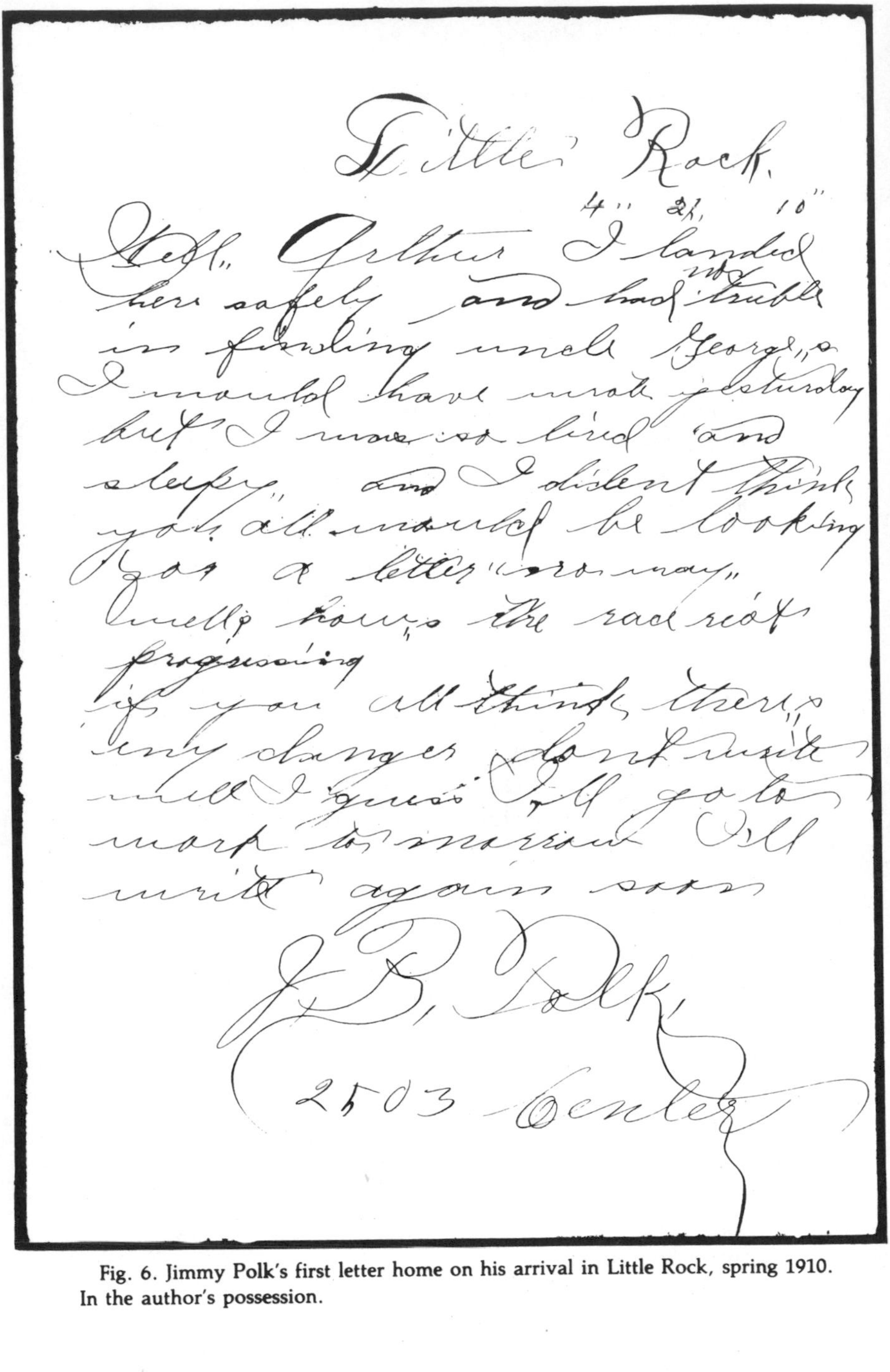

Fig. 6. Jimmy Polk's first letter home on his arrival in Little Rock, spring 1910. In the author's possession.

Other letters in the trunk are mostly from family members. The frequency and content of the letters from his brother Arthur, his sisters, and cousins suggest strong family ties. The family members often sent Jimmy money in amounts of two and five dollars. In fact, almost every letter mentioned the enclosure of a few dollars to help him out. The letters also expressed unusual sibling love and a deep concern for the safety, well-being, and protection of Spencer Polk's youngest son.

Jimmy's death resulted from some kind of trouble with whites in the Muddy Fork community. Nobody living who was there at the time will give specific details about what really happened. But from oral reports, from Jimmy's letters, and from a newspaper account of the incident, the story can be pieced together with some degree of accuracy.

The trouble began during the early part of 1910. Jimmy apparently left Muddy Fork in March and went to Atoka, Oklahoma. A letter to his sister Annie from Atoka dated March 12 indicates that he left home around that time. In February Jimmy had received a letter from Lyon Healy Instruments of Chicago telling him that the company was in receipt of his inquiry about ordering a fine violin. The letter is addressed to Jimmy at Muddy Fork. It appears, then, that Jimmy left home between the time he wrote about the violin in February and March 12, the date of his letter to Annie.

The letters also indicate that Jimmy left home to escape some difficulty he was having with unidentified white persons. His sister Alice wrote to him in Oklahoma, and a fragment of the letter bears this note on the subject:

> . . . on oath I mean the man that just started the tale. So you see there was no use of your running off at all.
>
> Ma is sending you $5.00. When you get it, the best thing you can do is come home. . . . We are very uneasy about you.[26]

In the same letter, Alice mentioned Mr. Blackwell's illness and offered to come out and stay with Jimmy and Blackwell until they were both well. Evidently this letter was written shortly after the time Jimmy wrote of Blackwell's illness in March 1910.

On April 17, Jimmy wrote his brother Arthur from Little Rock, where he had apparently gone instead of returning home.

Well, Arthur, I landed here safely and had no trouble in finding Uncle George's. I would have wrote yesterday but I was so tired and sleepy and I didn't think you all would be looking for a letter no way.

Well, how's the race riot progressing? If you all think there's any danger, don't write. Well I guess I'll go to work tomorrow. I'll write again soon.

J. B. Polk
2503 Center

A month later, on May 20, Jimmy wrote to Arthur:

I received your letter yesterday and was glad to get those $2.00 as I was in need of a slicker. I went right into town and bought me one. Because where I work a man has to tend to his work if it's raining down pitch forks!

I will draw a $30.00 check the last of this month and return some of your skullie! I certainly wish you could work here where I am. This is the easiest money I ever made. I am working at night. I am on dutie 11 hours but only work about 6 and sleep in the coaches the other 5. We get 18 cts. an hour. . . .

P.S. If you can, blow both my horns and see what those fire eaters will say.

On May 18, Arthur wrote to Jimmy in Little Rock:

Jim, Pa didn't get off Monday as I thought he would, but I know we are going today. And my other letter is sealed up so I am writing you another one.

Jim, if you get these letters write me at once. I am sending you a little stuff [money] in each one of them. Well, I ain't got time to write much. Now, don't forget to answer as soon as possible.

Jim, I have thought of a little stunt that I think you can work on those people here. You send two or three addressed envelopes. Get small ones and put them in a Government envelope and send them to me. I think I can locate Willie and I'll send them to him and he can send them to me. And those devils will think it's you sure.

References in the letters to Jimmy's having run away, to a "race riot," "fire eaters," "those people here," and "those devils" suggest that there was a racial incident involving Jimmy and certain whites at Muddy Fork during the time preceding his departure from home in March. The young man had surely not committed a serious crime, or that would have been mentioned in the papers, which at that time reported the least incidence of fighting, family squabbling, or unsocial behavior among blacks. The evidence of racial conflict involving Jimmy is corroborated by oral testimony, given below.

While Jimmy was in Little Rock, he worked at the Rock Island Railroad station. Train schedules dated 1910 and found in the trunk support this fact, and Jimmy wrote to his family about his job. A letter to his sister Emma dated April 30, 1910, gives the following information.

> This leaves me feeling fine. Hope Pa will get well soon. Tell him I'll send him a jug of good whiskey soon as pay day.
>
> I'm working at the Rock Island depot getting $54.00 per month. I don't much like the work but it's sure pay.
>
> I guess everybody wonders where I escaped to. I haven't very much time to go to church and be among the young people, but since I got a steady job, the gals all try to take me anyhow. I reckon I'll have to take me one of them to get the others to quit develing me.

On May 8, he wrote Alice, "I have been working almost every day since I came, but I just began working at the depot on the 27th of last month. I have a very easy job. I don't have any hard work at all. I'm cleaning cars." In a letter shortly after the one above, he mentioned that the work had grown particularly hard for "someone raised the way I was," but vowed to stick it out until summer.[27]

The family's constant reminders that they wanted him to come home no doubt influenced Jimmy's decision to leave Little Rock. A fragment of an undated letter from his brother Arthur reassures Jimmy of the family's concern: "Jim, if you come home any ways soon if you walk, let me know the way and I'll meet you up a piece." So, on a hot summer day near the end of June 1910, Jimmy Polk started for home. He had his small trunk with him, apparently intending to stay. He didn't walk, however, but boarded the train in

Little Rock. When the train stopped in Glenwood, Jimmy got off, and when he tried to get back on, the conductor refused to let him board. According to oral reports, Jimmy had words with the conductor. Perhaps Jimmy drew a gun on the man. He did have a gun in his possession, for it was one of the items kept for years in his trunk in the small room on the south wing of the house. What really happened will probably never be known, but sources say that Jimmy left Glenwood walking. He walked to Caddo Gap, where the family of Bud Bullock's wife lived. There he gave an account of what had happened. He was urged to stay at Caddo Gap until things quieted down, but, determined to return to Muddy Fork, Jimmy acquired a horse and set out for home. Somewhere in the woods between Glenwood and Muddy Fork, he was accosted by a group of white men and shot down. His body was left to rot in the leaves.[28]

The *Nashville News* carried this account of the incident on July 2, 1910:

JIM POLK KILLED

By Officers at Caddo Gap
Tuesday Night
Was Resisting Arrest
After Difficulty With a White Man
Was son of Spencer Polk
of Muddy Fork

News reached this city last Wednesday of the killing of Jim Polk, colored, at Caddo Gap by officers, while Polk was resisting arrest.

The negro had trouble with an engineer on the Gurdon and Fort Smith road, and when officers went to arrest him he showed fight, with the result that he was shot to death.

The oral reports differ markedly from the account carried in the newspaper. The story handed down in the family was that Jimmy had words with the conductor, who refused to let him board the train. In one of his letters, Jimmy had written that the railroad company was going to issue passes to all employees and that he intended to get one to go to California to see the Jack Johnson fight.[29] Perhaps he had a pass when he boarded the train in Little Rock and it was not accepted by the conductor when Jimmy tried to get back on in Glenwood. Perhaps Jimmy was wearing a gun. Jimmy loved guns, and he and his brother Arthur talked about guns in their letters. They discussed their marksmanship and sent each other pictures of the latest models of pistols available at the mail-order houses. Of course, Jimmy was a hunter and a trapper, and the ownership of a gun was considered a symbol of manhood. In one of his letters to Arthur shortly before his return, Jimmy mentioned buying guns for both himself and his older brother. He wrote in his last letter, dated May 20, 1910: "Say, have you got you that Savage Automatic yet? If you haven't, I can get you one if you want me to. I'm going to get me one pretty soon."[30]

So, with his Savage Automatic and a trunk full of love letters, valentines, and other brightly colored greeting and post cards, along with his clothes, Jimmy Polk boarded the train at Little Rock on his way to Howard County and home to Muddy Fork. Or maybe he was on his way to see Jack Johnson defend his heavyweight title in Reno, Nevada, on July 4, 1910. Although his intended destination may never be truly known, it is known that his trip ended in death in the deep woods somewhere south of Glenwood, where the train stopped and Jimmy got off or was put off.

In a rare moment when she talked of such things, Frances related the story to family members. She recalled that a certain white man, a friend of the family, came and told Spencer about what had happened and where to find the body of his youngest child. Spencer, Arthur, and Frances hitched up the wagon and rode to the scene. According to Frances, flies had attacked the body and the remains were too decomposed to move. The decision was made to bury Jimmy on the spot.[31] The trunk and gun were later recovered, the latter perhaps from the sheriff.

Jimmy's family contend that he was not allowed to get back on the train because he was a "Negro," and in those days blacks were not allowed to get off the train in small places like Glenwood. Others add that the trouble started over Jimmy's ticket, or pass, whichever he had. In any case, it appears that Jimmy's trouble started with the train conductor. Apparently the sheriff was notified of the trouble, and a group of white men gathered to look for Jimmy. The family was told that Jimmy had threatened the conductor with a gun. That he was hunted down and killed for an altercation with the train conductor was not an acceptable explanation for the family. One family member explained: "Jimmy was killed because he was brilliant and talented and poor whites picked on him and he went there [to Oklahoma and Little Rock] to get away from them. He had a gun and being colored, that was an excuse for murder in the view of poor whites at that time. He was young and restless and the whole incident was tragic."[32] What is particularly tragic is that Jimmy Polk was the victim of the racial attitudes that prevailed at the time—attitudes that meant death and destruction to a black male who dared to be brilliant and handsome at the same time he was dashing and restless. Jimmy didn't stay in his place.

During the period from 1900 to 1920, racial conflict, riots, and lynchings were rampant throughout the South and even in some parts of the North. Major riots occurred in Statesboro and Atlanta, Georgia, in 1904 and 1906, respectively, and in Springfield, Illinois, in 1904 and again in 1908.[33] Howard County, Arkansas, had had a major race riot in 1883,[34] and lynchings, beatings, and arrests of blacks were frequently reported in the state's newspapers.

In the year Jimmy Polk was killed, several similar incidents occurred in and near southwestern Arkansas. The Nashville News reported on January 22, 1910, that two blacks had been publicly hanged at Osceola before a crowd of 3,000. The two men had allegedly murdered a white couple on a boat the previous month. On February 5 a black man was shot in Hope while he was in the custody of the sheriff. He was accused of insulting a white woman he was working for. The situation had gotten so bad that the governor had instructed the sheriff to send for the militia to guard the man.[35] On March 8 of that same year, the Nashville News carried a story of the lynching of a black man in Dallas, Texas. Closer to home, on May 18, 1910, the News reported that a black man was lynched at Ashdown, and eight blacks were killed by a white mob in the vicinity of Palestine, Texas. On September 27, 1910, the same paper carried a story of the lynching of a white man and his two sons near Dumas, Arkansas. The white man was described as a complete "degenerate" because he had fathered two sons by a black woman and was trying to protect them. The perpetrators of the lynching were the sheriff and his posse, who had gone to the white man's home to arrest the two "mulatto" sons. All were brutally killed.

In reading the newspaper accounts, one can get the feel of the general animosity toward blacks that prevailed at the time. Willis D. Weatherford and Charles S. Johnson point out that one of the causes of racial antagonisms is "personal and group interest," and involves "significant group fear and loss of status, of loss of prestige, of loss of security, or all three." Weatherford and Johnson further explain how social status influences racial feelings: "The most bitter antagonisms manifested toward the Negro are shown most frequently by those elements of the white population nearest to the Negro in status. Racial antipathies are by no means as common between Negroes and socially secure Whites as between Negroes and Whites who are precariously situated socially. It is the question of status that explains much of the vehemence about 'keeping the Negro in his place,' and makes understandable the meaning to this class of a 'too smart nigger.' " As the progress of whites in a community deteriorates, racial antagonisms are heightened, and if blacks in that same community appear to be prospering, "resentment of the dominant group, particularly where the margin of dominance is shallow, may cause quite trivial incidents, and even suppositions, to burst forth suddenly and with unexplained violence."[36]

The inhabitants of Muddy Fork existed in a somewhat egalitarian society before 1900, but after *Plessy* vs. *Ferguson* the milk of human kindness from which whites and blacks drew common nurture began to dry up. Before 1900 the Polks in particular enjoyed a common status with the white community, and in terms of education, property, and social standing, Spencer Polk and his family were even superior to most of their neighbors. But the respect and good will that the family enjoyed were more in proportion to how they behaved than to who they were or what they owned. This was especially true for the male members of the family. The *News* referred to Spencer Polk as "one of the finest colored men in this part of the country." But Spencer's good character was measured in terms of his humility toward the mores established by the white community. Walter Westbrook, for example, reported that the Polk family stood up and waited on him while he sat at the table and dined alone. This kind of obeisance was not necessarily practiced in the Polk home before 1900, nor was it practiced entirely at a later period, when whites and blacks are known to have dined together in each other's homes. After Jimmy's death, an air of controlled tension was always present when whites were in the Polk home, and vice versa.

Thus the Polks were tolerated, respected, and admired—as long as they stayed in their place. "Their place" was to exhibit an attitude of humbleness at all times and to cater to the needs and desires of the white community. Jimmy Polk was a young man whose outward appearance and behavior reflected the immediate economic and social status into which he was born. He bore an air of arrogance and superiority, not only toward other blacks but also toward poorer whites.

Today, family members wonder why Spencer Polk did not pursue justice in the case of his son's death, which, if not outright murder, was certainly committed under questionable circumstances. The people who killed him knew who he was and, according to oral report, the man who came and informed the family of Jimmy's death was a member of the lynching party. The newspaper article noted that Polk "showed fight." That is hardly the term customarily used to indicate that a black man had pulled a gun or otherwise threatened the life or well-being of a white person. A few years later one of Bud Bullock's sons did indeed pull a gun on a white man and threatened to blow the man's brains out for withholding his wages. The man paid up and swore out a warrant for Bullock's arrest. Bullock got away with a fine, and there were no other repercussions from the incident.[37]

Jim Polk, unlike the Bullock man, was an "uppity nigger." He carried himself with a superior air and apparently disregarded the established mores that controlled the social and sexual interactions between blacks and whites in the community. For his indiscretions, he paid the ultimate price. And his father, Spencer Polk, having lived thirty years as a slave, had surely learned not to question the stain of man's inhumanity on the "quality of mercy" in an unjust land.

The Spencer Polk family, ca. 1900. Seated: John Spencer Polk and his wife Ellen; standing, L-R: Emma and her daughter Lillian, Arthur, Ben, Alice, Alice's daughter Pearl, Frances, and Annie.

John Spencer Polk (1833-1919) from a daguerreotype, ca. 1865.

The Spencer Polk house and family, ca. 1910. L-R: Ben, Arthur, Lillian, Pearl, Emma, Frances, Annie, Ellen, and Spencer.

Family members pose ca. 1910 with the column of cedars and log animal shelters in the background. The horses and mules are included as the family's show of wealth.

Alice Polk, dressed for school, ca. 1885.

Frances Polk, posed with a dining room chair.

Muddy Fork School group, ca. 1908. L-R, first row: Minnie Thompson, Pelly Dee Bullock, John Wesley Bullock, and Mattie Ann Bullock: second row: Annie Polk, Pearl Polk, Lillian Polk, and Mamie Thompson; third row: Arthur Polk, Jimmy Polk, and Oliver Thompson; fourth row: Hardy Murphy, the teacher. The Thompson children were the offspring of Eliza Willis Thompson and, allegedly, Allen Polk.

Mattie and Arthur Polk on their wedding day in November 1921. She was twenty-three, he was thirty-eight.

Arthur and Mattie Polk's first eight children, 1936. L-R: Cindy, Ruth (the author), Marjorie, Herbert, Julia, Ray, Dempsey, and Henry.

Above: the Spencer Polk house in 1936. Deterioration is evident. The ell room has been torn away and the shingles have been replaced by zinc roofing. Below: Arthur Polk with five of his ten children. L-R, seated: Ruth Patterson, Arthur, and Cindy Howell; standing: Julia Gilbert, Herbert Polk, and Marjorie Bland.

Above left: Louisa (Lou) Polk, oldest child of Peter Polk by his first wife, Cynthia. Above right: Mattie Polk, daughter of Peter Polk and his third wife, Sally Johnson. Below: Alonzo (Lonnie) Polk, son of Peter Polk and Sally Johnson, with his family. L-R, seated: Lucy Murphy Polk, Eva, and Alonzo; standing: Annie and Odell.

The author examines the tombstone of her grandfather, John Spencer Polk. In the background are the tombstones of Spencer's wife Ellen and their son Ben.

Artifacts from the Spencer Polk household. Clockwise from top: Jimmy Polk's trunk, a game board, a crochet needle, a carpenter's level, quilting cards, and a stoneware water jar.

Above left: archeologist Skip Stewart-Abernathy shows the author a stoneware sherd from an auger hole during the archeological survey of the Polk house site in December 1979. Above right: the south chimney, still standing a few months before the archeological survey. Below: one of the hand-hewn foundation logs, intact when the survey was conducted.

7. African Survivals and Scottish Airs

Traditions and folk customs in the Spencer Polk family represent a blending of cultures from Africa and Europe. The Scotch-Irish influence on the black Polks was demonstrated in many of their beliefs and customs, and it can be logically assumed that those traditions and folkways that cannot be shown to have had a European origin must have originated among the slave population or the Cherokee Indian people. Except for Spencer's and his brothers' early years with their mother Sally, there was little or no continued or widespread contact between the Polk slaves and the Cherokees. Moreover, there is no evidence in the oral history that the slave Sally passed on any Cherokee cultural traits to her offspring. Consequently, it seems likely that cultural elements in the family that cannot be accounted for by examining European culture derived from West African culture.

Elements of African culture were no doubt handed down from the several slaves that Taylor Polk owned from approximately 1835 to the end of the Civil War. There were also other slaves in southwestern Arkansas, some of whom may have been late arrivals from the west coast of Africa. Although the slave trade had been officially abolished in 1808, thousands of contraband slaves fresh from Africa continued to be brought into the lower colonies and newly settled states in the South up to the Civil War, as the opening of new lands increased the demand for slave labor. Even as southerners clamored for the reopening of the slave trade, newly imported Africans could be readily purchased in the markets of Florida, Texas, Louisiana, Mississippi, and Tennessee. As close to Arkansas as Memphis, a large number of Africans were available for purchase

as slaves during this period.[1] It is highly likely that some of these
new arrivals were brought into Arkansas, and there transmitted and
kept alive the culture of the homeland.

Cultural anthropologists such as Melville J. Herskovits and Roger
Bastide have clearly demonstrated cultural survivals among
Americans of African descent,[2] and there are many other attributes
of Afro-American culture that remain unexplainable unless one examines the history and cultures of West Africa. That some significant features of African culture survived among the slaves in
southwestern Arkansas, then, is not a far-fetched notion. More and
more scholars in the fields of anthropology, sociology, and archeology are making discoveries and drawing conclusions that show
the African influence on American culture. We know now that such
foodstuffs as watermelons, blackeyed peas, okra, gourds, and rice
were brought into the South with the African slaves. The produc-
tion, preparation, and use of these products were carried out by the
slaves, who were already familiar with and skilled in their use.[3]
Often the tools and utensils used in growing and preparing the products were made by the Africans. Moreover, the Africans' "ingenuity" in making use of natural materials on hand was no doubt given
free rein on the plantation.[4] The arts of basketry, quilt-making, and
pottery molding, and rice culture are just a few examples of how
the indigenous African ways of doing things were transplanted and
adapted to the New World culture. For example, it is evident that
"on the American plantation basketry was presented [by the
Africans] in purer form than most other crafts. . . . Adults taught
the art to their children exactly as it had been taught to them, so
that the method continued without interruption. . . . The making
of mats, fly whisks, brooms, and baskets remained unchanged."[5]
Like basketry, other cultural retentions were handed down in a more
or less pure form. The cultural traditions in the Spencer Polk family
reflect many elements that were just as surely African in origin as
others were unquestionably European.

It has already been pointed out that the Spencer Polk family was
an extended family, a traditional African family organization, as opposed to the nuclear family which is more evident among European
cultures. While the white Polks were a seemingly close-knit clan,
there is no evidence that the Taylor Polk household contained more
than one family of parents and children. Spencer's own connection

with the household was that of servant. It is evident from the research that the first Taylor Polk came into Arkansas with his family and set up a home, and that when his sons became adults, they established their own separate homesteads in the same vicinity.[6]

Spencer Polk's household, in contrast, from the earliest records up to the time the home was dissolved, contained two or more families at all times, including brothers and sisters, mothers and fathers, nieces, nephew, aunts, uncles, cousins, and grandparents. The house and its surroundings were structured in such a way as to accommodate multiple-family occupancy. When there were additions to the family, the house was expanded to accommodate them. These expansions to the original structure occurred at least three times: between 1870 and 1890 a hall and three additional rooms were added to the original one-room log structure; between 1890 and 1910 an ell room was added to the two rooms on the south wing; and in 1934 a second kitchen was added to the north wing—all in the African tradition of providing each woman in the household with her own living and cooking quarters.

While the organization of the family was distinctly along the lines of the African extended family, the everyday living practices and beliefs of the Polk family, as recalled by the present generation, were paradoxically European, no doubt derived from close association with the Scotch-Irish Polks. Moreover, it is clear that the black Polks adhered to the acceptable standard of assimilation into Euro-American culture imposed upon the slaves and descendants of slaves.

The black Polks took pride in the notion that they were ideologically far removed from any "taint" of African heritage. Their values were based upon the often-quoted homespun logic of "Poor Richard" and his almanac, along with the little green *Ladies Birthday Almanac*, which can be picked up at the Nashville Drug Store even to this day. The Polks lived by the Franklin adage of "Early to bed and early to rise, makes a man healthy, wealthy, and wise." Consequently, they never complained about working from "can to can't." They always believed that "cleanliness was next to godliness," if not a step ahead, and they kept the floors of the old log house spotless by scrubbing them with shuck mops and sand. The shuck mops were made by taking dry corn shucks that had been left intact after removing the corn ear, wedging the shucks into round holes that had been bored into a thick plank about sixteen inches long and

ten inches wide, and attaching a handle to the plank. Clean sand
from the creek sandbars was used to scrub the floors, along with
a bucket of water made potent by a good portion of homemade lye
soap. In a similar vein, the yard was swept clean by a "brush broom"
made from the thick foliage of a special hedge that grew in a small
patch in the back yard.

Inside the house, the rooms were kept warm by "chinking" the
cracks in the logs with mud plaster, and every so often the fireplaces
were given a new coat of white clay plaster around the jambs and
on the hearth. Clothes were washed by scrubbing them on a
washboard with lye soap and boiling them in a large iron pot. When
the wells became low in the summer and fall, the clothes were taken
to the creek bank, where a temporary wash area was set up, and
clotheslines were strung between the trees.

The strongest value with which the family was inbued was that
Polk was a name to be worn with dignity and pride, and all who
carried the name must show themselves to be both intelligent and
morally upright. Being intelligent meant reading and keeping up with
what was going on in the world. For this reason, the family members
all learned to read at an early age, often without the benefit of for-
mal schooling. Even in the hardest times when there was insufficient
food on the table, the family subscribed to three newspaper: the
Arkansas Gazette, the Nashville News, and the Kansas City Star.
They also subscribed to the Saturday Evening Post and the Pro-
gressive Farmer. In addition, Outdoor Life, Good Housekeeping, and
the Reader's Digest were delivered to the home during some periods.

The family members all read these publications, for the only other
reading materials in the house consisted of the literature books in
Emma's "library," which the children could "check out" only under
strict supervision; a Bible; and a "doctor's book," which was kept
hidden away in a box under the bed in Arthur's room because of
the pictures of human body parts. Exposure to the naked body was
strictly forbidden. Spencer's daughters continued to wear long-
sleeved, floor-length, high-collared dresses up to the day they died.

The Polks generaly did not espouse a specific religious doctrine.
In fact, like Taylor Polk, Spencer would send his family to
"preaching" but he did not go himself. There was a black church
at Muddy Fork during the early twentieth century, and the Bullocks
and other black families attended and were baptized into the African

Methodist Episcopal Church. The Polks, however, disdained such a "primitive" show of irrationality, and none of them was a member of the church until late in life, when they were introduced to the "Campbellite" or Christian Church. By the 1930s there was no church held for blacks at Muddy Fork on a regular basis. Occasionally a Methodist minister, Brother Thomas Hill, rode a red mule from Center Point to Muddy Fork to see about the small flock of Bullock members. The Polks—Arthur and his sisters and their children—seldom, if ever, attended.

The lives of Arthur's female relatives living in the south wing consisted of the dull routine of farm chores, sewing, quilting, and preparing meals. Occasionally they entertained a white visitor in the privacy of the "south room," the central room on the south end of the house. Emma, Frances, and Emma's daughter Lillian were sorely bitter, unhappy women who made little attempt to interact with Arthur's family, except to try to harrass his wife into leaving the premises. They seldom laughed, never played at games or sang a note of a song. Lillian would take a shotgun and go hunting during squirrel season; her son busied himself collecting arrowheads and prehistoric axheads from the surrounding hills and teasing his younger cousins. Emma would sometimes venture out of the south room and stand in the yard or in the apple orchard like a pale, silent statue; Frances trudged, stooped and gray-brown, through the cow paths, across the fields, and up and down the hallway of the house; Lillian would shoot out of the south wing like a threatening spring gust, draw a bucket of water from the well, and retreat back into the sanctum of the south room. The children would whisper and giggle about her "passing" for white when she went to the big cities on occasion. She didn't know they knew.

If the south end of the house was quiet and restrained, the north end was just the opposite. It was around the fireplace in the original log cabin room that the folklore of the family was primarily passed on. Spencer's son Arthur was a great storyteller, and he would gather his children around the fireplace and tell them hair-raising stories of murder and intrigue on the Arkansas frontier. He remembered the most intricate details of famous murder cases involving the white Polks, the Whisenhunts, and the Smalldens, who once owned a cotton gin at Muddy Fork and whose house site was just to the east of the Polk farm.

As if real-life stories were not enough to chill the blood, Arthur also told "ha'nt" stories about headless men and half-human creatures that once roamed the hills of Muddy Fork. Sometimes he would be joined in the telling of ghost stories by his wife's brothers, the Bullock men. The stories were often told around the fireplace in the wintertime, when the light of the fire shone on the tellers' faces and the dancing shadows from the firelight grew enormously tall and bobbed on the walls and ceiling in the back of the room, where the children's pallets were. Storytelling also took place in the summertime when the family gathered on the north end of the front porch on warm evenings after supper. The grownups would sit in cane-bottomed chairs and lean back against the wall, while the children sprawled in piles on the floor with the puppies and cats and a bucket of smoking rags to keep away the mosquitoes.

The stories usually centered around face-to-face encounters with strange and eerie happenings. There were a number of locations near the Polk and Bullock farms that were said to be "ha'nted." The old Smallden place in the east woods, the "Ha'nt Tree," or hanging tree, on the road to the cemetery, the Black Hill overlooking the Muddy Fork creek to the west, and the Indian mounds in the south woods were all said to yield up frightening apparitions if one dallied around their vicinity too long. At the Smallden house site, pink roses and crepe myrtle bushes beckoned the passing hunter, but an old abandoned well at the edge of the site was the dwelling place of a womanlike creature with flowing white hair. This creature had been seen more than once on a moonlit night, and each time had been mistaken at first for a person. In fact, Hubert Bullock reported that he had once mistaken the figure for Frances, who often roamed the woods at night looking for her cows; but just as he started to say, "Good evening, Miss Frances," the ghostlike creature walked gingerly off into the well!

The Ha'nt Tree was the tree on which the white folks had hanged black folks during slavery time, and if a person lingered around the tree, the moanings of the dead men could be heard. It was said that once Great Grandpa Mint Bullock had passed by the tree in a wagon late one night, and the ghost of a headless man got into the wagon and rode along with him for several miles.

The Black Hill, which is a part of the foothills of the Ouachita

Mountains, was once the dwelling place of another family whose log house stood for years after the family moved away. Once while hunting, Wesley Bullock stopped in the house to get out of a sudden thunderstorm. Something put him into a trance, and when he woke up, he was stuffed into the fireplace.

The old Indian mounds were the dwelling place of the dead, of course, and the children were taught to observe the mounds with great respect. If a person came upon the mounds in the woods, he was instructed never to walk atop them but to walk several yards around them, lest the spirits of the dead Indians come to life and avenge themselves on the intruder.

Another thing to avoid at all cost was a jack-o-lantern or will-o-the-wisp, a strange ball of light that one could see in the distance, especially on a dark summer night. If a person was out on the road alone, he could be easily misled into thinking that the mysterious beam was the lamplight coming from home. If he headed for the light, however, the beam would continue to get farther away and lead the unfortunate traveler into the forest. Once a person started following a will-o-the-wisp, he would go into a trance and would finally be led into complete oblivion.

Many were the times when the children sat on the porch of the old log house and were shown a will-o-the-wisp, bobbing and blinking across the pastureland to the west and finally fading away into the marshes of the creek bottom. The grownups would tell how one family member once returned home out of his head, his clothes in shreds, and his body scratched up after having followed a will-o-the-wisp one night on his way home.

The stories were told in the West African tradition for instruction as well as for entertainment.[7] The stories taught the young to be cautious of old abandoned house places, especially those that had rotting structures and unfilled wells. Such places were fairly numerous in the Muddy Fork community from the 1920s on and represented a real danger. The stories also taught the children not to dally when sent on errands or to the field to work, nor to wander off alone at night.

More specifically in the West African tradition were the stories of Bro' Rabbit. These stories as told in the Polk family included several that are well known, such as the "Tar Baby," "Bro' Rabbit

Makes Bro' Bear His Riding Horse," and the "Rabbit in the Briar Patch." Some of the stories had elements, however, that are not so well known. The Bro' Rabbit story was told as a series of events and not as several separate tales. In the stories as told in the Polk home, each story led into another incident, each following in logical sequence. All told, the stories made for hours of storytelling time, sometimes with not even a pause between episodes. For example, the Bro' Rabbit tales were told in the following fashion:

> After having been captured by the Tar Baby for hoarding the spring water during a drought, the rabbit was thrown into the briar patch by Bro' Bear. Rabbit decided to get back at Bro' Bear by telling the bear's girlfriend that Bro' Bear was just his [the rabbit's] old riding horse. The rabbit tricked the bear into giving him a ride, equipped with saddle, quirt, bridle, bit, stirrups, spurs and all. Embarrassed and enraged when the riders finally came to a halt after galloping by Miss Bear's house, Bro' Bear went out stalking the Rabbit. Bro' Rabbit eluded the bear by running up a hollow tree. The bear got Frog to watch the tree while he went to get a cane to twist the rabbit out. While the bear was gone, the rabbit tricked the frog into looking up into the hollow, kicked trash in his eyes, and while Frog went to wash out his eyes, escaped. When the bear returned, he and the frog had an episode over the fact that Frog hadn't done his job. Then the bear decided to trick the rabbit by playing sick. He knew the rabbit was compassionate, though dangerously mischievous. Bro' Bear took to his bed and sent word out that he was dying. Bro' Rabbit knew it was a trick, however, but decided to play along. He prepared some medicine and took it to the bear. The medicine, Bro' Rabbit explained, was called nyip nyip and was a sure cure for anything. The nyip nyip was really a concoction of red hot pepper that set the bear on fire. The Bear grabbed the rabbit around the neck and was about to kill him for sure, but the rabbit pleadingly explained that he had made a mistake; that the medicine he intended to get was nyam nyam. Nyam nyam was really a paste made with stinging nettles, and when the bear took it, he was devastated with pain. The contortions of the bear served only to delight the terrible Rabbit.[8]

The stories would go on and on until the small ones had to be carried to their straw pallets in the back of the room. The stories were told primarily by Arthur's wife, Mattie, and were probably handed down to her by her father's people. The source of these stories has been traced to Africa by several scholars. Richard Dorsen cites several African sources for the animal stories in black American folklore in his introductions to specific tales.[9] An interesting element that supports a West African origin in these tales is the use of the linguistic terms "nyip nyip" and "nyam nyam". The pronunciation of the ng sound at the beginning of these words is common among the languages spoken by the Akan people. For example, among the Akan of Ghana there is a word "nyame" which means God, and the common Akan name Nyamekye means "God's gift."[10] Furthermore, Herskovits cites the term "nyam-nyam" in a list of Jamaican correspondences to Surinam speech found in the taki-taki idioms of the West Indies.[11] Interestingly, the ng sound at the beginning of certain words was observed in the speech of Mattie Bullock Polk's father, Bud Bullock, whose father Mint had come "straight from Africa." Bullock pronounced the word "no" as "nyo," and the term "nyaah" for "no" is a common Afro-American expression.

In addition to telling the "ha'nt" tales and the Bro' Rabbit tales, the family practiced some folk beliefs and superstitions that probably derived from both African and European cultures. They adhered to the signs that predicted the weather, such as "Evening red and morning gray/Speed the traveler on his way." A ring around the moon meant inclement weather ahead, and a new moon with its tip pointed toward the earth meant flooding rains. On the other hand, a new moon sitting upright like a bowl meant that a drought was imminent. A storm could be averted if someone "split" the cloud with an ax. That is, if a threatening cloud appeared, a member of the household was directed to go to the woodpile, take the chopping ax, aim it at the cloud by holding it high in the air overhead, make a swooping chop, and bring the axhead down into the ground. The cloud was supposed to "split" or break up automatically and the storm would pass over. This is an African retention recognized by most cultural anthropologists.[12]

The main source of weather information was the *Ladies Birthday Almanac*. The family used the almanac to determine when to plant certain crops, as indicated by the changes in the moon. The time to spay cattle and hogs or to mark them by cutting notches in the ears or by cropping off the tail was determined from the explanations of the Zodiac signs found in the almanac. No cutting of animals was done unless the signs were right, which meant that the signs must be in the lower extremities of the arms and feet, rather than in the vital organs of the bowels, heart, or head. A person's hair was also cut by the signs. Hair must be cut when the moon was full in order to assure proper regrowth.

Other beliefs emphasized in the family were the following:

• Tying a bag of asafetida around a baby's neck would ward off colic and teething pain. (African origin)

• Sweeping the feet of a person with a broom would cause the person never to marry. (European origin)

• Cutting a baby's hair before the first birthday would stunt the child's growth. (European origin)

• If you wound a "love vine" around over your head three times and tossed it onto a bush, you would surely find a lover if the yellow tendril continued to grow on its new host. (European origin)

• After combing the hair, you should always burn the strands that come out in the comb. If a bird collected your hair to build a nest, you would have a headache until the bird's eggs hatched. (European origin)

• A screech owl crying near the house meant someone in the family would die. (African origin)

• A whistling woman and a crowing hen always came to no good end. (European origin)

• If a cat slept with the children, it could "steal" a child's breath away. (African origin)

Unlike many Afro-American families in the rural areas of the South, the Polk family did not believe in "hoo doo," witches, and other forms of the supernatural that went beyond the realms of logic, except the ones mentioned above. Even those listed were not wholly adhered to. It was taught that personal causation superceded any long-standing belief that had not been demonstrated through experience.

In addition to their folklore, everyday practices, and beliefs, the Polks enjoyed a musical tradition that represented a cultural mix of slave seculars and Scottish ditties. On the one hand, the family passed on chants and songs that were popular among Afro-Americans and which no doubt had an African-American origin. On the other hand, the Polks actively participated in the musical tradition of the whites in the Muddy Fork community, with the Polk women attending the square dances and the male members of the family providing the music and "calling" the sets. At least two of Spencer's sons were musically inclined. Jimmy Polk not only played the fiddle but owned a fine violin that is still in the possession of a family member. Jimmy's interest in fiddles is evident from the material found in his small trunk, which included a mail order form for violins and a letter from a music company official responding to his inquiry about the cost and quality of the company's products. It is said by family members that Jimmy played for dances held by whites, and it is recalled that other Polk men, including Spencer himself, could call square dance sets. [13]

Spencer's son Arthur had a beautiful tenor voice, and the members of the household always knew when things were going well, for Arthur walked around singing folksongs and doing his Scotch-Irish version of a popular Afro-American musical innovation called "scat." Two of Arthur's favorite songs were "Cindy" and "Sally Good'n." His affinity for the latter song may derive from the fact that his grandmother was named Sally, and he named his youngest daughter "Cindy," perhaps after the song. Although "Cindy" has come down as a popular country song, "Sally Good'n" is not so well known.[14] Two different versions of the song are found in folklore records, and the version Arthur Polk sang contained portions from both:

> O' I had a piece o' pie
> And I had a piece o' puddin',
> I give it all away
> To see Sally Good'n.

> I looked up the road
> N' I seen Sally comin',
> I thought to my soul
> I'd kill myself a-runnin'.

In his high tenor voice, Arthur would sing the lyrics over a couple of times, and then he would "scat" the sounds of the violin:

Diddle, diddle, dum
A-dum, dum a-diddle,
Diddle, diddle, dum, dum
A-dum dum, a-diddle.

Dee, dee, a-dum dum a-diddle
Dum dum, a-dum dum
A-dum dum, a-diddle.

In a similar manner, Arthur would render his versions of "Cindy,"
"Turkey in the Straw," "Old Dan Tucker," and many other folksongs
that were handed down from his Scotch-Irish ancestry. Arthur's
children were taught other songs, such as "She'll Be Comin' 'Round
the Mountain," "Oh, Susannah," "Nellie Gray," and "The Old Gray
Goose Is Dead." The spirituals were taught to the children by their
mother and by the few teachers who came to Muddy Fork to teach
during the summer. Group singing was a favorite pastime for the
girls and their mother. In the mid-1930s Mrs. Annie Epperson White,
the granddaughter of Taylor Polk, let the family have a used foot-
pedaled organ, and often the big room of the old log house was filled
with the sound of music. Occasionally white neighbors requested
that Mattie Polk bring the girls to visit and sing their repertoire of
folk and religious songs.

Although slavery was seldom discussed in the family, some of
the slave seculars were familiar. These were taught in terms of what
the slaves thought about themselves and their situation, and were
repeated to reflect the gravity of the slave condition, as in the following "chant":

Run, nigger, run
The patter rollers get you,
Run, nigger, run
It's almost day.

Run, nigger, run
The patter rollers get you,
Run, nigger, run
You better get away.

For pure humor, another secular was sometimes voiced:

> Nigger in the woodpile
> Can't count to 'leb'm,
> Th'owed him in a feather bed,
> Thought he went to heab'm.

These ditties were never spoken outright, but whispered and giggled over during play. The term "nigger" was considered a derogatory word and was seldom heard in the household, or in the community for that matter, by whites or blacks.

While the music in the Polk home reflected a combination of Afro-American and Euro-American influences, the real "soul" music of the family came from the Polk children's matrilineal side. The descendants of the Bullock slave family were nearly all accomplished musicians, playing the guitar, violin, piano, French harp, and organ by ear. Arthur's brother-in-law John Wesley Bullock made violins, carving them out of a tree trunk in traditional West African fashion. But unlike the Polks, whose musical propensities were mostly in the Scotch-Irish vein, the Bullocks played the blues. On occasions when the Bullock family members came to visit their sister's family, they brought their guitars and played and sang "The Saint Louis Blues" and "Drink Muddy Water, Sleep in a Hollow Log." They even brought their wind-up Victrolas and danced the "Snake Hips," did the "Breakdown," and soloed on the "Buck Dance" to the music of then-popular blues recordings.

Another area in the cultural tradition of the Polk family is reflected in the games the children played, the toys they used, and other amusements with which family members entertained themselves. Prior to 1936, when the Polk children first entered public school, the family was almost completely isolated from black people other than immediate family members. After the 1920s, only two black families resided at Muddy Fork, the Polks and the Bullocks. Therefore, the games and other recreational activities of the family represent cultural attributes that were handed down directly from parents to children and reflect cultural survivals for at least three generations. The first of these generations was, importantly, a slave generation represented by both Spencer Polk and Mint Bullock. It is more than probable that some of the games and recreational activities had their origin among the slaves or even farther back, among West African cultures.

One of the games which appears to have had an African origin was the game of hull-gull. No reference to the term "hull-gull" has been found, but there is a once-popular Afro-American dance called the "hully-gully." Hull-gull was a counting and guessing game played in the following manner: Two players sat facing each other. The first player would pick up a handful of "pieces" from his own personal stock. While he held the pieces concealed in his fist, the game proceeded:

> 1ST PLAYER: Hull-Gull!
> 2ND PLAYER: Handful!
> 1ST PLAYER: How many?
> 2ND PLAYER: Five [or any number he chose].

The first player then opened his hand, revealing his pieces. If there were more than the number guessed, the first player repeated the action. If there were fewer than guessed, the second player had to pay the first player the difference between the number of pieces guessed and the number held in the hand. If the second player guessed the exact number of pieces in the hand, the first player had to pay his opponent all of the pieces he held and give up the lead to the second player. The game continued until one player ran out of pieces, or until both grew tired.

Hull-gull pieces were made, as in present-day African games, from the seeds of a local wild fruit. The pieces were acquired by picking the hard, green berries from a vine that grew among the corn in the bottom fields. The berries were peeled, exposing hard, white, concave seed kernels, which, with their serrated edges, closely resemble cowrie shells. The seed kernels were allowed to dry in the sun and made excellent pieces for handling by small hands. The game was similar in both the way it was played and the use of seeds as pieces to the traditional game of owari played in Ghana. Owari utilizes seeds as pieces and a special game board or receptacle, and it teaches concentration, mathematical skill, and manual dexterity. The game is known by other names and found throughout West Africa and in parts of the eastern hemisphere.[15]

Another popular game the Polk children played was a "counting out" game that utilized a nonsense verse that was chanted. The origin of the game is left to speculation, but the limericks are well remembered. Any number of players could participate by sitting in a circle. The "leader" started the game by chanting and pointing to each player in turn at each word:

> Wild brow limba lock
> Five geese in a flock
> One flew east
> One flew west
> One flew over the Cuckoo's nest.
>
> My father lived on Brandy Hill
> He had a hammer and nine nails
> He had a cat-o-nine-tails.
>
> Tom whup Dick
> Blow the bellows
> Good old man
> Go!

The player to whom the "leader" pointed on the last word, "Go!" was "out", and was removed from the game. The lead passed to another player until all players were "out." If the leader pointed to himself on the word "Go," he too was "out." The counting was done very rapidly up to the last line; consequently, it could not be ascertained beforehand just where the last syllable would fall. The object of the game was to be the last one left sitting in the circle.

A game played by the Polk children and identified as having a definite African origin was "Chick-A-My, Chick-A-My Crainy Crow," or "What Time, Old Witch?" In this game, the players would walk around the "witch," who sat in the middle of a circle alone. The players, representing a hen and her chickens, would chant as they trooped around the witch:

> Chick-a-my, chick-a-my Crainy Crow,
> I went to the river to wash my toe,
> When I got back
> My black-eyed Susan was gone.
> What time, Old Witch?

The witch would answer with any number from one to twelve. If she answered twelve, however, that was the signal that she was going to leap up and catch one of the chickens. The captive would then take over the lead as the "witch" and the chanting would go on, varying only on the last line to indicate that another "chicken" was gone:

> When I got back
> My brown-eyed Lucy was gone.

In *Folk Beliefs of the Southern Negro*, Newbell Niles Puckett explains that in "Chick-A-My, Chick-A-My-Crainy Crow," "we have a possible survival not only of belief in witches but also apparently of cannibalism, since the 'old witch' steals the children [chickens] from the leader and pretends to cook them."[16] By the time this game reached the Polk children, however, the motif of cooking the children had fortunately been lost. There is a difference between cooking symbolic "chickens" and practicing cannibalism, a concept that has not been handed down among Afro-Americans. Another probable meaning in "Chick-A-My-Crainy Crow" might be connected with the selling away of one's children or loved ones during slavery, for the idea of stealing or kidnapping the children was strong in the version of the game played by the Polk children.

To ascertain the exact origin of these games will require further research. The games were peculiar to the Polk family, however, for the white children at Muddy Fork with whom the Polk children played did not know these games, and neither did the black children at Center Point, where the Polk children first attended public school. At Center Point the children played the traditional Afro-American games of "Little Sally Walker," "Lost My Handkerchief," and "Walking on the Green Grass."

In addition to counting games, the Polk children were entertained by homemade toys. A special toy that had an African origin was the "bull roarer," which Arthur Polk made for his children. A "bull roarer" is a musical instrument common among African and other non-Western cultures. The West African writer Chinua Achebe mentions the instrument in his works.[17] The bull roarer was made by whittling a thin piece of wood, about six inches long and two or three inches wide, into a special shape with a hole carved in one end. A piece of twine was tied through the hole, and when the string was whirled around rapidly, the piece of wood made a loud, roaring sound. Arthur Polk knew the exact shape and size to carve the bull roarer in order to produce the right sound.

A favorite summer pastime for the young was propelling a "hoop and pad" up and down the lanes between the Bullock and Polk farmsteads. A "hoop and pad" was made by taking an iron band from a worn-out wagon wheel hub and rolling it along the ground with a paddle. The wheel was kept upright by the paddle, which was made from a short strip of wood or a stick to which was attached a tin flap on one end. The tin flap was often made from a flattened snuff box, which was nailed to the stick, curved around to fit the narrow band of iron, and maneuvered in such a way as to steer the rolling wheel along the desired route.

Other homemade toys included the "bean flip," cornstalk horses, corncob dolls, and a variety of whistles. The "bean flip" was a slingshot made from a forked tree branch, with rubber bands made from old inner tubes attached as straps. The ammunition was held in a piece of leather cut from a cast-off shoe and tied to the rubber bands to form a small slingshot. Small rocks were used for ammunition, and the toys were used for target practice or to shoot birds for food.

The making of cornstalk horses was both a skill and an art. The "horses" were soon discarded rather than used to play with, so the main purpose in making them was to see who could make the best horse. Dry cornstalks were stripped of the hard covering, and, using the soft center for the body and head, the horse was put together by thin strips made from the hard outer stalk. The strips of stalk were cut into desired lengths, sharpened on the ends, and used as pins to attach head and body, or used in larger strips for legs, tail, and ears. Careful details of ears, eyes, legs, and tail provided for individual creativity and personal imagination.

Corncob dolls were made by using a cob for the body and making the head from a goldenrod plant that formed, in the middle of the stalk, a large round tumor that turned brown and hard in the fall of the year. The round tumor was broken off with a long stem on one end. The stem was pushed into the soft center of the cob, forming a perfect neck and head. The head was then adorned with cotton for hair and bits of paper for eyes, nose, and mouth. The cob body was then dressed in the fashion that could best be devised by using scraps of cloth, ribbon, and threads. The girls would vie to see who could design the most fabulous fashions for her individual family of dolls. Store-bought dolls were seldom brought home, but when they were they were soon cast aside in deference to the children's own creations.

Common twine provided another source for toys. Forming designs and playing tricks with string made for hours of entertainment for the Polk children. String was used to make a "Jacob's Ladder" and a "cat's cradle," which were intricate designs threaded between the fingers of both hands. String was also used to "cut off" one's fingers; this was done by looping the thread through the fingers, thus cutting them off. "Spinning buttons" were made by threading twine through the holes of buttons, winding it up, and then pulling the elasticized twist of twine back and forth to spin the button with a buzzing sound. It was a real trick to be able to tie a knot in a string without turning loose the ends of the string. Of course, live "kites" were improvised by tying a string to the leg of a captured June bug and setting the green and gold creature free to fly the limits of its hand-clutched tether.

Arthur Polk was adept at making a variety of toys, household equipment, and farm implements through his ability in hand carving, a skill he learned from his father, Spencer Polk. Arthur made whistles that really worked from both switch cane reeds and turkey quills. He also taught the boys how to make intricate bird traps by carving a trigger for the trap out of three thin strips of wood, notched and set together in the shape of the number 4. A heavy board was set at a forty-five degree angle on the ground, with the board resting on top of the trigger. To attract the birds, sorghum seeds were strewn underneath the heavy plank and tied to the end of the trigger. When the birds gathered under the plank to feed, their pecking on the grain attached to the trigger would spring the trap, the plank would fall, and the birds would be pinned beneath. Sometimes the children would tie a long string to the trigger and sit and watch for the appropriate time to spring the trap while the birds fed. The trapped birds were, of course, used for food.

Arthur Polk also taught his sons how to make rugged trucks and wagons using sapling poles and pieces of lumber confiscated from the Wisdom sawmill[18] for the chassis and matched rounds sawed from green tree logs for wheels. The boys modeled their wagons on pictures in the Sears Roebuck catalog and the occasional log trucks and wagons that lumbered past the house on the way to the sawmill. The vehicles the children made were big and sturdy, with trailers and beds, and they rode them, self-propelled, down the steep hill behind the house.

The children also amused themselves by playing horseshoes and holding cockfights. Once they learned that two roosters would fight over territory, Arthur's sons developed cockfighting into a rather ingenious enterprise. Since there were three separate flocks of chickens on the farm—their mother's, Emma's, and Frances's—the boys had no trouble finding antagonists for their cockfights. At first they would confiscate the rooster from Frances's or Emma's flock and take him over to their mother's yard for an exciting fight until the women came screaming and yelling to the rescue of their respective birds. With the help of their mother's youngest brother, Robert Bullock, the boys would sometimes kidnap the rooster from their Grandmother Viney's flock and put on a bout with the rooster in their mother's yard. Finally, they persuaded their mother to let them raise their own roosters, and they even ordered thoroughbred game fighting cocks from the mail-order house. When the roosters grew so familiar with each other that they wouldn't fight, the boys simply disguised them at will, using make-up of different colored paste made from soot and red, yellow, and white clay. The paste would be dabbed on the neck feathers to create a strange new rooster, and the fight would be on!

Although cockfighting was frowned upon by the boys' parents and was considered an utterly distasteful and barbaric practice by the Polk women, when the boys got their own roosters a good cockfight was sometimes enjoyed by all. The fight would be stopped before serious injury or death to the fowls could occur, and filing of the roosters' spurs was strictly forbidden.

Hunting and trapping for birds and small animals, and fishing along the banks of the Muddy Fork provided recreation as well as much-needed food for the family. The children were taught to use a gun at a very early age, and although Arthur himself never fished or hunted, his sons, great-nephew, niece, and daughters all hunted for squirrels and rabbits and fished in the creek. The males also trapped for mink, 'possum, and coon. The pelts from these animals were sold at Nashville, and the 'possum and coon were sometimes roasted with sweet potatoes to provide a family meal. Rabbit was hung up the chimney on a rod and smoked for several days in a fashion that is used to preserve meat in the West African round houses today.[19] Birds were also smoked in this manner.

One unique practice used to catch birds was "bird thrashing." In the fall of the year, piles of brush from cleared land became a nesting place for blackbirds and brown thrush. Armed with sticks and lanterns, both children and adults would surround the brush pile at night. At a given signal, everybody would begin to beat upon the pile, and when the birds flew out, they would be blinded by the lantern light, making them easy prey to be knocked down and caught. The captured birds would then be taken home, dressed, put on a long stick, and roasted over the coals in the fireplace or hung up the chimney and smoked a few days for future dining.

Although African survivals in the form of music, religion, speechways, and folkways have been well documented, and although more recent scholarship has identified retentions in the making of pottery and wood carving, the contributions of Africans to the development of farming practices have not been so well emphasized. It is very evident, however, that "Africans and their New World descendants made important contributions to the development of American agriculture."[20] This comment is particularly true for the growing of rice in the South Carolina lowlands, but it could also apply to farming in the wilderness of pioneer Arkansas. The farming practices and practical crafts observed on the Polk farm reflected a blending of cultures, to be sure, for most of these practices had become universal by the mid-nineteenth century. From whatever source, however, they represent long-standing traditions among Arkansas's first families, black as well as white.

The Spencer Polk family, for example, employed the slash-and-burn method of preparing land for planting, just as it is done in West Africa today.[21] In the late fall or early spring, the dried growth on the land would be burned to produce fertilizer, it was thought, the rubble turned under, and the new crops planted. This method was also used to prepare "new ground." Trees and undergrowth were cut, piled, and burned in a fashion employed by subsistence farmers for generations in West Africa. Often the new ground was used for sweet potatoes or watermelons. In such cases, the soil was prepared in traditional African fashion by heaping up mounds of earth into which the tubers, slips, or seeds were planted. In Africa, this method is used to prevent the torrential rains from carrying away or dispersing the newly planted crops.[22] This practice could not have been practical or necessary in Europe, where neither the food crops nor the climatic conditions warranted it.

The Polks' technique of winnowing blackeyed peas was very similar to the way rice was prepared in West Africa, using special "rice fanners," shallow woven baskets. A large blanket or sheet was placed on the ground, the dried legumes were placed in a pile in the center, and the heap was beaten with sticks until all the peas separated from the hulls. The hulls were removed, leaving only the fine chaff among the grain. Using shallow pans, the peas were scooped up, held high in the air, and slowly poured back down upon the spread. The chaff was carried away by the breeze, and the process was repeated until clean peas were obtained. This is another practice which is observed in much of West Africa today, sometimes in remote areas uninfluenced by modern Western techniques. It was also the method used by African slaves and their descendants on the plantations of South Carolina and Georgia in the nineteenth century and beyond.[23]

In the case of practical crafts, it is highly likely that the skills Spencer Polk passed on to his sons were ones he learned from African slaves. Weaving from cane and bark is indigenous to Africa,[24] and Spencer's surviving son Arthur knew these skills well. He knew exactly which kinds of trees yielded the best bark for weaving baskets and chair bottoms and backs, and he knew how to carve ax handles, singletrees, wagon spokes, and barrel staves. He also hewed shingles and split rails in the European mode. Both the Polk and the Bullock males knew how to make furniture from rattan, including long chaises and three-legged stools, crafts that strongly suggest a West African carry-over. In some West African societies, young men are still required to learn the craft of making rattan furniture as a part of their training during initiation.[25]

Other examples of African retentions handed down in the Polk family include the use of herbs and other natural substances for practical purposes. The family grew a variety of herbs in the family garden, including dill, garlic, mustard, catnip, sage, poppies, and shallots. There was also a mint patch and a calamus bed across the road in front of the house. In addition to these herbs, the family used bark and seeds from various trees and plants, including red oak and slippery elm bark, sassafras, and spicewood. These were used to make teas and tonics for various ailments such as the common cold, tonsillitis, and fever. Flaxseeds were often placed in the eye for dislodging irritants, and, like their West African ancestors, members of the family chewed on sticks to keep their teeth clean or to rearrange their dip of snuff. The sticks were chosen from the branches of the sweet gum tree, just as West Africans use a specific tree from which to glean their chewing sticks for personal use or to peddle in bundles in the marketplace today.[26] Hickory bark was used for dyeing cloth, and this practice, along with the use of wooden bowls, may have been one of the few carry-overs from the Cherokee Indians.[27]

The trunk which Jimmy Polk left behind contained items that further reveal cultural retentions from the past. Two hand-crafted checkerboards suggest the family's propensity for games at some early period in time. One of the boards is a plain pine slab about two feet long and one foot wide with the checker squares drawn in slate and blackened with boot black. The other is more finely constructed of a perfect square, with the design stained in blue-black ink. One side has spaces of the same number as the checkerboard side, only the spaces are round spots instead of squares. Also in the trunk was a hand-carved crochet hook with an intricately grooved end that mirrors the West African tradition of embellishing everyday objects with artistic design.

The children's father, Arthur, was a many-talented man who not only made things with his hands but also recited poetry and retold historical events for the education of his young ones. He loved to entertain the children by standing on his head, and when he shaved it was a family event. He usually let his mustache grow thick and long, and his beard often covered his face. But then occasionally he would cut all the hair from his face, much to the delight of the children, who were accustomed to seeing his upper lip covered with hair. When he decided to shave the hair from his face, he would start by putting a kettle of water on the stove to heat. This action would usually go unnoticed. When the water started to boil, he would fill a wash pan full of the hot water, take his shaving cup and brush down from the medicine cabinet, approach the small mirror that hung next to the window by the fireplace mantel, and command, "Bring me my razor strop!" This was the signal to gather round and witness the seldom-seen metamorphosis of the man called "Papa." The razor strop could be anywhere in the house, for it was used for whipping as well as for shaving. But when Arthur started to shave, everybody knew that the strop had to be produced, so it was always somewhere in sight. Once he received the strop from some small hand, Arthur hung the strop beside the mirror and then retrieved his long shiny razor from its hiding place in the medicine cabinet. Removing the razor from its case, he would begin to hone it up and down on the strop in slow but deliberate motions. By this time, every eye in the north room was upon him, for all knew that the thick, dark mustache and stubbled beard were coming off, and a strange new man would be their father for the next few days.

In addition to gathering herbs and barks for medicine, on occasion Arthur Polk would gather ingredients and make a churn of spirit beverage. An interview with members of Arthur's family, Julia Polk Gilbert and Herbert and Preston Polk, provides an account of this last activity:

QUESTION: Back to the attic. I can remember the bottles that were up there. Do you know what kind of bottles they were?

GILBERT: Well, they were very strange—some of them were green and some were sort of brown.

QUESTION: Were they wine bottles?

H. POLK: Whiskey bottles! [He was in his "cups" at the time, himself.]

P. POLK: They were wine and vinegar bottles.

QUESTION: You know, there were the remains of a vineyard up there, and I got the idea somewhere about wine making.

H. POLK: Well, all right, then!

QUESTION: And then there were the hops. Do you remember the hop vines?

GILBERT: Around by the gate to the garden fence.

QUESTION: They didn't just grow up there?

GILBERT: Somebody planted them there. And I got the idea that maybe 'way, a long time ago they either made some type of home made brew and bottled it. You know, they either made wine or wine and beer. Remember how Papa made those churns full of home brew?

QUESTION: I don't remember—

GILBERT: [Incredulous] You don't remember Papa's churns of home brew that he would set beside the fire and have the cloth over it and a string tied around it! And that mellow scent would come out—

QUESTION: Oh, yes!

GILBERT: Well, that was his jug of home brew, but, now, he didn't make that in later years. That was 'way back when I was very small. And he'd have that churn setting there. But we knew that we weren't to touch it; it wasn't for us. But Papa'd have it sitting there by the fire [fireplace] with a rag over it and string wrapped around the rag. And we could smell it. You could hear it, you know, bubbling—fermenting.[28]

Arthur also tended the bees in the back yard. This practice was no doubt handed down in the white Polk family. The first reference to bees in the research came from the probate record of the Taylor Polk estate. When Polk's estate was settled in 1885, a set of "bee gums" was sold to James Polk, Taylor's son. Oral reports indicate that Spencer acquired the bee gums for his youngest son Jimmy, and when Jimmy was killed, the lot of attending the bees fell to Arthur.[29] Assisted by his sister Frances, Arthur would take a bundle of smouldering rags for a smoke screen and approach the bees with little or no covering over his face and hands. He and Frances would take dishpans and buckets and gather the honeycomb from the hives. The honeycomb would be drained, the honey stored in stone jars, and the beeswax melted down for use in patching leaks in pots and pans and water buckets. Arthur also knew how to attract a swarm of bees. Occasionally the bees would flee from their hives for one reason or another and swarm on a nearby tree. When that happened, Arthur and Frances would track them down, find the queen, and return her to the hive. Then, taking cowbells, which they rang loudly to attract the bees, they would lure the swarm right back to the back yard.

When the hives fell into disrepair and the bees went away for the last time in the last 1930s, Arthur showed his children how to gather honey from "bee trees." These were hollow trees in the woods where bees often made their home. Cautioning the children never to harm the bees by cutting the tree down or using fire, as some neighbors did, Arthur taught his offspring to use the smouldering rags, just as he had used them in the yard. Often the same tree provided honey for the family year after year.

The art of making mud masonry was another skill handed down from the past. From time to time the chimneys and fireplaces of the house and the furnace of the sorghum mill had to be repaired extensively. At such times, Arthur Polk would go to a certain part of the creek bottom and collect a sticky white clay for making "mud cats," or daubing, with which to hold together the stones of the chimney or furnace. The clay would be mixed with water to a thick consistency, and wisps of long, thin grass around which to form the "cats" would be folded into the clay. The "cats" were patted and kneaded into long, oval shapes and placed between layers of limestone rocks to hold the stones together. The "mud cats" were mixed in shallow pits dug out of the earth especially for that purpose. Mud houses in West Africa are put together in a similar fashion, using mud and grass. From whatever source this ancient skill derived, it was not practiced among other residents of Muddy Fork, and was observed by oral sources only on the Polk farm.

The Polks had a strong propensity to name their children after relatives or other important people. The importance of naming practices in African societies has been well documented, and the Polks unwittingly reflected the African influence in the naming practices handed down in the family. Because of the physical and psychological closeness of Spencer Polk to his father, unlike many other former slaves, the black Polks retained the owner's surname after Emancipation. That in itself is important to note, but it is in the bestowing of given names that elements of the African naming system can be observed.

In her study of the Promisedland community, Elizabeth Rauh Bethel found that "while family names established lineage in a general sense, a given name was also a vital component of a child's identity. Because babies were often named for relatives and parents, given names were part of a family tradition and linked the newborn with a specific elder member of the family."[30] Naming among Africans and Americans of African descent is often the most important and most significant occurrence surrounding the birth of a baby. The

Polks adhered to a seemingly long-established practice of naming children, especially males, after relatives or other important people. Spencer's sons Charles, Benjamin Franklin, and James were all named after members of the white Polk family, and both Douglass and Arthur, after famous people. In Arthur's family, most of the male children were named for significant people. The names of two of Arthur's sons, William Henry and Clay, were common names among the white Polks; and Arthur chose "Jack Dempsey" and "Herbert Hoover" as names for two other sons.

Among African societies, one practice is to give the newborn child a name from the "living-dead," or the ancestors. To become an ancestor, of course, one must have led an exemplary life of heroism in one's actions, leadership in the group, and benevolence toward others. Naming a child after an ancestor was done in the anticipation that the child would be endowed with the traits and characteristics of the person after whom he or she was named.[31] Thus, naming a child for a president or a great prizefighter showed the parent's hopes for greatness for his own offspring.

One important characteristic of African naming practices was that the naming of a child sometimes took several days or even months.[32] In the case of Arthur Polk's fifth son, who died in infancy, the baby had not been named after three months. The whole family was waiting for Arthur to decide on the name, since the father had first priority in choosing a name. On the event of the child's death, a name had to be given to the doctor who had finally arrived and pronounced the baby dead. With all eyes on him, wondering what he would say, Arthur stood briefly, head bowed. Then he said solemnly but firmly, "His name is Arthur." It was the reverse of necronymic naming, or the naming of a child after a dead family member.[33] It was the first time the family members knew the father's choice of a name for the now-deceased baby.

Among the Polks, the one who gave the name was almost as important as the name itself. Often a name, or one of two or three names, given a child was chosen by a grandparent, aunt, or uncle. Sometimes girls were named after favorite aunts or grandmothers, but unlike the naming practices among some whites, girls were seldom named for their mothers.[34] In the case of his oldest daughter, Julia Ann, Arthur chose to name her for his aunt Julia

Murphy, but the Ann was added for both the mother, Mattie Ann, and Arthur's youngest sister, Annie.

Finally, among the several cultural traditions handed down in the Polk family, their habits of speech present some of the most interesting. The children of Spencer Polk spoke a variety of speech that was a combination of backwoods hillbilly and Scottish-Irish brogue with hardly a trace of black English. They said "aye-aye" for "yes" and "skidday" for "get up" or "move over," called children "chaps," and referred to themselves and everyone else as "a body." They called a switch for whipping children a "withe," and they always ended exclamatory sentences, whether talking to persons or animals, with the distinctive "Sir!" They said "a-tall" instead of "at all," and they sat on the "gallery" instead of the "porch." Some things happened "of an evening" instead of "in the evening," and everything was bound to happen "d'rectly."

8. The Last Remove

The dissolution of the Spencer Polk homestead at Muddy Fork can be attributed to several factors. First, one must consider the change in social conditions in the Muddy Fork community following *Plessy* vs. *Ferguson*, the Supreme Court decision that sanctioned separation of the races. The attitudes of egalitarianism between black and white residents of the community diminished, and some degree of veiled antagonism and animosity toward blacks flourished among the poorer class of whites. This change is evident in the numerous newspaper accounts of violence perpetrated against blacks from 1900 through 1930. In reporting these incidents, local newspapers were extremely negative toward blacks in tone, using terms that were often derogatory and pejorative. The *Nashville News*, for example, reported that a "crazy negro" was arrested for fighting in 1910, and another black man was described as a "typical flat nose African type."[1]

Added to the changing attitudes was the fact that after Spencer's death, white neighbors began to borrow the modern farm implements from Arthur and never returned them to him. Arthur would not ask to have the implements returned for fear of arousing the animosity of the borrowers.[2] As a result, by the mid 1930s most of the large farm equipment—the disk plows, listers, middlebusters, harrows, and hayrakes—had been carried away by the neighbors.

A third reason for the decline of the homestead was that there was no regular school at Muddy Fork for black children to attend. The final abandonment of the family home came about when Arthur's wife Mattie sent the four youngest children to boarding school in Nashville and soon followed them there herself.

These conditions, combined with the Great Depression, caused debilitating social and economic problems which the family was never able to overcome. When Arthur Polk married in 1921, the family was fairly well off. They often boasted that all of the Polk women—Arthur's sisters—had money in the bank at Nashville when the crash came in 1929. Yet even before the Depression years, the condition of the family had begun to deteriorate. In a household of seven adults and a growing number of children, the problems of providing food, clothing, shelter, and education were magnified by the fact that there was only one adult male worker. Subsistence was the order of the day, and Arthur, his sister Frances, and his wife Mattie managed to maintain some continuity in raising farm products, livestock, and poultry enough to keep the family from starvation.

The children were taught as they grew older to plant and hoe and gather in the crops. They also learned early to care for livestock, milk the cows, and collect firewood for the cookstoves and fireplaces. Each fall a small amount of cotton was garnered to sell for cash to pay the taxes on the farm and to buy food staples such as flour and sugar, and necessities such as shoes for the adults and cloth to make garments for the children. Some of these items were purchased at the county seat, Nashville, during the semiannual trips in the fall and spring, and others were bought from peddlers who made their weekly or monthly routes through the townships. Often eggs and chickens, blackberries and muscadines were gathered and traded to the peddlers, who not only had their large trucks lined with shelves of goods from the town, but also had chicken crates and egg boxes decked out on top of their vehicles.

The provision of food was taken care of by growing truck crops and maintaining two family gardens. The truck crops included sweet potatoes, watermelons, turnip greens, collards, Irish potatoes, peas, cantaloupes, and sorghum. The original family garden, located to the north of the house, was tended by Arthur's sisters, and the second garden across the lane in front of the house was maintained by Arthur's wife Mattie. The children helped work in both gardens, where a variety of vegetables were grown, including cabbage, beans, onions, beets, eggplant, artichokes, kale, English peas, lettuce, okra, cucumbers, tomatoes, peppers, summer squash, cushaw, and pumpkins. Peach, pear, apple, plum, and persimmon trees grew in scattered orchards and abounded on the hillsides to provide additional foodstuffs.

In addition to the fruits and vegetables grown on the farm, the family gathered wild blackberries, huckleberries, muscadines, and possum grapes for making pies and jellies. Hazelnuts, hickory nuts, walnuts, pecans, and chinquapins were gathered from the woods and stored under the house for the winter months. When food was really scarce, the children gathered "red haws" (hawthorne berries), crabapples, maypops, and mulberries.

To supplement the family provisions of food and to buy clothing and oil for the lamps, Arthur and his children sometimes hired out to the white families in the neighborhood. Arthur would not allow his children to hire out often, and he or Mattie always went with them unless it was to help Mrs. Annie White (Annie Epperson White was the granddaughter of Taylor Polk) and her husband, Jack White. It was evidence of his latent fears that Arthur would not allow the children to go to the fields alone with other white families.

While most white families were no more able to hire labor than the Polks were during the Depression, some white families found help necessary in chopping and picking cotton. When Arthur and his family hired out, it was as much in the spirit of helping their neighbors as for the purpose of making money. Often the Polks traded their labor for commodities such as peas, corn, and potatoes, for hardly anyone at Muddy Fork had cash money during the Depression years of the late 1920s and 1930s.

The ability to provide an education for the children had become one of the gravest problems the Polks faced by the mid-1930s. The black families at Muddy Fork had diminished to only two households, and it became increasingly difficult to engage a teacher to come to such a remote area to teach one family of children. At the turn of the century there had been a flourishing school at Muddy Fork, according to oral accounts, and the school had been maintained during the first quarter of the century. Land was set aside for the school, which had evolved from a brush arbor school around 1900 to a frame schoolhouse erected by 1910, according to old photographs. Real estate tax records show that taxes were levied against a schoolhouse and a church adjacent to the northern section of the Spencer Polk property in Section 17, and against a negro church adjacent to the southern perimeter of the property in Section 28.[3] Evidently the school and church located in Section 27 are one and the same building, referred to by residents as the Polk

Meeting House. The tax records of 1925 describe the location of the schoolhouse, church, and cemetery as follows:

Polk Cemetery: SE 1/4 NE 1/4 Section 27, 2 acres

School House: NW 1/4 NE 1/4 Section 27, 1 acre

Church: NW 1/4 NE 1/4 Section 27, 5 acres

Spencer Polk owned 40 acres of land in the NW/NW section of the same plat,[4] and this is no doubt the school and church and meeting house once used by both whites and blacks. There is no listing in the tax records of a school for blacks, but there is an entry for a "negro" church and a "Poor Farm" located in the NE/SE and NE/NE portions of Section 28, land that had once been owned by Ives Polk, who was married to Spencer's sister Eliza, and by George Clemens, who was married to Ellen Polk's sister Julia Murphy Clemens.[5]

Apparently the church and school were housed in the same building, and there were separate buildings for blacks and whites after 1900. It is also evident that a school at Muddy Fork had existed as early as 1880, for all of Spencer's school-aged children were attending school, according to the census taken that year. The spot where the arbor school had been located was often pointed out to Arthur's children by their mother and father, who had both attended the school. In addition, a group picture taken around 1908 shows a school building in front of which the children and their teacher are standing. A second school building located south of the Spencer Polk property was constructed in the mid-1920s, according to oral reports, although a search of school records at the archives in Little Rock did not yield any information on either school. A teacher's record book is extant, and a picture of the building, taken in 1936, shows it to have been the typical "little red schoolhouse." It was a one-room building, painted red, with a board-and-batten exterior, a door in the center of the front facade, another door on the left corner in the back, and two windows, evenly spaced one on each side of the building. Inside were long wooden benches, and a crude speaker's stand stood in the center of the back of the room to be used when there was "preaching."

By the mid-1930s the main problem in holding school was in acquiring a teacher. Occasionally one was hired to come and teach for a month in the summer, and some of these teachers are well remembered by the Polk children. One of the first was a Mrs. Nealey Coulter, who taught for a short period in the late 1920s.[6] In the summer of 1933 a Miss Nona Green from Tollette came to Muddy Fork to teach, and in 1935 a Miss Bessie Crofton took on the task of teaching the Polk children. The teachers usually lived in the south rooms with Arthur's sisters, and on nice days the teacher and children walked the short distance to the schoolhouse. On rainy days classes were held in the south rooms.

The students attending these one-month terms were Arthur and Mattie Polk's first seven children, and much later one of Mattie's nephews, Alphonso Bullock, whose parents, Hubert and Phoebe Bullock, moved back to Muddy Fork for a short while in 1934. Emma's grandson James was privately tutored by the teachers and no doubt by Emma herself.

When Bessie Crofton was the teacher (she was, in fact, the last of the teachers at Muddy Fork), she put on an elaborate closing-day program and invited school officials and her relatives from Nashville to come to Muddy Fork and witness the event.[7] It was during the preparations for the program that Miss Crofton and the children decided to name their school "Maple Valley School," and for the closing program the children were taught a school yell that went as follows:

> With a vee vo,
> With a vi vo,
> With a vee vo, vi vo vum,
> With a vum get a rat trap
> Bigger than a cat trap,
> Vum get a cat trap
> Bigger than a rat trap,
> Anybody ask us who we are:
> Maple Valley! Maple Valley!
> Rah! Rah! Rah!

The oldest child, William Henry, sang Joyce Kilmer's "Trees," and the younger children recited short poems. Among those recited were two that show the teacher's inventiveness in making learning relevant. One of the girls recited:

When I grow up I mean to be
A school teacher, you see.
I'll get a hick'ry three feet long
And whip the boys when they do wrong!

Another expostulated:

What are you looking at me for?
I didn't come to stay.
I just came to tell you
That it's closing day!

After Miss Crofton's tenure, it became impossible to get another teacher to make the journey to Muddy Fork for a whole month, and the children did not attend school the next year or so. Then in 1936 a Mr. R.C. Childress, who was the supervisor of education for blacks in the State Department of Education, heard about the plight of the Polk children. He, along with a young social worker, Miss Inolia McIntosh, who later became Childress's second wife, made the trip from Little Rock to Muddy Fork to see what could be done about getting the Polk children into public school.[8] As a result of their efforts, the school district at Muddy Fork was consolidated with the Dunbar High School District at Center Point, and a system of transporting the Polk children to the school there was devised.

When Mattie Polk explained that there was not sufficient clothing for the children to attend public school, Miss McIntosh gathered a truckload of used clothing and shoes from white residents in Nashville and Little Rock, and then assisted Mattie in making over the mostly adult garments into child-sized dresses, coats, trousers, and shirts. Some of the high-heeled slippers were cut off at the heels and transformed into low-heel shoes for the young girls.

In the fall of 1936, shortly after the ninth child was born, the seven older children began attending school at Center Point, riding the fifteen or so miles over the hardly passable dirt roads in a pickup truck which had been boarded up at the sides and covered with a tarpaulin. Mr. John Sypert drove the truck from Center Point to Muddy Fork, picked up the children, and returned them home in the evening. Because of the condition of the roads, the trip often began before daylight and ended during the twilight. During periods of heavy rains, the vehicle would often get stuck in the mud and remained stuck for hours until some chance driver, usually of a log truck, came along to help get it out of the mire. At other times during inclement weather, the truck could not make the trip at all. During this same period, white children at Muddy Fork were attending school at Nashville, traveling the distance in a new yellow school bus.

The Polk children proved to be excellent students, and although they had had little schooling before 1936, they were all placed in grades according to their age, with Henry, the oldest at fourteen, in the seventh grade, and Ruth, the youngest at six, in the first grade. Since there were seven children, there was one at each grade level at Dunbar, and they all excelled in their respective classes.

In spite of the fact that the children were at last attending public school, the winter of 1936 was one of the worst the family ever experienced. In September, Mattie gave birth to her ninth child, a big baby boy with a full cap of straight black hair and wide-set blue-black eyes. The child soon became plump and pink-cheeked, and since the last child was four years old and the three youngest children all girls, the new baby boy was the delight of all the children. Awaiting the time when Arthur would name the child, the family referred to their little brother as simply "the baby."

But the winter was so hard in 1936. The crops had been poor that year; the hogs had died with the cholera that summer; teenaged "turkey hunters" had mischievously shot most of the turkeys, which they came upon as the flock wandered about in the woods near Thanksgiving; and the chickens had dwindled down to a couple of old roosters and a few setting hens. Consequently, the family diet consisted mostly of cornbread and sorghum molasses. The weather had become extremely cold by December, and the freezing wind whistled through the chinks in the logs of the north wall. Arthur and Mattie and their nine children often found themselves pushing and scrounging around the fireplace to keep warm.

On days when it was particularly cold and all the food was gone, the children would cry and quarrel among themselves. Arthur would pace the floor in the back of the room and cry out in an anguished voice, "There are just too many of us. We're going to all starve to death." Or he would state prophetically, pathetically, "I believe we could make it if there weren't so many of us."

At such times, the author recalls, she felt in her six-year-old's way that it was her father's wish that some of them would go away. Not particularly a favorite of anyone's, she felt strongly that it was she who was in the way and causing the family's problems, In fact, she felt that her father did not love any of them very much, since he thought they were all "too many."

And then the Baby became ill. He took a cold in his chest in mid-December and began to run a high fever. Viney Bullock, Mattie's mother and a full-blooded Choctaw Indian, brought a poultice of some odd concoction to put on the baby's chest, and Mattie procured some strong-smelling salve from the peddlar to rub on the small one, but the Baby only got worse. His lips and cheeks turned red as flame, and by the third or fourth day of his illness he began to struggle for breath. It was spasms, Ma Viney said, and she and Mattie took turns holding the baby on their laps by the fire all night long.

Sometime after midnight Mattie told Arthur to go for a doctor. The closest doctor lived at Dierks, about seven miles away, and the closest neighbor who had a telephone was Elbert Chaney, who lived about a mile away through the deepest woods. Arthur went to the Chaneys' and telephoned to Dierks for the doctor, who arrived at the house just as day was beginning to break. The gray-clad man took the baby from its mother's arms, laid the child across his lap, and listened to the small chest with a stethoscope. It was double pneumonia, the doctor said, and after a few moments of listening, the doctor raised his head and pronounced that the baby was dead.

Mattie's face crumpled up like a much-used brown paper sack, and she went to the back of the room and knelt by the bed as if in prayer. Arthur went to the bed and knelt beside her, and from him came the strangest "oooo-hoo-hoo-hoo." Ruth thought that her father was laughing—that he was happy the baby was dead and there would not be too many of them any more. She went and stood by her parents and began to laugh, too. Her mother raised her tear-stained face and spoke sharply. "Ruth! Stop that!" "But Papa is laughing," the child cried, thoroughly confused now. "No, child," her mother spoke in quiet pain, "your father is crying."

For Ruth it was the first encounter with the death of a family member, and, more importantly, it was the life-long affirmation that their father loved them all. She had never heard her father cry before, nor did she ever hear him cry again.

During the fall of 1937 no transportation was available to take the children to Center Point, and Mattie pursuaded her husband to move to a location nearer the school. In the middle of the winter, therefore, Mattie and Arthur packed their belongings and their children onto a wagon and moved to Center Point. They moved into the home of a distant relative, Jonah Anderson, a widower, and his adolescent son Carl. The Andersons lived on a small farm a few miles south of the Dunbar school building. John Sypert again took the children to school in his truck, for there was only one school bus to transport children to the black school. Most children in Center Point walked to school, except for those who lived too far away, in Pea Ridge or Under the Hill.

Although Arthur moved his family to Center Point, he actually never moved there himself. He returned to Muddy Fork to care for his sisters. He would journey to Center Point each week to take supplies and firewood, and then return to Muddy Fork, traveling the distance in a wagon.

Life at Center Point proved even harsher than at Muddy Fork. There was no money, no barns of grain, no smokehouse, no place to hunt, and no room to escape from the crowded hunger of nine empty mouths. Mattie and her eight children existed on the scant provisions Arthur brought from Muddy Fork, and she managed to acquire a small amount of foodstuff from a white neighbor, a woman who lived in a big red brick house a few miles from the Anderson farm. The children called the woman "Old Yellow Legs," for she had some kind of ailment that required applications of sulphur to her legs. Mattie would walk to the woman's home and do small chores and milk the cows in exchange for a portion of the milk and other items of food. The children, all adults now, still remember and laugh about how they practically lived on "red haws," and how they dug turnips out of the frozen earth and ate them raw, just as Scarlet O'Hara did in *Gone with the Wind*.

The school situation at Center Point proved totally unsatisfactory also, for during the winter months a basketball game was held every week at Nashville or Lockesburg or some other nearby town. Everybody else at the school would go, including the driver of the Polk children's vehicle, and the children were left at the school alone until late at night, when the busload of basketball enthusiasts returned. Once, the children decided they would not stay at the school and set out walking for the Anderson home, got lost, and ended up near Nashville. Someone saw them walking along the road, and they were fortunately picked up and delivered to their anxious mother.

After only a few short months at Center Point, the Polks returned to Muddy Fork in the early spring of 1938. The children attended school intermittently at Center Point for the next four years. One year they did not attend at all. After John Sypert stopped driving the children to school, it was difficult to get anyone to make the trip. One year, an attempt was made to transport the children along with children living Under the Hill and at Dierks. The truck was driven by a young man named Buster Wesson, who lived Under the Hill. There he collected his brothers and sisters and the children of Thomas Boles, drove to Dierks and picked up several children from the sawmill quarters, and then circled on around to Muddy Fork to pick up the Polk children. Again, the route was difficult because of the condition of the roads, and the driver made the trip on an average of three days a week. The last attempt to deliver the Polk children to Dunbar was undertaken by the young principal of the school, Ray Coulter, who drove his own personal car to collect the children. After 1942, however, no further attempts were made to transport the children to Center Point.

As a consequence of poor attendance, none of the Polk children graduated from Dunbar High School at Center Point. In 1938 Arthur's sixth son and tenth child was born, and the oldest son entered the CCC camp at sixteen, having completed the ninth grade. In 1940 he volunteered for the army, and in 1943 the next two sons followed his example. Then, in the spring of 1945, Arthur's oldest daughter, Julia, and the fourth son, Herbert, decided to seek their fortunes in California. They journeyed to Los Angeles, where they were assisted in finding jobs by their relatives, descendants of Douglass Polk.

By 1945, then, Arthur and Mattie Polk's five oldest children had left Muddy Fork. There were four younger children left at home, and none was attending school. Mattie, however, was determined that at least some of her children should have a chance to acquire an education, which meant completion of high school. She began to seek help from the Howard County Supervisor of Schools, Cecil E. Sheffield. After numerous trips to Nashville, she finally persuaded Sheffield to take action. Sheffield and school officials of the

Childress School District in Nashville devised a plan to consolidate the Muddy Fork District with the Childress District.

The Childress School District was named after Dr. R.C. Childress of the State Department of Education, the same man who had started the Polk children on their road to public education.[9] Childress School District at Nashville was one of only three or four all-black districts in the state, having a school board elected by the black community and a black superintendent of schools.[10] The president of the school board at Childress was C.P. Kelley, and the superintendent was G.W. Weddle. The Childress School Board, Superintendent Weddle, and County Supervisor Sheffield all agreed to provide room and board for the Polk children in lieu of transportation.[11]

Consequently, in the fall of 1945 the four youngest Polk children were placed in the home of Bess and Lydia Gill on Ansley Street in the New Addition of Nashville. The school was only one block from the Gill home, and the school district paid the Gills for a room for the four children and provided eight dollars a month with which the children were to buy food. The oldest of the four children was Marjorie, who at sixteen entered the tenth grade. Ruth at fifteen entered the ninth grade; Cindy at thirteen entered the seventh; and Preston at seven entered the first grade.

The four children began regular school attendance for the first time, except for Ruth, who had spent two years attending L'Ouverture High School in McAlester, Oklahoma, while living there with her mother's youngest sister, Mrs. Georgia Jones. Mr. Weddle took the children under his protective "wing" and put them all on the free lunch program, gave them school commodities to supplement their small allowance, and often bought them food from his own resources. He taught both Marjorie and Ruth to type, setting up a chart in front of them, placing their fingers on the right keys, and commanding them to "go to it." When they learned to type, he paid them a small fee to act as his "secretary," first Marjorie, then, when she graduated, her sister Ruth.

The four children lived one year with the Gills and then moved into a regular boarding house with a Mr. Wiley Kelly on Hutchinson Street. There they had two rooms and shared the kitchen with other students and teachers who also lived in the house.

The first of Arthur and Mattie Polk's children to finish high school was Marjorie, who graduated from Childress High School in 1948.

The following year Ruth graduated as valedictorian of her class. The third daughter, Cindy, married in 1948 and did not finish school. The youngest son, Preston, was sent to Washington, D.C., to live with his oldest brother Henry in 1949, and graduated from Spingarn High School there in 1956.

In 1948, after Marjorie graduated, Mattie decided to leave Muddy Fork and go to Nashville to live with her children. She wanted to be certain that her baby boy Preston would have a chance to finish school after the girls all finished or married and went away. So she took up residence with the children at the Kelly boarding house, and began to urge her husband to leave Muddy Fork also.

When Mattie left the Polk home at Muddy Fork, only Arthur and his ailing sister Frances were left behind. After Emma died in 1943, her daughter Lillian never returned to Muddy Fork, and Lillian's son James had long since left home, his mother and grandmother having gotten him into the 10th Cavalry in 1936. Arthur's sister Annie was married and living in Columbus, and Alice was living with her daughter in Texas.

When Frances's illness reached the point where Arthur could not attend to her needs, her sister Annie took her to live and subsequently die at Columbus. With Frances's departure, Arthur was completely alone, and he was finally pursuaded to leave the house and join his wife in Nashville, where she had rented a house on Hutchinson Street. In 1952 they moved into a house which they had bought and transported to a lot on South Front Street.

When Frances left the house, her sister Annie took the four-poster rope bed, the spinning wheel, the hand-woven baskets, and other cherished articles with her to Columbus, from whence they have subsequently disappeared. Arthur took with him the small trunk that had belonged to his brother Jimmy, a few of his farm implements, the old anvil and grindstone, and other items. Most of the furnishings were left in the house, however, and before Arthur could transport them all to Nashville, vandals carted off everything, including the zinc roofing on the house and buildings. With the roofing gone, the house and barns soon began to deteriorate, and although Arthur returned to the site to prop up walls and lay planks over the holes in the roof, the house crumbled within a few short months.

Life at Nashville proved to be exciting and fulfilling for Mattie, but Arthur was never happy away from the old home place. While his wife joined the New Light C.M.E. church, sang in the choir, and attended school functions, Arthur busied himself raising a truck crop of potatoes, corn, watermelons, and cantaloupes. He also took pride in the few flowers he grew in the small yard, including sweet peas and roses he had transplanted from Muddy Fork.

Arthur and Mattie had no income except for money given to them by their children and the small amount Mattie made as a helper at the Benson Nursing Home for a while. When Arthur's two nieces began to urge him to sell the land at Muddy Fork, he had no choice but to agree, although it broke his heart to part with the only place he had ever considered "home." Unable to pay the taxes, Arthur knew they would lose the land, and when his sister Annie consented to sell the place, he consented also. The entire 480 acres were sold to the Dierks Lumber Company in 1959. Company officials verbally promised Arthur and his family that they would always have access to the land to hunt and fish, and were free to visit the home site whenever they desired. Through the years, Arthur and his children continued to visit the site of the home, and whenever any of the family members return to Arkansas for a visit now, a trip to Muddy Fork is always a part of their itinerary. The land is at present a part of the vast holdings of the Weyerhaueser Company.[12]

9. For Generations to Come

The descendants of the slave Sally and her master, Taylor Polk, have now reached the seventh generation. Four of these generations lived in the house at Muddy Fork built by Spencer Polk and occupied by his children and his children's children. Spencer's son Arthur represented the longest surviving descendant to carry forward the Polk name, and he was also the last to occupy the homestead at Muddy Fork. Arthur also produced the largest number of immediate descendants of Spencer and Ellen Polk. All of Arthur's children except the last two grew to adolescence or adulthood at Muddy Fork. The following details of their lives are germane to this study in tracing the family to the present generation.

William Henry (1922-1967)

William Henry, Arthur's first-born son, was named for a succession of white Polks named William, and for his great uncle, Henry Murphy. He was a husky, dark-complexioned child, and his mother said that when he was born the Polk women took him to the south room to scrutinize his features.[1] They decided he was too dark to be a Polk and never allowed him (or any of the other children, for that matter) to call them "aunt."

The Depression years were especially hard on the Polk family, and in 1938, at age sixteen, Henry enlisted in the Civilian Conservation Corps in order to help out the family. He was stationed at a camp in Charlotte, Arkansas, and the family received an allotment of $22 a month for his service. After a year at the camp, he worked at the Arlington Hotel in Hot Springs as a bellhop, and in 1940 he enlisted in the regular army's 29th Quartermaster Division.[2] During World War II he was stationed in Australia, where he lost an eye when a cable on a tank he was pulling flew back and stuck in his face. He retired from the army after twenty years of service in 1960. After his honorable discharge, Henry worked for the Bureau of the Census in Washington, D.C. He never married and had no children.

Jack Dempsey (1923-)

Born only a year after his older brother William Henry, Jack Dempsey was named for the then world heavyweight boxing champion. With an olive complexion and straight black hair, Arthur's second son was more acceptable to the Polk women, who tended to dote on him, and it was clear that he was his father's "favorite" son. It was for Dempsey that the family's second car, a Model-A Ford, was purchased around 1940.

With World War II in progress, Dempsey volunteered for the army in 1943, shortly after he reached his eighteenth birthday. He served in the 92nd infantry as a military policeman and spent most of his service career in the Fort Batallion 211 in California. He reached the rank of sergeant, and was honorably discharged in 1945.[3] In 1949, he married Charlean Davis of Nashville, and they had three children, a son Dennis and two daughters, Sharon and Christine. Charlean has since died. Dempsey and his children and grandchildren live in Washington, D.C.

Raymond Clay (1925-1983)

Mattie Bullock Polk probably named her third son after Arthur's cousin Clay Murphy, who had wanted to court her in her youth. Named Clay at birth, this son of Arthur Polk was nicknamed "Baby Ray" by his great-grandmother Mary Berryman, who was visiting her daughter Viney at the time of the child's birth. As a result he grew up being called Ray, and that is the name that was officially recorded on army entry records. During the 1940s when he had to prove that he was indeed named Clay, he changed his name to Raymond Clay.

Following in his brothers' footsteps, Ray volunteered for the armed services in February 1943, when he was only seventeen years old. He achieved an outstanding military record as squad leader for the Army Quartermaster Corps. He reached the rank of corporal and was cited for marksmanship during initial boot training. He served in the battle zones of the campaigns of Normandy, Northern France, and the Rhineland. One of his assignments was removing the dead and wounded from the field. Although the army did not consider him to have seen "action," he was wounded in the leg by shrapnel on the battlefield near St. Louis, France, in the summer of 1944. For his efforts he received the American Campaign Medal, the Army Occupation Medal, and the World War II Victory Medal. He reinlisted after separation from the army at Camp Roosevelt, France, in 1945, and was honorably discharged with commendations for excellence and efficiency as a soldier in 1947.[4]

Ray married Dorothy Jean Moore of Nashville in 1950, and became the father of two sons, Marshall Polk of Washington, D.C., and Wayne Polk of the United States Air Force. He contracted multiple sclerosis in 1962, and after a long struggle with the illness died in a Washington hospital on August 28, 1983. His widow and grandchildren still live in Washington.

Julia Ann (1926-)

Julia, they said, looked just like the Polks. Fairer in complexion than either of the boys before her, she was the apple of her father's eye and fondly acceptable to his sisters. It was she who most often went to the south room to carry messages and check books out of Emma's library to read to the other children. As the oldest daughter, it was she who took on much of the responsibility of helping her mother with the younger children and directing them in household chores and work in the fields.

Julia married first Hurtis Hendrix of Graves Chapel, Arkansas, and later Lorse Gilbert of San Diego, California. She is the mother of six sons, John Arthur, Marquin Anthony, Stanley, Douglass, Julius Eric, and Oliver. She has one grandson, Anthony Julian. She and her family all reside in San Diego.

Herbert Hoover Hadley (1927-1983)

Born with blue eyes that soon turned hazel colored, Herbert looked just like his father Arthur, except that his hair was sandy red, unlike that of any of the Polks, all of whom had very black hair. Like his three older brothers, Herbert volunteered for the armed services after spending a short period of time in Los Angeles during the World War II years.

In 1946, approaching the age of nineteen, Herbert joined the 93rd Engineer Construction Batallion, and later served in the 135th Engineer Batallion as a unit leader in Transportation Operations. He was stationed in the Philippine Islands, Guam, Japan, Korea, and Vietnam. He was actively involved in the Korean conflict during the early 1950s and received the Commendation Ribbon with Metal Pendant for meritorious service in 1951. He was cited while serving in the Corps of Engineers of the 77th Engineer Combat Company as a Combat Construction Specialist. His meritorious service was rendered near Haman, Korea, when he supervised the construction of a four-mile auxiliary route through rice paddies and rugged mountains under intermittent sniper fire. He was able to complete the route in three days.[5]

Herbert spent twenty years in the service and retired May 31, 1966, with honor and distinction. While stationed in Japan he met and married Fukue Kodama, and his children by that marriage are Spencer Herbert, Raymond Kasi, and Janiece. Herbert died of a heart attack on July 18, 1983. His widow, children, and grandchildren live in Los Angeles.

Marjorie Helen (1929-)

Marjorie was named by her aunt Frances, and family members said she looked like the aunt who named her. With long, black, wavy hair, Marjorie was always said to be the most beautiful of all the children. The first of Arthur's children to finish high school, she joined her sister Julia in Los Angeles soon after graduation in 1948. There she met and married Lloyd Bland of San Antonio, Texas, who has since died. Marjorie has three daughters, Cherise Helene, Charlotte Marie, and Rebecca, and a granddaughter, Candice. Charlotte is employed with Johnson Products Company and lives in Chicago. The other family members live in Los Angeles.

Ruth (1930-)

Arthur's seventh child and third daughter was named by her mother, who chose the name of the heroic Hebrew woman of the Old Testament as a suitable model for a mother's hopes for her own child. Ruth was the second of the Polk children to graduate from high school, and just before her graduation she brought gladness to her mother's eye by eloping with the school principal, Thomas Edward Patterson of Jefferson, Texas. That was in 1949, and after attending first Wiley College in Marshall, Texas, and then A.M. and N. College in Pine Bluff, Arkansas, Ruth became a schoolteacher in the school at Nashville where her husband was principal. Later the couple moved to Little Rock, where Ruth taught in the public schools and later became a school administrator. Ruth is the mother of four children, a daughter Valerie (deceased), and three sons, Thomas Edward, Jr., Kenneth Aaron, and Tracey Desmond Dallas. Thomas and Kenneth live in Little Rock, and Tracey is serving in the navy aboard the USS Inchon. Ruth has three grandchildren, Kuan Kenneth, Kia Kyanna, and Thomas Edward III.

Cindy Lee (1932-)

If Julia was the apple of her father's eye, this youngest girl child of Arthur's, "Cindy Babe" as he called her, was the center, the core, of all of his paternal affection. He coddled and spoiled her when she was a baby, and when she grew older his eyes would always light up when she came into his presence. Needless to say, he was not pleased when she ran away and married Ira Howell, Jr., of Nashville when she was only sixteen and Ira not many years older.

The couple moved to Fresno, California, in the 1950s, where Cindy resides with her children and grandchildren. She is the mother of two sons, Michael Henry and Charles, and six daughters, Monica, Linda, Sandra, Marsha, Rose Marie, and Nancy.

Arthur (Sept.-Dec. 1936)

Arthur's fifth son contracted pneumonia soon after his birth and died at only three months of age.

Range Preston (1938-)

The last child born to Arthur and Mattie Polk is the image of what
Spencer Polk must have looked like in his youth. One of the tallest
of Arthur's sons, Preston is well over six feet, with the broad
shoulders and heavy black beard of his grandfather. Several days
after he was born, Arthur announced the name he had chosen. Not
having any other male members of the family with the names Range
or Preston, the older children queried their father as to where he
got them, but he never told them. It was a secret he took to his grave.

The youngest child was sent to Washington, D.C., when he was
fifteen years old. There he lived with his oldest brother Henry and
attended Spingarn High School, graduating in 1956. After finishing
high school, Preston enlisted in the navy and served twenty years,
retiring with honor from the military in 1978.[6] He is married to the
former Lois Capps, and they live in Virginia Beach, Virginia. They
have no children.

Of Spencer's Polk's ten children, only three besides Arthur had
children: his oldest son Douglass and his two oldest daughters, Em-
ma and Alice. Douglass Polk had one son, Willie, and one daughter,
Essie. Willie Polk apparently left no heirs, but Essie married a John
L. Graves and they had seven children, only one of whom, Mrs.
Faye Knott, is still living. Mrs. Knott lives in Los Angeles, along
with her children, Jacquelyn, Patricia, Bennie Knott, Jr., and
Wallace.[7] All of these individuals have children, and their grandchildren, along with the grandchildren and great-grandchildren of
Mrs. Knott's deceased brothers and sisters, represent the seventh
generation of Polks derived from Sally and her master, Taylor Polk.

Emma Polk had one daughter, Lillian, who married Edward Shelton in Oklahoma in 1917.[8] Lillian, who died in 1982 at the age of
eighty-six, had one son, James, now a retired army officer. Alice
Polk had one daughter, Pearl, who at eighty-seven is the oldest living descendant of Spencer and Ellen Polk. Pearl married the late
Patrick Henry Murphy in 1916, and they had five children, four of
whom are now living. They are Dr. John Brown Murphy of San
Antonio, Texas; Mary Ellen Jackson of Anahuac, Texas; Maxine
City of Los Angeles, California; and Patrick Henry Murphy, Jr., of

Austin, Texas. All of them have children of their own. Mrs. Pearl Murphy lives with her daughter Mary Ellen Jackson in Anahuac. The other descendants of Sally the slave girl and Taylor Polk can be identified through Sally's son Peter, since very little information has been found on her son Frank and her daughter Eliza. Frank Polk is said to have gone west in the 1850s with Taylor Polk's son Anderson. Recently it has been discovered that Frank's descendants included a daughter, Beatrice Johnson of Los Angeles, California, whose children and grandchildren also reside in Los Angeles.[9] Eliza married Ives Polk (no relation) and moved to Texas. Eliza and Ives Polk had two children, Henry and Susannah, about whom no other information has been found.

Peter Polk had a comparatively small family. He was apparently married three times and the offspring from two of these unions can be identified. His first wife, whom he took during slavery time, was named Cynthia, and they had a son named Thomas and a daughter named Louisa, or Lou. From oral accounts by Mrs. Eddie Lee Wilson and her niece, Mrs. Beatrice Knight of Fort Smith, Arkansas, and from a document left by Lou Polk's son, Semmie Clardy, Peter Polk's wife Cynthia was sold away from him to slave owners coming into Arkansas from Texas. Clardy wrote: "Since my grandmother had been sold as a slave from her husband, the half-white Polk, her new master settled in Hot Springs, Arkansas, and my grandmother became Cynthia Preston. She remarried without a divorce after slavery, since slave marriages did not count anyway."[10] Cynthia Polk was pregnant when she was sold, and Lou Polk was born in a covered wagon en route from Muddy Fork to Hot Springs. Clardy goes on to report that when Lou, his mother, was four or five years old, "a Methodist minister on his circuit from Hot Springs to Center Point discovered and made connections of the two families. My grandfather [Peter Polk] had remarried, but was glad to make the journey of seventy-five miles by wagon to get his daughter."[11]

Peter Polk apparently kept Lou with him as a member of his household, for she is listed in the "Index to Howard County Marriage Records" as having married Barney Clardy of Howard County in 1885.[12] Lou Polk Clardy had several children, including her son, Semmie, who left the family history, another son, Curtis, and three daughters, Eddie Lee Wilson, Alice Deloney, and Nellie

Piggee. Their children and grandchildren live in various parts of the United States. Mrs. Eddie Lee Wilson, the only surviving child of Lou Polk, resides in Fort Smith, Arkansas, and has no children.

Peter Polk later married a woman named Jennie, whose tombstone at Muddy Fork declares that she is the wife of Peter Polk. Jennie Polk died in 1882.

In 1884, Peter married Sally Johnson, a widow with two sons, John and Grant Johnson. Peter and Sally Johnson had three children, Alonzo, Mattie, and Nobie. Alonzo Polk married Lucy Murphy, Ellen Polk's niece, and they had three children, Odell, Annie, and Eva. Odell Polk resides in Washington, D.C.; Annie Polk Craft lives in Newport, Arkansas; and Eva Polk is deceased. Peter's daughter Mattie married first R. Claude Sanders of Center Point, and they had three sons, Rupert, Garland, and Worthy. Rupert Sanders lives in Los Angeles, Garland Sanders in New York, and Worthy Sanders in Center Point, Arkansas.

Nobie Polk Clardy, the daughter of Peter Polk, lived to be the oldest descendant of Sally and Taylor Polk. Her husband was Detroit Clardy of Center Point, and the couple had several children, five of whom are still living. They are Joe Wheeler Clardy of Denver, Adell Clardy Mamby of Center Point, Leon Clardy of Los Angeles, D.C. Clardy of Center Point, and Hutson Clardy of Los Angeles. Nobie Polk Clardy died at Nashville, Arkansas, in 1984 at the age of ninety-three.

Peter Polk left Muddy Fork after he married Sally Johnson in 1884, and bought a small farm at Center Point, where he raised his last family. His wife sold the land he owned at Muddy Fork to put his son Alonzo through college.[13]

Of the descendants of Sally and her master Taylor Polk, most have been ordinary men and women, for the most part morally strong and intelligent. None has ever been imprisoned or committed any serious crime, as far as is known, and a significant number have been outstanding in their respective fields. Several have made excellent schoolteachers, with three receiving the Ph.D. degree in the field of education. Many of the Polk men have had commendable military careers, one reaching the rank of major in the army during the 1940s, a time when black army officers were few in number. Other family members have attained success in the fields of medicine, law, business, and commerce. Following is a list of individuals in the Polk family who have become successful in a variety of professions:

Recipients of the Ph.D. degree

Dr. John Brown Murphy of San Antonio, Texas (great-grandson of Spencer Polk)

Dr. Constance Craft Dees of Normal, Alabama (great-granddaughter of Peter Polk)

Dr. Ruth Polk Patterson of Little Rock, Arkansas (granddaughter of Spencer Polk)

Education (schoolteacher or college professor)

Emma Polk (daughter of Spencer Polk), deceased.

Alonza Polk (son of Peter Polk), deceased.

Eddie Lee Wilson-Johnson (granddaughter of Peter Polk), Fort Smith, Arkansas.

Dr. John Murphy (great-grandson of Spencer Polk), San Antonio, Texas.

Annie Polk Craft (granddaughter of Peter Polk), Newport, Arkansas.

Dr. Ruth Polk Patterson (granddaughter of Spencer Polk), Little Rock, Arkansas.

Dr. Constance Craft Dees (great-granddaughter of Peter Polk), Normal, Alabama.

Barbara Craft Stephens (great-granddaughter of Peter Polk), Detroit, Michigan.

Joan Craft Henry (great-granddaughter of Peter Polk), Center Point, Arkansas.

Adele Clardy Mamby (granddaughter of Peter Polk), Center Point, Arkansas.

Roland Piggee (great-grandson of Peter Polk), Stamps, Arkansas.

Medical doctor

Dr. Norman Polk (great-grandson of Peter Polk), Hawaii.

Dr. Dwight Gregory Stephens (great-great grandson of Peter Polk), California.

Appellate judge

The Honorable Glenn Johnson (step-grandson of Spencer Polk), Chicago, Illinois.

Lawyer

Loretta Polk (great-granddaughter of Peter Polk), Washington, D.C.
Donald Deloney (great-grandson of Peter Polk), Washington, D.C.

Military Officer

Major James E. Shelton, retired (great-grandson of Spencer Polk), Reno, Nevada.

Corporate/business manager

Charlotte Marie Bland (great-granddaughter of Spencer Polk), Chicago, Illinois.
Karen Jones (great-great granddaughter of Peter Polk), Richmond, Virginia.

Occupational therapist

Valerie Ellaine Patterson (great-granddaughter of Spencer Polk), deceased.

Legal assistant

Douglass Hendrix (great-grandson of Spencer Polk), San Diego, California.

Computer programmer

Julius Eric Hendrix (great-grandson of Spencer Polk), San Diego, California.

Systems analyst

Marquin Anthony Hendrix (great-grandson of Spencer Polk), San Diego, California.

Shipwright

Stanley Hendrix (great-grandson of Spencer Polk), San Diego, California.

Greyhound bus operator

John Arthur Jones (great-grandson of Spencer Polk), San Diego, California.

Fireman

Michael Henry Howell (great-grandson of Spencer Polk), Fresno, California.

Postal supervisor, mail clerk

Patrick Henry Murphy, Jr. (great-grandson of Spencer Polk), Austin, Texas.
Odell Polk (grandson of Peter Polk), retired, Washington, D.C.

Journeyman lineman and musician

Thomas Edward Patterson, Jr. (great-grandson of Spencer Polk), Little Rock, Arkansas.
Kenneth Aaron Patterson (great-grandson of Spencer Polk), Little Rock, Arkansas.

Air traffic controller/airlines manager

Harry Lee Jones, Jr. (great-great grandson of Peter Polk), New York City
Charles Howell (great-grandson of Spencer Polk), Fresno, California.

Airline stewardess

Stephanie Coleman (great-great granddaughter of Peter Polk), Chicago, Illinois
Pamela Stephens (great-great granddaughter of Peter Polk), Chicago, Illinois

The individuals identified above represent only those descendants of Peter and Spencer Polk whose lives have come to the author's attention. It is not an all-inclusive listing, for there are undoubtedly other descendants of Peter and Spencer Polk who are also noteworthy. It is not possible at this time to name all of the fine men and women, boys and girls who carry the bloodline of Sally and Taylor Polk, although all branches of the family tree have been recognized.

The Polks descended from Sally and her master Taylor Polk are relatively few in number, and considering that many of them are only one or two generations removed from slavery, their accomplishments are ones of which the family can be proud. Considering, furthermore, that many of these individuals and/or their parents and grandparents began their lives in the community of Muddy Fork, an isolated area far removed from direct access to social and educational opportunities, their achievements are, indeed, outstanding.

Spencer Polk's brothers, Peter and Frank, and his sister Eliza left Muddy Fork before the turn of the century, and apparently all died before 1900; but Spencer remained in the community to live his life to a ripe old age. Most of the older descendants of Spencer and his brother Peter interviewed for this book remember Spencer as a symbol of inspiration and family pride. They especially recall his keen intellect, kindheartedness, and warm generosity. Those who don't remember the man personally recall their parents' and grandparents' references to Spencer Polk in the same vein. It is the author's hope that this account of his life, both the beautiful and the sad, will serve as a source of motivation and encouragement to the younger family members, to their children, and to future descendants of the Polks of Muddy Fork for generations to come.

10. Archeology and Artifact

Today, as one crosses the modern concrete bridge that spans the Muddy Fork Creek, the gentle rise of a hillside comes into view. If it is springtime, the hillside is still covered with yellow daffodils and jonquils. In spring and summer, japonica and crepe myrtle bushes still blush invitingly deep pink to butterflies and wild honeybees. Above the many-colored flowers, thick growths of poplars, brushbroom bushes, English dogwood, and wild honeysuckle suggest that this ancient garden was once a place of human habitation. If one stops to examine the site more closely, vestiges of architecture reveal themselves. Two piles of limestone rocks that were once huge chimneys sprawl several yards apart. The remains of gigantic oak logs, mostly rotted shells now, lie in contorted array but still suggest the outlines of a rectangular foundation. Nearby, a circular heap of moss-covered earth surrounds a wide chasm that used to be the well. This is all that remains of a once self-contained farmstead and the center of activity in a thriving nineteenth-century settlement.

Even today, though, more than a century since Spencer Polk and his friends and neighbors rolled out of the forest the giant oak logs with which he constructed his first log cabin, there are hundreds more clues left behind on that hillside and preserved in the attics of his descendants to tell the final chapter of this early American family. An examination of the site of the Spencer Polk homestead by the Arkansas Archeological Survey in 1979 unearthed some of those clues and added new insights on the Spencer Polk family as an example of early Arkansas life.

In 1978, when the original project on the Spencer Polk homestead began, the idea of collecting artifacts and using archeological techniques to explore Afro-American history and culture was virtually unheard of. In fact, only since the 1920s has the use of artifacts from everyday life in America become popular as a method of historical research. Historians of the past had held tenaciously to the idea that only written sources were useful for documentation of historical research. They relied upon a "scientific" definition of history that "ignored completely the artifactual evidence of the national past."[1] Since the 1920s, however, collecting and preserving the nation's material culture has become a national pastime. Since the restoration of historic Williamsburg in the 1930s, historic preservation programs have become a significant vehicle for recording and documenting the everyday life of ordinary Americans.

During the past two decades, the use of archeology to gain information about the past by examining earth-bound objects such as bits of pottery, building fragments, and food remains has resulted in "greater knowledge about past human behavior." In understanding American material culture, "visual data" have become as important as "verbal data" in historical research.[2] The use of archeology in the study of Afro-American culture is especially vital because of the lack of authentic written records. Information that can be gleaned from archeology and artifact study can contribute a great deal toward "defining the total picture of black lifeways in America."[3] For this reason, historians, cultural anthropologists, and archeologists are at last giving needed attention to black American material culture, as evidenced by site surveys of the places where African-Americans have lived, worked, and been buried from the period of slavery up to the present time. Examples of recent archeological work on Afro-American sites are the excavation of a slave cabin at Cumberland Island, Georgia;[4] examination of the site of a black community at Parting Ways, Massachusetts;[5] excavations at several sites in Florida;[6] and the site survey of the McKindra plantation in Conway County, Arkansas.[7]

The original project on the Spencer Polk homestead began with a proposal to the Arkansas Endowment for the Humanities to develop a paper describing the log house that Spencer built and discussing the background of the occupant. The research findings

were to be augmented by a slide presentation on the visual evidence
of the homestead. The proposal included a search for family pictures and household items that would be photographed and made
into slides.

The project was approved and funded by the Arkansas Endowment for the Humanities in February of 1978. Shortly after the project was funded, Bill Worthen, director of the Arkansas Territorial
Restoration, suggested that an archeological survey of the house site
might be possible. He had photographed log dwellings throughout
the state and had taken shots of the remaining evidence of the Spencer
Polk house. Worthen recommended Dr. Leslie "Skip" Stewart-
Abernathy, an archeologist with the Arkansas Archeological Survey,
as the person to contact about the Polk site.

Dr. Abernathy agreed to assist in the project, and a second phase
of the research, including the archeological survey, was proposed
and funded in the spring of 1979. The second phase of the project
also called for a public exhibit of the artifacts collected, and Lucy
Robinson, director of the Old State House in Little Rock, agreed to
display the items there when the project was completed.

The archeological examination of the Spencer Polk house site was
conducted in the fall of 1979 by the Arkansas Archeological Survey
at the University of Arkansas at Fayetteville. The survey was directed
by Dr. Stewart-Abernathy and the survey team was made up of Dr.
Abernathy and his assistant, Mike Swanda of Ouachita Baptist
University at Arkadelphia, Arkansas. They were assisted by Parker
Westbrook of Nashville, Arkansas, and the author. Westbrook's
sister, Lucille Westbrook, made trips to the site to provide the team
with much welcomed coffee and doughnuts at mid-morning.

The survey team first arrived at the site on the icy cold morning
of December 7, 1979, and spent the next four days mapping out the
area and identifying significant points such as foundation rocks,
fireplaces, trash dumps, and kitchen areas. For the author, the examination of the site was an adventure in traveling back in time,
and for a few short hours the abandoned hillside and the people who
had lived there seemed to come to life again under the skillful prob-
ing of the archeologist and his companions.

The first task of the survey team was to clear away enough of
the undergrowth to gain access to the site. Among the flowers and

shrubs were thick growths of small poplar and cottonwood trees, vines, briars, and tall weeds. At the time when the proposal to examine the site was written, the chimney at the south end of the house was still standing intact. During the few months prior to the survey, however, intruders converged on the site and hauled away the entire chimney and fireplace, leaving only a few of the stones under a pile of mud mortar that had held the chimney together. In order to get to the site, the invaders had to cut a path wide enough for a vehicle to enter from the main road. As a consequence, the larger poplar and cottonwood trees had been cut down, and their trunks criss-crossed the lower portion of the house site. The obstruction from the fallen trees limited the workers' activities to the northern section of the foundation. By the end of the first day, the area had been cleared sufficiently so that the archeologist's drafting table and other equipment could be set up, and measurements and pictures could be taken of the emerging foundation timbers and fireplace hearth.

On the second day of the survey, the team began to pull artifacts from auger holes, using a metal detector to locate objects. In almost every sample, sizable bits of pottery, china, and glass fragments were extracted, some of which the archeologist identified as very "fancy stuff." On the night before, the team were the guests of the Westbrooks in Nashville. Parker and Lucille Westbrook were two of the most enthusiastic supporters of the Polk family project. Their father, Walter Westbrook, had been a neighbor of Spencer Polk at Muddy Fork at the turn of the century, and Parker and Lucille were the ones who persuaded their father to consent to be interviewed for the project. The Westbrooks had invited the team to their home the night before for dinner in Parker's newly reconstructed log cabin in the backyard of their home on North Main Street. After dinner the group was taken to the main house to admire the Westbrooks' collection of antiques, among which was proudly displayed a set of Alfred Meakin china. The next morning at the Spencer Polk site, one of the first real "finds" was a large piece of whiteware with the inscription "Royal Ironstone China—Alfred Meakin-England."

One of the most surprising discoveries was the presence of a cellar near the north fireplace hearth, a feature the archeologists had not expected to find in the Polk structure. Noticing clean white sand in the auger holes, they began to excavate a shallow pit. They discovered a six-by-six-foot area lined with sand from the creek bed. The cellar was probably constructed when the original log cabin was built. By the 1920s the area beneath the fireplace was not clearly identified as a cellar, for the original pit was not apparent at that time. There were four short planks in the floor directly in front of the hearth, however, that could be removed fairly easily by pulling out the loose nails that held them in place. At that time the area was used for storing sweet potatoes and dried walnuts and hickory nuts in the winter. The cellar area could be gotten to either by lifting the boards in the floor to remove items or by entering from the outside through an opening next to the chimney to place items in the storage area. It was not even referred to as a "cellar" after the 1920s, but only as the place "under the house" where things were stored to keep dry and warm, including sometimes Old Lady, the dog, and her new litter of puppies.

Of the nearly two hundred items pulled from the site, only a few were intact, including glass bottles, plowshares, and a Model-T Ford oil dipstick. Most items were fragmented by use and decay. Those bits and pieces under the earth show, however, that although he was a former slave and lived most of his life in seeming isolation from the rest of the world, Spencer Polk had access to and took advantage of the modern world market. The artifacts, both collected and excavated, show that the Polk family at Muddy Fork enjoyed at times a rather high standard of living for the rural backwoods of the South. They combined in splendid harmony the very old and the very latest in the way of Victorian decorative and useful arts. While the head of the household slept on a rope bed made by slaves, his daughters' dresses were adorned with fancy glass buttons that could have been imported from Europe. The way the members dressed in family pictures shows that they were able to buy the latest fashions in ladies' and men's wear. A car crank and radio batteries preserved in the dirt show that the Polk family enjoyed some modern conveniences long before they became available to the majority of rural Americans.

The archeologist's report of the survey sheds further light on the character of the Spencer Polk homestead and the significance of the Polk family history to a better understanding of Arkansas and American farm life:

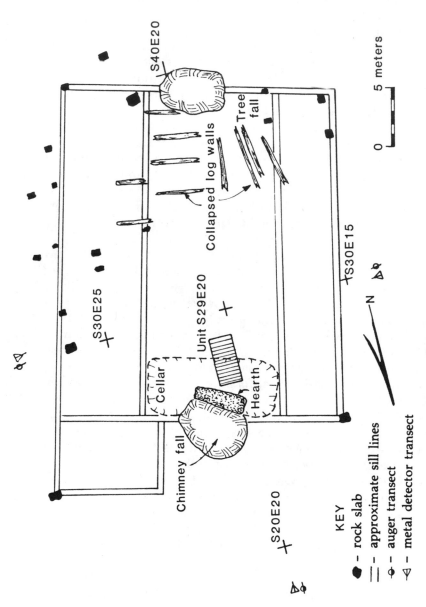

KEY

● – rock slab
‖ – approximate sill lines
⟁ – auger transect
▽ – metal detector transect

S40E20

S30E25

S30E15

S20E20

Unit S29E20

Cellar

Hearth

Chimney fall

Collapsed log walls

Tree fall

N

0   5 meters

Fig. 7. A scaled drawing of the Spencer Polk house site, based on the archeological survey made in 1979. Drawing by "Skip" Stewart-Abernathy.

Arkansas Archeological Survey

Statement of Significance: The Polk Site, 3H096

In November, 1979, a team from the Arkansas Archeological Survey under my direction conducted an archeological reconnaissance at the Polk site, 3H096. This is a farmstead located on the Muddy Fork River in central Howard County that was occupied from about 1875 to about 1953. During this reconnaissance the site was mapped, informant interviews were conducted, auger and metal detector transects were undertaken, a surface collection was made, and a 1X2 meter test pit was excavated to sterile soil. This effort was carried out as a part of a project conducted by Dr. Ruth Polk Patterson and funded by a grant from the Arkansas Endowment for the Humanities.

Analysis of artifacts and other data recovered is still underway. At this point it is already evident that several statements can be made as to the local and regional significance of this archeological site.

First, although the site has been damaged by the widening and paving of a road running through the stead and by insensitive clearing of the margins of the roadway, the portion of the farmstead containing the house is in excellent condition. Although the house itself no longer stands, the house plan can be reconstructed by the extensive evidence of stone underpinnings, the presence of chimney columns at both the north and south ends of the foundation area, and by the presence of portions of the hewn log fabric of the structure itself. The subsurface record of activity in the house and in the surrounding yard remains intact. Initial work indicates that further work would produce evidence of patterning created by construction and use of outbuildings, gardening, water storage, discard behavior, and laundry activity. The presence of a cellar, an unusual feature for vernacular architecture in Arkansas, under the northern portion of the house, confirmed by test excavations, indicates that enormous numbers of artifacts exist as fill for the cellar. These artifacts, even though they are only the broken and decaying remnants of the objects used in the house, provide an extraordinary data base for further understanding of rural life in southwest Arkansas.

Second, the Polk site is significant because it is one of the few historic sites recorded in Howard County. The Polk site represents a long tradition of small farmers utilizing the rolling hills and riverine bottom lands for mixed farming. Advantages of the Polk site include that we know its exact location, its exact condition, and we have available a lengthy oral record of activities of farm management, social interaction, changes in material culture, and family life that occurred there. Although it is likely that other farmstead sites exist in the area, it is also likely that they have been more heavily disturbed by later construction, agriculture, or timbering. Finally, given state-wide research priorities, limited funding, the lack in the state of enough personnel trained in the evaluation of historic sites, and the demands placed on archeologists to salvage sites endangered by intensive agricultural practices in eastern Arkansas, by rapid residential development near urban centers, and by looters who see artifacts only as something to be sold, it will likely be several years before extensive work is done on historic sites in the area. We know today that the Polk site is an important one worthy of preservation.

Third, and perhaps most important, the Polk site represents one of the few farmsteads occupied by blacks that have been studied in Arkansas, and for that matter in the United States. Spencer Polk, founder of the farmstead, was a freed slave who had been born in 1833 and who had strong ties with the Taylor Polk family of plantation owners in Howard County. The effort undertaken by Spencer Polk, his wife Ellen Murphy, and their descendants to build new lives as free farmers is a laudable adventure, no less interesting because it was an effort that was being duplicated all over Arkansas and the South. The Polks became respected members of rural society, prosperous within the context of the Muddy Fork region, and remembered today by blacks and whites in the Nashville area. The Polk site therefore exists at the beginning of the 1980s as a strong reminder of the self-sufficient black farm family and as a strong counterpoint to the stereo-typical images of Uncle Tom and the ghetto gang member. As an archeological site, it represents a unique site in our knowledge that can enable archeologists and historians to better understand the lifeways and contributions of rural blacks outside of the tenant farmer context. At the Polk site there is an enormous amount of information about the life of ordinary people. The heritage of Arkansas is a strong one and based in the lives of ordinary people white and black. The Polk site in its present conditions is an outstanding example of that heritage.

Skip Stewart-Abernathy[8]

During the first phase of the project on the Spencer Polk family in 1978 and 1979, artifacts that had been handed down in the family were collected. Descendants of Spencer Polk had kept in their possession several important objects that reflect the socioeconomic status of the family as well as their personal tastes and general lifestyles. The items collected dated from the pre-Civil War period up to the 1930s. Among the objects collected from family members were photographs, household items, personal items, documents, and letters. These, along with the artifacts unearthed during the archeological survey, were placed on exhibit at the Old State House Museum in Little Rock from November 1, 1980, through March 1981. The museum exhibit was accompanied by a lecture on the significance of the items to the Polk family. Among the most important objects collected from the family were the following:

A portrait of Spencer Polk. Set in an eighteen- by twenty-inch frame of gold and silver leaf, the portrait is an eight- by ten-inch tintype softly tinted and placed beneath a light blue mat with an oval window. Taken when Spencer was a young man, the portrait dates from the 1860s and was taken to Columbus by Frances when she left Muddy Fork in 1950 to live with her sister Annie. Annie took the portrait to Austin, Texas, where it was left in the care of her niece, Pearl Murphy, who gave it to the author for the exhibit.

A twenty-inch-high pottery jar. Made of low-fired, unglazed earthenware with the number 7 on the shoulder, this large water container could have been made by African slaves. It is similar to Ghanaian vessels described by anthropologist Leland Ferguson in his discussion of Colono-Indian vessels, which he argues were actually produced by African slaves. There were many such vessels of various sizes in the Polk household, but this was the only one that has survived intact. The author brought the jar to her home in Little Rock when her parents died in the 1960s.

A *small trunk*. This trunk belonged to Jimmy Polk and had been in his brother Arthur's possession since Jimmy's death in 1910. Arthur kept the trunk close by his bed at all times and never let anyone go near it. When Arthur died in 1964, his daughter Ruth, the author, took the trunk to her home in Little Rock, where its contents remained undisturbed until the Spencer Polk project began in 1978. The trunk measures 26 by 16 by 14 inches, with a rounded top, and is made of tin reinforced by strips of wood. The trunk was filled with memorabilia that became a major part of the museum exhibit.

A *carpenter's level*. The level was found in Jimmy's trunk and is presumed to have belonged to Spencer Polk, who was a carpenter as well as a blacksmith. The level appears worn from much use and probably dates from the 1860s. This level was never used by Arthur, for none of the family members had ever seen it before his death. Furthermore, Arthur had his own set of larger levels. The presence of this twelve-inch level in the trunk suggests that it held some special sentimental value.

A *china cup and saucer*. Acquired from Pearl Murphy, the cup and saucer had been taken from Arkansas to Texas by Annie Johnson, who had collected several household items when she took her sister Frances to live with her at Columbus. The cup is made of heavy white china bordered with gold roses around the top. On the left side are large red and yellow roses above a band of deep rose-colored tint. On the bottom of the cup are the partially obscured letters "ANT. . . ." The saucer is made of lightweight china with roses and cornflowers on two sides, and its twelve sides are rimmed with gold.

Two hand-made game boards. The game boards in Jimmy's trunk appear to be extremely old. One of the boards is a twelve- by twenty-four-inch pine plank with a checkerboard drawn on one end. The other is a twelve-inch square with a checkerboard on one side and round dots on the other. The boards were no doubt handed down from Spencer Polk's days, for none of the family members played checkers during the last decades of the home's occupancy.

A hand-made crochet hook. Carved out of what appears to be hickory wood, the hook is six-and-a-half inches long, tapered and curved to a perfect hook on the end.

A lady's bonnet. Made of black broadcloth, this intricately hand-stitched bonnet was made by Emma for her mother Ellen. Still looking as new as the day it was made, it is the type of bonnet worn by farm women to shade the face from the sun. The quilted crown framed the face, and straps tied under the chin held the bonnet securely on the head.

Three whiskey bottles. These bottles reflect the Polk men's love of good whiskey. One is a pint-sized bottle with the label "Old Watermill, distilled and bottled by Old Kentucky Distillery, Incorporated, Louisville, Kentucky." The other two are half-pint bottles, one with a bubble in the glass on the side and the other with an embossed clear-glass bottom and burgundy shoulders. The name "S.W. Willis" is scrolled diagonally across to the upper part of the latter. Two of the bottles have glass and cork stoppers, and the other has a metal screw-on top.

A stoneware churn and a pitcher. The churn is eighteen inches high and eight inches in diameter. It has two lids, one for covering the churn and the other with a hole in the center for the churn dasher to fit through when churning milk. Made of white stoneware with a blue stripe and manufacturer's label, the churn matches the ten-inch-tall pitcher used for serving milk at the table. The churn and pitcher belonged to Mattie Polk and date from the 1920s.

A cedar chest. When the WPA began to improve the roads in Howard County in the late 1930s, the highway crews eventually made their way to Muddy Fork. The workers came with bulldozers and graders to widen the road in front of the Polk home. The new road cut the dusty wagon trail down into the earth, forming a high bank on each side between the columns of cedars. In many places the roots were severed, and some of the trees died. Finally, in the early 1940s, the road crew announced that the trees would have to be cut down. The trunks of the fallen cedars were sold to a neighbor, who wanted to make cedar chests from the timber. In exchange, he made a cedar chest for Arthur's wife Mattie. Though crudely made, the chest became one of her prized possessions.

Quilting cards. Many a quilt was made in the home with this set of spiked boards with handles used for stretching out the fibers of raw cotton. The cotton was spread between the top and bottom sections of the quilt for padding.

Greeting cards. Jimmy Polk's trunk contained a collection of greeting cards, most of which were in color, but one series of which was in black and white. Most were designed as postcards, and several had been mailed to Jimmy and bore stamps and postmarks.

Miscellaneous items. The trunk also contained the letters to and from Jimmy and those from Mattie Bullock Polk to Arthur Polk quoted in chapter 6. The letters from Mattie to Arthur were in a red leather case with the inscription "Ropps Commercial Calculator" on the outside. On the inside flap of the case was the following inscription in Arthur's handwriting:

ARTHUR POLK
In case of accident please notify
J.S. Polk
Howard Co. Muddy Fork, Ar.

In addition to the letters, the case contained a tax receipt dated March 31, 1909, and two poll tax receipts dated March of 1908 and 1911. Other items in the case were a pale blue envelope with decorative script addressed to Mr. Adolphe Ebert, 227 Calle Vallencia, Espagne Barcelona. Finally, the case contained a woman's pink silk handkerchief bordered in deep rose with gray hummingbirds sipping at rosecolored tulips. The handkerchief probably belonged to Mattie, for her sister, Willie Bell Maxwell, has often spoken of the beautiful and expensive gifts Arthur bought Mattie during their courtship.

The archeological survey turned up an additional collection of items from the Polk home. These have been categorized by the archeologist according to where they were found:

Surface objects. These included one china wall fragment with a light blue pattern, decalcomania whiteware, dating from 1880 to 1950; a small plowshare; and a large metal crank, possibly from a tractor. Since no tractors are known to have been in the vicinity, the crank could have been intrusive.

Household dump sites. The dump sites yielded several plain wall and rim sherds; one rim sherd with pattern, decalcomania, dating from 1880 to 1950; one base fragment with a black band; and one base fragment with "Royal Ironstone China" and the maker's mark, Alfred Meakin, England, dating from about 1897-1913 (the peak period of prosperity for the Polk family).

Metal detector test sites. Auger transects yielded several clear white and colored wall and rim sherds; several bottle fragments; lamp globe fragments; brown and natural stoneware fragments dating from the 1830s; horseshoes; wire nails and cut nails; bone, glass, and shell buttons; beads; window glass; a school slate; and a Model-T Ford oil testing rod.

Cellar fill. Excavation of the cellar pit yielded a clear base sherd with a "V 7" mold mark, dating from 1910 to 1950; a dark green wall sherd, 1800-1900; an aqua bottle wall/base with " . . . thing syrup" on the side post, 1860-1900, possibly Evan's teething or soothing syrup, as advertised in a Peekskill, New York newspaper; one whole brown six-sided bottle, six centimeters high with the mold mark 7"S&D"29 on the base and "Sharp & Dohms Baltimore" on the sides, post-1903; two graphite pencil cores; a bone-handle brush, and a prehistoric lithic (stone) tool, late Archaic novaculite.

The collection of items from both family members and the survey shows that the Polk family used many household items that had been handed down from the period of slavery. The stoneware jars and jugs, the game boards, the crocheting needle, the carpenter's level, and the wire nails were all relics from the earliest days of the household or items that Spencer Polk had used in his youth and acquired from his former master. The presence of whiskey and medicine bottles and decorative spongeware on whiteware indicates that the family made use of mail-order services from faraway cities and had at one time the money to buy the best that was available.

Along with the examination of the house site in December of 1979, the survey team visited the Muddy Fork cemetery where Spencer Polk and others of his family are buried. There among the pine trees and under the growths of ivy and dogwood are the tall tombstones of Spencer, his wife Ellen, and their son Ben. Small markers and boulders identify the spots where other family members are buried. Farther down in the woods and outside the protective fence of the white cemetery is the grave of Taylor Polk.[9] Looking eerie and formidable in the darkened shadows of the forest trees, Taylor Polk's grave is a huge rectangle of dark stones carefully piled up to form a once ostensible mausoleum. For some reason the masonry of the tomb is strangely reminiscent of the piles of stones that mark the spots where Spencer Polk's chimneys and sorghum mill furnace once stood. Perhaps it was Spencer Polk himself who constructed the ominous shrine to the only white Polk known to be buried at Muddy Fork. Spencer was the last adult Polk male to be buried there. The size and quality of the three Polk markers in the black section of the cemetery are further evidence of the eminence of the Spencer Polk family in the Muddy Fork community.

Spencer Polk, born a slave, was typical of most individuals of African descent in Arkansas in the 1830s. The circumstances of his birth, however, were unusual. Like most bondsmen in America, his freedom came only when the great strife ended. As a free man, however, the relationship he had with his former master gave him advantages in acquiring land and establishing a homestead that his fellow African-Americans did not typically have. The homestead he established stood out as a central place in the community in which he lived and raised his family. The house he built was a typical example of vernacular architecture, but at the same time it portrayed the unusual background and personality of the founder.

The magnitude of the Spencer Polk farmstead and the lifestyle of its inhabitants show that instead of ignorant backwoods people whose lives were untouched by "civilization," the black Polks of Muddy Fork were indeed in touch with the march toward modernity. The founder of the homestead and head of the family, although his name has not been recorded in history books, was a man whose contributions to his community were no less important because of his anonymity. Finally, Spencer Polk's life and that of his family remind us that, as Arkansans, as southerners, and as Americans, all of our lives are intertwined, intermingled, and connected by the bonds of the past, whether those bonds were forged in slavery or linked by divine nature, which has bestowed upon us all a heritage that was once, and must forever be, free.

Appendix

Descendants of Sally, a Slave, and Her Master, Taylor Polk

I. PETER POLK, 1827-ca. 1900 (m. Cynthia, ca. 1850; m. Jennie, ca. 1870; m. Sally Johnson, 1884)
  II. Thomas Polk, 1853-1872
  Louisa Ellen Polk, 1865-1949 (m. Barney Clardy, 1885)
    III. Sally Clardy, 1886 (d. in infancy)
    Alice Clardy, 1888-1921 (m. Simon Deloney, 1911)
      IV. Edgar Ervin Deloney, 1911 (m. Odessa Neal, 1934)
        V. Hazel Deloney, 1935 (d. in infancy)
        Ruby Deloney, 1936 (m. ___ Richardson, nd.)
        Curtis Deloney, 1938
      IV. Mattie Lou Deloney, nd. (m. Cecil Neal, nd.)
        V. Joyce Neal, 1941-
        Wilma Neal, 1944-
        Anita Neal, 1950-
      IV. Arthur Deloney, nd.-1939
        Luther Deloney, 1915- (m. Jewel ___)
        V. James Deloney, 1946-
        Luther Deloney, Jr., 1957-
        Rhonda Deloney, 1959-
        Van Deloney, 1962-
      IV. Simmie Deloney, nd. (m. Earline Dinlap, nd.)
        V. Donald Deloney, nd.
        Paula Deloney, nd.
        Tracy Deloney, nd.
      IV. Robbie Deloney, nd. (m. Haskell Scoggins, nd.)
        V. Alice Scoggins, nd.
        William Scoggins, nd.
      IV. Simon (Jack) Deloney, nd. (m. Florence ___, nd.)
    III. Emma Clardy, 1890 (d. in infancy)
    Willie Clardy, 1892 (d. in childhood)
    Nellie Dean Clardy, 1884-1977 (m. Ernest Piggee, 1914)
      IV. Lelvan Piggee, nd.
      Robert A. Piggee, 1917- (m. ___)

IV. Robert A. Piggee (*continued*):
   V. Diane Piggee, 1940–
      Onita Piggee, 1942–
IV. Barney Piggee, 1919–   (m. _____)
   V. Anthony Piggee, 1951–
      Barbara Piggee, 1953–
      Patricia Piggee, 1956–
IV. Alonzo Piggee, 1921-1974 (m. _____)
   V. Wynne Piggee, 1951–
      Donna Piggee, 1953–
IV. O.B. DuBois Piggee, 1923–
      Roland Piggee, 1925–   (m. Maxine Owens, 1952)
   V. Rozalyn Piggee, 1953–   (m. Theandrew Clayborn, 1976)
      VI. Jeroid T. Clayborn, 1983–
   V. Edgar Piggee, 1955–
      Aundre F. Piggee, 1959–
      Carlos D. Piggee, 1963–
IV. Londell Piggee, 1927-1980 (m. _____)
   V. Tina Piggee, nd.
IV. Eddie Louise Piggee, 1938–
      James Marvin Piggee, nd.
      Ernestine Piggee, nd.
III. Simmie Clardy, 1896-1964 (m. Letha Gamble, 1919)
   IV. Nettie Adele Clardy, nd. (m. LeRoy Stephens, nd.)
      V. Dwight D. Stephens, nd.
         Stephanie Adele Stephens, nd. (m. _____)
         VI. Gregory Coleman, nd.
      V. Pamela Yvonne Stephens, nd.
   IV. Annie Beatrice Clardy, nd. (m. _____ Jones, nd.)
      V. Eric Curtis Jones, nd. (m. Anna Mae Mays, nd.)
         VI. Jean Jones, nd.
            Erica Jones, nd.
            Nicholas B. Jones, nd.
            Bradley M. Jones, nd.
      V. Karen Annette Jones, nd.
         Harry L. Jones, nd. (m. _____)
         VI. Malik Rashad Chenault Jones
      V. Carl L. Jones, nd. (m. _____)
         VI. Tameki Beatrice Jones, nd.
            Terrell Anthony Jones, nd.
   IV. James L. Clardy, nd. (m. Katherine _____, nd.)
      V. Deborah Clardy, nd. (m. _____ Glasser, nd.)
         VI. Mellisa Glasser, nd.
      V. Lea Clardy, nd. (m. _____ DeVaughn)
         VI. Damon DeVaughn, nd.
            Dana DeVaughn, nd.

V. James Clardy II, nd.
III. Roy Clardy, 1896 (d. in childhood)
Floy Clardy, 1900 (d. in childhood)
Lanie Clardy, 1902 (d. in infancy)
Freddie Leander Clardy, 1904-nd. (m. _____)
    IV. Doris Lee Clardy, nd. (d. in infancy)
III. Eddie Leona Clardy, 1904 (twin to Freddie) (m. _____ Wilson;
m. Lonnell Johnson, 198__)
Alonzo Curtis Clarky, 1907-1945 (m. Olivia Edwards, nd.)
    IV. Leonard Clardy, nd.
II. Alonzo Polk, 1885-19__ (m. Lucy Murphy, 1912)
  III. Odell Polk, 1913 (m. Lucille Norman, 1944)
    IV. Norman Odell Polk, 1945
    Loretta Polk, 1956
  III. Annie Polk, 1917- (m. Curtis Craft, 1938)
    IV. Constance Craft, 1939- (m. Ernest Dees, 1961)
      V. Gregory Dees, 1962-
      Jeffrey Dees, 1971-
    IV. Barbara Craft, 1941- (m. Charles Thompson, 1959; m.
Tao Stephens, 1968)
      V. Cynthia Thompson, 1960-
      Sharon Thompson, 1961-
      Angela Stephens, 1970-
    IV. Joan Craft, 1943- (m. Lindsey Henry, 1964)
      V. Karen Henry, 1966-
      Kimberley Henry, 1969-
    IV. Curtis Craft, Jr., 1947- (m. Reanetta Jones Hunt, 1982)
      V. Christopher Curtis Craft, 1984-
  III. Eva Polk, 1919-1967 (m. James Shelton, 1942; m. Melwood
Brown, 1950)
    IV. Eddie Shelton, 1944- (m. Rosa _____)
      V. Eva Marie Shelton, 1967-
      Tony Shelton, 1973-
    IV. Donald Brown, 1951-
II. Mattie Polk, 1888-1971 (m. Claude Sanders, 1911; m. Robert Whit-
more, 1937; m. Ben Scoggins, 1954)
  III. Rupert Sanders, 1911- (m. Dolly _____, nd.)
  Garland Sanders, 1914- (m. Gaytha Sylver, 1962)
    IV. John Sanders, 1966-
  III. Worthy Sanders, 1919-
II. Nobie Polk, 1891-1984 (m. Detroit Clardy, 1909)
  III. Burlee Clardy, 1910- (m. Ernest Nelson, 1930)
    IV. Winifred Nelson, 1931- (m. W. Cook, nd.)
      V. Winston Cook, nd.
      Ronnie Cook, nd.
      Mercede Cook, nd.
    IV. Dora Nelson, 1933-

II. Nobie Polk (*continued*):
 III. Henry Clardy, 1912-1982 (m. Justine Whaley, 1969)
   Hilbert Clardy, 1914-1938
   Hudson Clardy, 1918-   (m. Francis Milton; m. Darlene _____)
   IV. Scharice Clardy, nd.
 III. Joe Wheeler Clardy, 1920-   (m. Verneice Jackson, 1942)
   IV. Ralph Clardy, nd. (m. _____)
     V. Ralph Clardy, Jr., nd.
       VI. Stephanie Clardy, nd.
     V. Pamela Clardy, nd.
   IV. Lynn Clardy, nd.
     Betty Clardy, nd. (m _____ Jones, nd.)
       V. Stephen Jones, nd.
       Crystal Jones, nd.
 III. Adell Clardy, 1923-   (m. John Mamby, 1945)
   IV. Theresa Mamby, 1966-
 III. D.C. Clardy, 1925-   (m. Jocelyn Wood, 1974)
   IV. Bruce Clardy, nd.
     Jason Clardy, nd.
     David Clardy, nd.
 III. Leon Clardy, 1929-   (m. Dorothy _____, nd)
   IV. Pamela Clardy, nd.
 III. Archie Lee Clardy, 1938-1947

I. FRANK POLK, 1829-nd. (m. Emma _____, nd)
 II. Beatrice Polk, nd. (m. James Johnson, nd.)
  III. Beatrice Johnson, nd.
   John Johnson, nd.
   Sarah Johnson, nd.
   Emily Johnson, nd.
   Sunshine Johnson, nd.
   Wynn Johnson, nd.

I. JOHN SPENCER POLK, 1833-1919 (m. _____ Turrentine, nd.; m. Ellen
Murphy, 1867)
 II. Douglass Polk, ca. 1860-1920 (m. Josie Simpson [or Gibson], 1881)
  III. Willie Douglass Polk, nd.
   Essie Lela Polk, nd. (m. John Louis Graves, nd.)
    IV. Richard Avery Graves, nd.
      Fay Johanna Graves, nd. (m. Bennie Knott, nd.)
        V. Patricia Knott, nd.
        Jacqueline Knott, nd.
        Bennie Knott, Jr., nd.
        Wallace Knott, nd.
    IV. John Louis Graves, Jr., nd.
    IV. Alvin Spencer Graves, nd.
      Willie Mae Graves, nd. (m. _____ Lewis)
        V. Anita Mae Lewis, nd.

IV. Miriam Myrtle Graves, nd.
Gloria Elizabeth Graves, nd.
II. Allen Polk, 1860-ca. 1900
Emma Jane Polk, 1869-1943 (m. J.R. Blackwell, 1907)
   III. Lillian Polk, 1896-1982 (m. Edward Shelton, 1917)
      IV. James Edward Shelton, nd.
II. Charles Polk, 1872-ca. 1900
Alice Polk, 1875-1953
   III. Pearl Polk, 1895-　　(m. Patrick Henry Murphy, 1916)
      IV. John Brown Murphy, 1919-　　(m. Edwina King, 1942)
         V. John Edwin Murphy, 1959 (m. Glenda Jackson)
      IV. Mary Ellen Murphy, 1921-　　(m. Arthur T. Jackson, 1945)
         V. Carmen Diane Jackson, 1947-
         Arthur James Jackson, 1953-　　(m. Cynthia Gouletas, 1984)
         Nina Gail Jackson, 1954-
      IV. Maxine Murphy, 1925-　　(m. Leonard C. City, 1952)
         V. Leonard Glenn City, 1955-
         Elaine Yolanda City, 1961-
      IV. Patrick Henry Murphy, Jr. 1933-　　(m. Harriet Moore, 1963)
II. Benjamin Franklin Polk, 1878-1916
Mary Frances Polk, 1881-1952
Chester Alan Arthur Polk, 1883-1964 (m. Mattie Ann Bullock, 1921)
   III. William Henry Polk, 1922-1967
   Jack Dempsey Polk, 1923-　　(m. Charlean Davis, 1948)
      IV. Dennis Polk, 1952-　　(m. Edith James, nd.)
         V. Jason Polk, 1978-
         Gerald Polk, 1980-
         Jackie Polk, 1982-
      IV. Sharon Polk, 1955-
         V. Vernell Jones, 1976-
      IV. Chris Polk, 1959-
         V. Katrina Perry, nd.
   III. Raymond Clay Polk, 1925-1983 (m. Dorothy Jean Moore, 1950)
      IV. Marshall Polk, 1953-　　(m. Cynthia N. Ceasar, 1974)
         V. Raymond Chioke Polk, 1976-
         Candice Taleta Polk, 1978-
      IV. Wayne Polk, 1955-
   III. Julia Ann Polk, 1926-　　(m. Hurtis Cullus Hendrix, 1950; m. Lorse Gilbert, 1974)
      IV. John Arthur Jones, 1946-
      Marquin Anthony Hendrix, 1949-
      Stanley Hurtis Hendrix, 1952-
      Marvin Douglass Hendrix, 1954-
      Julius Eric Hendrix, 1958-
      Lorse Oliver Gilbert, 1967-

II. Benjamin Franklin Polk (continued):
   III. Herbert Hoover Hadley Polk, 1927-1983 (m. Fukue Kodama,
        1952)
       IV. Spencer Herbert Polk, 1953-   (m. Sherri Newman, 1978)
           V. Miyako Polk, 1974-
           Kikuyo Polk, 1977-
           Kyosho Polk, 1980-
           Takashi Polk, 1982-
       IV. Raymond Kasi Polk, 1960-   (m. June Smith, 1984)
           Janiece Kaye Polk, 1961-   (m. Norman DeBase, 1983)
   III. Marjorie Helen Polk, 1929-   (m. Lloyd Bland, 1950)
       IV. Cherise Helene Bland, 1952-   (m. Lauren Young, 1981)
           V. Candice Young, 1981-
       IV. Charlotte Marie Bland, 1954-
           Rebecca Bland, 1962-   (m. Eric Grattan, 1984)
   III. Ruth Polk, 1930-   (m. Thomas Edward Patterson, 1949)
       IV. Valerie Ellaine Patterson, 1950-1977
           Thomas Edward Patterson, Jr., 1951-
           V. Thomas Edward Patterson III, 1982-
       IV. Kenneth Aaron Patterson, 1953-   (m. Marilyn Nicholson,
           1974)
           V. Kuan Kenneth Patterson, 1977-
           Kia Kyanna Patterson, 1980-
       IV. Tracey Desmond Dallas Patterson, 1965-
   III. Cindy Lee Polk, 1932-   (m. Ira Howell, Jr., 1948)
       IV. Monica Teresa Howell, 1949-   (m. Charles Dozier, 1966)
           V. Michelle Levette Dozier, 1967-
           DeShawn Sheree Dozier, 1970-
       IV. Henry Michael Howell, 1951-   (m. Betty Ranee Rainey,
           nd.)
           Charles Edwin Howell, 1952-
           Linda Kay Howell, 1955-
           Sandra Anita Howell, 1957-
           Marsha Ann Howell, 1958-
           Rose Marie Howell, 1963-
           Nancy Charmaine Howell, 1965-
   III. Arthur Polk, 1936 (d. in infancy)
        Range Preston Polk, 1938-   (m. Lois Capps, 1969)
   II. Anna Mae Polk, 1886-1968 (m. Floyd Johnson, 1922)
       James G.B. Polk, 1889-1910

I. ELIZA POLK, ca. 1838-1920 (m. Ives Polk [no relation], 1870)
   II. Susannah Polk, nd.
       Henry Polk, nd.

Notes

Chapter 1. Crooked Marks on the Landscape

1. Robert Duffy, *Beginnings: Historic Architecture in Arkansas* (Little Rock, 1980), 1-15.

2. Oral reports by several sources, corroborated by family portrait, ca. 1910.

3. From notes on a description of the buildings taken by the author and interpreted by archeologist Skip Stewart-Abernathy during the archeological survey of the site in 1979.

4. Paul M. Gaston, *The New South Creed* (New York, 1970), 135.

Chapter 2. The Wilds

1. Alex Haley, from a lecture on his research for *Roots* presented at Central High School, Little Rock Ark., 1976.

2. Mrs. Frank M. Angellotti, "The Polks of North Carolina and Tennessee," Part 1, *New England Historical and Genealogical Register* 77 (1923): 134-40.

3. Angellotti, "The Polks of North Carolina and Tennessee," Part 2, *New England Historical and Genealogical Register* 78 (1924): 37-38.

4. Walter L. Brown, *Our Arkansas* (Austin, Tex., 1958), 118-19.

5. Hot Spring County Index to Deeds, p. 239, Hot Spring County Courthouse, Malvern, Ark.

6. Ronald Vern and Ronald Teepler, eds., *Arkansas Sheriff's Census, 1823 & 1829* (Salt Lake City, 1976), p. 32; copy at Arkansas History Commission.

7. U.S. Bureau of the Census, *1840 Population Schedules of Arkansas*, on microfilm at Arkansas History Commission.

8. A comparison of several maps of Arkansas on display at the Old State House established that the Polk settlement appeared in three different counties between 1808 and 1850.

9. *Colton's Arkansas, 1858* (map), Arkansas History Commission, Little Rock. See also *A New Map of Arkansas with Its Canals, Roads, and Distances* (Philadelphia: S. Augustus Mitchell, 1849).

10. Montgomery County Record Book of Deeds, Montgomery County Courthouse, Mt. Ida., Ark.

11. Montgomery County Marriage Records, Montgomery County Courthouse, Mt. Ida, Ark.

12. Lacy Porter McColloch, "Alfred Clay Hale, Native Son and Man of Destiny," *Arkansas Historical Quarterly* 35 (Autumn 1976): 251.

13. Mack A Guinn, letter to the author, Jan. 14, 1981.

14. Interview with Mack A. Guinn, Mt. Ida, Ark., Sept. 9, 1982.

15. "Caddo Cove," *Southern Standard*, Aug. 16, 1884, p. 2.

16. Hot Spring County Tax Assessment Records, 1830-1860, Hot Spring County Courthouse, Malvern, Ark.

17. Orville Taylor, *Negro Slavery in Arkansas* (Durham, N.C., 1958), 24.

18. Ibid.

19. Ibid., 25.

20. Angellotti, "Polks of North Carolina and Tennessee," pt. 1, 220.

21. Clarence Alan Carter, comp., *Territorial Papers of the United States, vol. 19, Arkansas Territory, 1819-1825* (Washington, D.C., 1932), 388.

22. Ibid., 842-69.

23. Interview with Mack Guinn, Mt. Ida, Ark., Sept. 9, 1982.

24. Taylor, *Negro Slavery in Arkansas*, 30.

25. Oral reports handed down by Polk family members and verified by interview with Mrs. P.H. Murphy, Spencer Polk's oldest living descendant, Austin, Tex., Dec. 1979.

26. Dallas T. Herndon, *Centennial History of Arkansas* 1 (Chicago, 1922), 55-64.

27. *A New Map of Arkansas with Its Canals, Roads, and Distances*, (Philadelphia: S. Augustus Mitchell, 1849).

28. John L. Ferguson and J.H. Atkinson, *Historic Arkansas* (Little Rock, Ark., 1966), 58.

29. Hot Spring County Tax Assessment Records.

30. Oral reports handed down in the family and corroborated in an interview with Mrs. P.H. Murphy, Austin, Tex., Dec. 1979, along with information in a letter to the author, dated March 10, 1978, from Spencer Polk's second-oldest living descendant, a granddaughter who desires to remain anonymous.

31. Angellotti, "Polks of North Carolina and Tennessee," part 2, 37.

32. Interview with Mrs. Willie Bell Bullock Maxwell, Center Point, Ark., July 15, 1979. Mrs. Maxwell is a descendant of Leander "Mint" Bullock, a slave owned by Blount Bullock, Taylor Polk's neighbor. She is also the sister-in-law of Spencer Polk's son Arthur.

33. Angellotti, "Polks of North Carolina and Tennessee," part 2, 37.

34. Oral reports handed down in the family and corroborated by interview with Mrs. P.H. Murphy, Dec. 1979.

35. Hot Spring County Tax Assessment Records.

36. Ibid.

37. Taylor, *Negro Slavery in Arkansas*, 54.

38. Ibid., 56.

39. Corroborated by the interviews with both Mrs. Murphy and Mrs. Maxwell.

40. Mrs. P.H. Murphy, letter to the author, Nov. 9, 1978.

41. Taylor, *Negro Slavery in Arkansas*, 194.

42. Hot Spring County Tax Assessment Records. Also supported in Angellotti, "Polks of North Carolina and Tennessee," part 2, 37.

43. Interview with Jack Dempsey Polk, Washington, D.C., Oct. 25, 1979. Mr. Polk is a grandson of Spencer Polk and son of Arthur Polk, Spencer's only son to survive him. Jack Dempsey Polk said his maternal grandfather, Harrison Bullock, was the first to reveal information to him about his paternal grandfather's lineage. Then, according to the interview, Mr. Polk approached his father, Arthur Polk, concerning the relationship of Spencer Polk to Taylor Polk, and Arthur confirmed, though reluctantly, that Spencer Polk was indeed the son of Taylor Polk.

44. Interview with Mrs. Willie Bell Maxwell, Center Point, Ark., Oct. 23, 1979.

45. Hot Spring County Tax Assessment Records.

46. Taylor, *Negro Slavery in Arkansas*, 194.

47. W.E.B. Du Bois, *The Souls of Black Folk* (New York, 1969), 44.

Chapter 3. The First Remove

1. Montgomery County Tax Record Book for 1840, Montgomery County Courthouse.

2. Interview with Mack Guinn, Sept. 9, 1982.

3. Montgomery County Tax Records, 1849-1867, Montgomery County Courthouse.

4. After 1850, no records of Taylor Polk appear in Montgomery County documents, and the 1850 slave census shows him living in the township of Muddy Fork in Pike County.

5. *Colton's Arkansas, 1858."*

6. Montgomery County Probate Records, Montgomery County Courthouse.

7. Pike County Tax Records for 1834-1875, on microfilm at Arkansas History Commission.

8. Ibid.

9. Le Roy Williams, "Slavery in Arkansas," unpublished article submitted to the author as a part of the research for this project.

10. Florence R. Beatty-Brown, "Legal Status of Arkansas Negroes before Emancipation" *Arkansas Historical Quarterly* 28 (Spring 1969): 6-12.

11. Jacob Trieber, "Legal Status of Negroes in Arkansas before the Civil War," *Arkansas History Commission Publication* 3 (1911): 179.

12. Taylor, *Negro Slavery in Arkansas*, 188, 189.

13. Interview with Jack Dempsey Polk, Washington, D.C., Oct. 25, 1979.

14. Cane and bark weaving and the use of rattan and cowhide to make chairs and stools are indigenous African crafts. Spencer's surviving son Arthur and his father-in-law learned most of these skills from their fathers, who no doubt learned them from other slaves on the plantation. Articles made in the same manner were not observed in the households of whites at Muddy Fork. The logical conclusion is that either whites never had those skills to pass on to the former slave population, or the skills had died out among the white residents, which is unlikely in an isolated area such as Muddy Fork.

15. Interview with Mrs. Pearl Murphy, Austin, Tex., Dec. 12, 1979.

16. Description from tintype portrait of Spencer Polk, ca. 1865.

17. From an unpublished manuscript by Raymond Clay Polk of Washington, D.C., written around 1955 and in the possession of the author.

18. *Biographical and Historical Memoirs of Southern Arkansas* (Chicago: Goodspeed Publishing Co., 1890) 253-308.

19. Interview with Mrs. Pearl Murphy, Austin, Tex., Dec. 12, 1979.

Chapter 4. Oh, Give Me Land

1. Letter to the author, dated March 10, 1978, from an elderly granddaughter of Spencer Polk who wishes to remain anonymous.

2. Interview with Mrs. Pearl Murphy, Austin, Tex., Dec. 12, 1979.

3. U.S. Bureau of the Census, *1880 Population Schedules of Arkansas*, on microfilm at Arkansas History Commission, Little Rock.

4. Interview with Willie Counts, Lockesburg, Ark., Aug. 19, 1979; and interview with Pearl Murphy.

5. Pike County Tax Records for 1867, on microfilm at Arkansas History Commission.

6. Howard County Record of Deeds, Book 25, p. 147, at Howard County Courthouse, Nashville, Ark.

7. Copy of original Homestead Patent No. FC537, Certificate 537, Application No. 1611, U.S. Department of the Interior, Bureau of Land Management.

8. Claude Oubre, *Forty Acres and a Mule: The Freedmen's Bureau and Black Land Ownership* (Baton Rouge: Louisiana State Univ. Press, 1978), 87, 26-30.

9. Ibid., 37-38, 95-103.

10. Ibid., 103, 104.

11. Ibid., 109, 190.

12. Examination of deeds now owned by Weyerhaueser Co., Hot Springs, Ark. Thompson Epperson was apparently George T. Epperson, as no other reference to Thompson Epperson has been found.

13. U.S. Bureau of the Census, *1880 Population Schedules of Arkansas*.

14. Interview with Mrs. Pearl Murphy, Austin, Tex., Dec. 13, 1979.

15. U.S. Bureau of the Census, *1880 Population Schedules of Arkansas*.

16. Howard County Record of Deeds, Book 118, p. 173.

17. Copy of original Homestead Patent No. HC7561, Certificate 7561, Application No. 13301, U.S. Department of the Interior, Bureau of Land Management.

18. Howard County Personal Property Tax Records, Howard County Courthouse.

19. From examination of probate records of the Taylor Polk estate, Howard County Courthouse.

20. From the Sales Bill of Personal Property of Taylor Polk, deceased, filed Sept. 20, 1885, Howard County Courthouse.

21. Interview with Walter Westbrook, Nashville, Ark., Sept. 18, 1978.

22. Oral reports handed down by Polk's descendants.

23. The presence of rock flakes and tools found and identified in the archeological examination of the site suggests that the place was inhabited by Archaic people some three thousand years ago, according to archeologist Skip Stewart-Abernathy.

24. McCulloch, "Alfred Clay Hale," 251.

25. According to the archeologist, the concrete hearth could not have been a part of the original structure because cement represents a much later architectural feature.

26. Interview with Walter Westbrook, Nashville, Ark., Sept. 18, 1978.

27. The house as seen from a family portrait, ca. 1910.

28. U.S. Bureau of the Census, *Population Schedules of Arkansas-1880.*

Chapter 5. Within and Without the Veil

1. U.S. Bureau of the Census, *Twelfth Census of the United States, 1900, Schedule No. 1: Population*, on microfilm, Arkansas History Commission, Little Rock.

2. U.S. Bureau of the Census, *Population Schedules for 1910*, on microfilm, Arkansas History Commission.

3. From oral reports handed down by Polk family members.

4. Herndon, *Centennial History of Arkansas*, 3: 819.

5. Interview with Jack Dempsey Polk, Washington, D.C., Oct. 25, 1979.

6. Interview with Mrs. Julia Polk Gilbert of San Diego, granddaughter of Spencer Polk, Los Angeles, Cal., Aug. 7, 1979.

7. Interview with Taylor Wilson, nephew of Spencer Polk, Lockesburg, Ark., Dec. 27, 1982.

8. Interview with Walter Westbrook, Nashville, Ark., Sept. 18, 1978.

9. Interview with Mrs. Willie Bell Maxwell, Center Point, Ark., July 15, 1979.

10. From oral reports handed down by Polk family members.

11. Interview with Adell Clardy Mamby, Center Point, Ark., July 6, 1982.

12. U.S. Bureau of the Census, *Population Schedules for 1880.*

13. *Nashville News*, July 2, 1910, on microfilm, Arkansas History Commission.

14. *Howard County Advocate*, May 3, 1883, in possession of Lucille Westbrook of Nashville, Ark.

15. Interview with Mrs. Willie Bell Maxwell, Center Point, Ark., July 15, 1979.

16. Charles W. Chesnutt, *The Wife of His Youth and Other Stories* (Ann Arbor, Mich., 1969), 1-3.

17. Leon Litwack, *North of Slavery* (Chicago, 1961), 182-83.

18. Edward Byron Reuter, *The American Race Problem* (New York, 1927), 64-96. See also Arthur de Gobineau, "Essay on the Inequality of the Races" (1854), in *Gobineau, Joseph Arthur, Comte de, 1816-1882: Selected Political Writings*, ed. Michael D. Biddiss (New York, 1917), 97-144.

19. Du Bois, *Souls of Black Folk*, 122: "The second thought streaming from the death ship and the curving river is the thought of the older South—the sincere and passionate belief that somewhere between men and cattle, God created a tertium quid and called it a Negro."

20. Both the slave census of 1850 and the national census of 1880 identified blacks on the basis of skin color as Black or Mulatto in an attempt to "count" the number of Africans in America who had white mixture. The separation of family members into distinct "classes" was no less dehumanizing than the apartheid practices in South Africa today.

21. Eugene D. Genovese, *Roll, Jordan, Roll* (New York, 1972), 429-30.

22. Ibid.

23. Joel Williamson, *New People: Miscegenation and Mulattoes in the United States* (New York, 1980), 50-51, 15.

24. Ibid., 92.

25. Ibid., 67.

26. Genovese, *Roll, Jordan, Roll*, 430.

27. C. Vann Woodward, *The Strange Career of Jim Crow* (New York, 1960), 41.

28. Ibid., 42-43, 74-99.

29. Interview with Walter Westbrook, Nashville, Ark., Sept. 18, 1978.

Chapter 6. One Seed Becomes a Singing Tree

1. Letter to the author from a granddaughter of Spencer Polk who wishes to remain anonymous.

2. Loren Eisely, *Darwin's Century* (Garden City, N.Y., 1961), 264-65.

3. Mrs. Pearl Murphy, letter to the author, May 17, 1979.

4. Interview with Mrs. Willie Bell Maxwell, Center Point, Ark., Aug. 1979.

5. Howard County Marriage Records, Book B-1, p. 363, Howard County Courthouse, Nashville, Ark.

6. Mrs. Fay Knott, letter to the author, Aug. 1984.

7. Homestead Certificate No. 7561, Application No. 13301, Patent No. HC7561, U.S. Department of the Interior, Bureau of Land Management.

8. Oral reports from several sources corroborate these details.

9. Related by several Polk and Bullock family descendants.

10. Howard County Marriage Records, Book H, p. 202.

11. Jimmy Polk, letters to family members found in trunk, now in the possession of the author.

12. Howard County Marriage Records, Book K, p. 493.

13. It was well known in the Polk family that certain members passed for white on occasion, and still do.

14. Interview with Walter Westbrook, Nashville, Ark., Sept. 18, 1978.

15. Interview with Mrs. Julia Polk Gilbert, Los Angeles, Cal., Aug. 7, 1979.

16. *American Educator Encyclopedia*, 1965 ed., s.v. "Arthur, Chester Alan," p. 360.

17. Howard County Tax Assessment Records, 1880 through 1909, Howard County Courthouse.

18. Interview with Mrs. Julia Polk Gilbert, Los Angeles, Cal., August 7, 1979.

19. Letters from Mattie Ann Bullock to Arthur Polk are in the possession of the author.

20. Interview with Mrs. Willie Bell Maxwell, Center Point, Ark., Aug., 1980.

21. Mrs. Annie M. Johnson, letter to the author, Nov. 12, 1979.

22. Interview with Mrs. Pearl Murphy, Austin, Tex., Dec. 12, 1979.

23. Emma Polk, letter to Jimmy Polk, n.d., found in Jimmy Polk's trunk.

24. Ophelia Walton, letter to Jimmy Polk, Sept. 1908.

25. Ibid.

26. Alice Polk, letter to Jimmy Polk, n.d.

27. Jimmy Polk, letter to Arthur Polk, May 20, 1910.

28. Accounts of Jimmy Polk's death were given at different times by several descendants of Spencer Polk, including Pearl Murphy, Jack Dempsey Polk, and Julia Gilbert. Mrs. Murphy and Mrs. Maxwell were both living at Muddy Fork at the time Jimmy was killed.

29. Jimmy Polk, letter to Alice Polk, May 8, 1910.

30. Jimmy Polk, letter to Arthur Polk, May 20, 1910.

31. Interview with Mrs. Julia Polk, Gilbert.

32. Mrs. Pearl Murphy, letter to the author, April 27, 1983.

33. For a general overview of racial conflict during the period from 1900 to 1920, see John Hope Franklin's *From Slavery to Freedom*, 4th ed. (New York, 1974), 322-27.

34. *Arkansas Gazette*, Aug. 12, 1883.

35. *Nashville News*, Feb. 5, 1910.

36. Willis D. Weatherford and Charles S. Johnson, *Race Relations: Adjustment of Whites and Negroes in the United States* (Boston, 1934), 58-59.

37. Interview with Jack Dempsey Polk, Washington, D.C., Oct. 25, 1979.

Chapter 7. African Survivals and Scottish Airs

1. Franklin, *From Slavery to Freedom*, 135-37.

2. Melville J. Herskovits, *The Myth of the Negro Past* (Boston, 1958); Roger Bastide, *African Civilizations in the New World* (New York, 1971); and Alan Dundes, ed., *Mother Wit from the Laughing Barrel* (Englewood Cliffs, N.J., 1973) are among the scholars who have established the basis for studies on African survivals among Americans of African descent.

3. Judith Wragg Chase, *Afro-American Arts and Crafts* (New York, 1971), 55-57.

4. Ibid.

5. Ibid., 59.

6. There are many references to the white Polks in county tax records which reveal their landholdings and places of residence from 1808 to 1890 in Montgomery and Howard counties.

7. Mbye Cham, lecture, University of Illinois, Urbana-Champaign, 1978.

8. This version of the tales was told by Mattie Ann Bullock.

9. Richard Dorsen, *American Negro Folktales* (Greenwich, Conn.), 16. Although Dorsen insists that most of the tales in his collection have been traced to European origins, he reluctantly admits that 10 percent of the tales have West African correspondences.

10. Ogonna Chuks-orji, *Names from Africa* (Chicago, 1972), 61.

11. Herskovits, *Myth of the Negro Past*, 282.

12. Newbell Niles Puckett, *Folk Beliefs of the Southern Negro* (Chapel Hill, N.C., 1926, 420. Puckett explains that in Africa "the Northern Gold Coast natives consider rain to be in possession of a man of the tribe, who, if the rain is too abundant, mounts his roof and threatens the rain with a knife or other implements."

13. The author recalls that Mrs. Annie M. Johnson, Spencer Polk's youngest daughter, often spoke about the calling of sets by her father and brothers.

14. Two versions of "Sally Goodin" appear in Vance Randolph, ed., *Ozark Folksongs* (Columbia, Mo., 1949). Randolph cites the two versions as having been sung by Mrs. Carrie Barber of Pinewell, Mo., in 1922, and Mrs. Lillian Short of Cabool, Mo., in 1940.

15. "Games from Africa," unpublished teaching materials distributed by the African Studies Center, Univ. of Illinois, Urbana-Champaign.

16. Puckett, *Folk Beliefs of the Southern Negro*, 56.

17. Chinua Achebe, *Things Fall Apart* (Greenwich, Conn., 1959), 172.

18. A sawmill owned by one Lon Wisdom was set up on the Taylor Polk lands adjacent to the Spencer Polk farm for several years during the 1920s and 1930s.

19. Robert Farris Thompson, "African Influence on the Art of the United States," in Amistead L. Robinson, et al., eds., *Black Studies in the University* (New Haven, Conn., 1969), 127.

20. John Michael Vlach, *The Afro-American Tradition in the Decorative Arts* (Cleveland, O., 1948), 8.

21. Mary Lee Wiley and David Wiley, *The Third World: Africa* (West Haven, Conn., 1973), 61.

22. Interview with Dr. Aba Touray, Fourah Bsy College, Freetown, Sierra Leone, West Africa, July, 1979.

23. Chase, *Afro-American Arts and Crafts*, 59.

24. Daryll Forde, *African Worlds* (London, 1954), 106.

25. Interview with Dr. Aba Touray.

26. The chewing of sticks is indigenous to African cultures. I observed this parctice in Sierra Leone, Ghana, Liberia, and Senegal. In Sierra Leone the sticks are broken from the tumbic tree, which has a natural lime flavor. In Senegal and Ghana the sticks were being sold in bundles on the streets.

27. Daniel Littlefield, *The Cherokee Freedmen* (Westport, Conn., 1978), 6.

28. Interview with Mrs. Julia Gilbert and other family members, Los Angeles, Cal., Oct. 1979.

29. Corroborated by several Polk family members.

30. Elizabeth Rauh Bethel, *Promisedland: A Century of Life in a Negro Community* (Philadelphia, 1981), 146-47.

31. John S. M'Biti, *African Religions and Philosophy* (Garden City, N.Y., 1970), 154.

32. Bethel, *Promisedland*, 146-47.

33. Herbert G. Gutman, *The Black Family in Slavery and Freedom, 1750-1925* (New York: Vintage Books, 1976), 186-201.

34. Ibid.

Chapter 8. The Last Remove

1. *Nashville News*, Oct. 9, 1910.

2. Interview with Jack Dempsey Polk, Washington, D.C., Oct. 25, 1979.

3. Assessment and Extension of Taxes against Real Property in Howard County, Arkansas, for the Years 1908-1909, Howard County Courthouse, Nashville, Ark.

4. Assessment and Extension of Taxes against Real Property in Howard County for the Year 1925, Howard County Courthouse.

5. Howard County Real Estate Tax Book for 1875, Howard County Courthouse.

6. Interview with Jack Dempsey Polk, Washington, D.C., Oct. 25, 1979.

7. The school program was recalled by Polk family members who had participated in it.

8. Interview with Mrs. Inolia McIntosh Childress, Little Rock, Ark., April 1979.

9. A history of the school is included in the 1949 Childress High School yearbook, edited by the author.

10. T.E. Patterson, associate executive director of the Arkansas Teachers Association, once the superintendent of the Childress District, indicated that other all-black districts existed at the same time in Tollette, Rosston, Minifee, and Magnolia, Ark.

11. The practice of providing room and board in lieu of transportation was not a common one. G.W. Weddle often told the author how difficult it had been to work out the agreement with the county supervisor, Cecil Sheffield.

12. Documents transferring the Spencer Polk and Taylor Polk properties to the Dierks Lumber Co. and subsequently to the Weyerhaueser Co. were examined at the Weyerhaueser Co. offices in Hot Springs, Ark.

Chapter 9. For Generations to Come

1. Interview with Mrs. Julia Polk Gilbert, San Diego, Cal., August 1983.

2. Telephone interview with Herbert Polk, July 15, 1983.

3. Interview with Jack Dempsey Polk, Washington, D.C., Oct. 25, 1979.

4. Military records of Raymond C. Polk, examined at his home in Washington, D.C., March 1983.

5. Military records of Herbert H. Polk, mailed to the author from Los Angeles, Cal., June 1983.

6. Interview with Preston Polk, Little Rock, Ark., Aug. 1983.

7. Interview with Mrs. Fay Knott, Los Angeles, Cal., Aug. 1983.

8. Howard County Marriage Records, Book M, p. 481, Howard County Courthouse, Nashville, Ark.

9. Mrs. Fay Knott, letter to the author, May 8, 1984.

10. S.B. (Semmie) Clardy, unpublished manuscript, sent to the author by Joe Wheeler Clardy of Denver, Col.

11. Ibid.

12. Howard County Marriage Records, Book 82, p. 255.

13. Interview with Mrs. Adell Clardy Mamby, Center Point, Ark., July 12, 1983.

Chapter 10. Archeology and Artifact

1. Thomas J. Schlereth, "Material Culture Studies in America, 1876-1976" in Thomas J. Schlereth, ed., *Material Culture Studies in America* (Nashville, Tenn., 1982), 13-15.

2. Robert Ascher, "Tin Can Archeology," in Schlereth, *Material Culture Studies in America*, 325.

3. Robert W. Neuman, *Geoscience and Man* (Baton Rouge, La., 1982), 22.

4. Ibid.

5. James Deetz, *In Small Things Forgotten* (Garden City, N.Y., 1977), 147-53.

6. Robert Ascher and Charles H. Fairbanks, "Excavations of a Slave Cabin: Georgia, USA," in *Historical Archeology* (Lansing, Mich., 1971), 3.

7. Lawrence Gene Santeford and William A. Martin, "The Conway County Water Supply: Results of Archeological Survey and Testing and a Historical Survey of a Proposed Reservoir Area in Conway County, Arkansas" (Fayetteville, Ark., 1980), 174-82.

8. Unpublished report, Arkansas Archeological Survey. Submitted to the author in Jan. 1981.

9. Lucille Westbrook, Howard County historian, corroborated the grave site as that of Taylor Polk; it is located alongside a second tomb believed to be that of his second wife, Jane.

Bibliography

Books

Achebe, Chinua. *Things Fall Apart*. Greenwich, Conn.: Fawcett Publications, 1959.

American Educator Encyclopedia, s.v. Arthur, Chester Alan. Lake Bluff, Ill.: United Educators, 1965.

Ascher, Robert. "Tin Can Archeology." In *Material Culture Studies in America*, Thomas J. Schlereth, ed. Nashville, Tenn.: American Association for State and Local History, 1982.

_____, and Fairbanks, Charles H. "Excavation of a Slave Cabin: Georgia, USA." In *Historical Archeology*. Lansing, Mich.: Society of Historical Archeology, 1971.

Bastide, Roger. *African Civilizations in the New World*. New York: Harper and Row, 1971.

Bethel, Elizabeth Rauh. *Promisedland: A Century of Life in a Negro Community*. Philadelphia: Temple Univ. Press, 1981.

Biographical and Historical Memoirs of Southern Arkansas. Chicago: Goodspeed Publishing Co., 1890.

Brown, Walter L. *Our Arkansas*. Austin, Texas: Steck Co., 1958.

Carter, Clarence Allen, comp. *Territorial Papers of the United States*, vol. 19, *Arkansas Territory, 1819-1825*. Washington, D.C.: Government Printing Office, 1932.

Chase, Judith Wragg. *Afro-American Arts and Crafts*. New York: Van Nostrand Reinhold Co., 1971.

Chesnutt, Charles W. *The Wife of His Youth and Other Tales*. Ann Arbor, Mich.: Univ. of Michigan Press, 1969.

Chuks-orji, Ogonno. *Names from Africa*. Chicago: Johnson Publishing Co., 1972.

Deetz, James. *In Small Things Forgotten*. Garden City, N.Y.: Anchor Press, 1977.

Dorsen, Richard. *American Negro Folktales*. Greenwich, Conn.: Fawcett Publications, 1967.

Du Bois, W.E.B. *The Souls of Black Folk*. New York: Alfred A. Knopf, 1903. Reprint. New American Library, 1969.

Duffy, Robert. *Beginnings: Historic Architecture in Arkansas*. Little Rock: Arkansas Historic Preservation Program, 1980.

Dundes, Alan, ed. *Mother Wit from the Laughing Barrel*. Englewood Cliffs, N.J.: Prentice Hall, 1973.

Eiseley, Loren. *Darwin's Century*. Garden City, N.Y.: Doubleday, 1961.

Ferguson, John L., and Atkinson, J.H. *Historic Arkansas*. Little Rock: Arkansas History Commission, 1966.

Forde, Daryll. *African Worlds*. London: Oxford Univ. Press, 1954.

Franklin, John Hope. *From Slavery to Freedom*. 4th ed. New York: Random House, 1974.

Gaston, Paul M. *The New South Creed*. New York: Alfred A. Knopf, 1970.

Genovese, Eugene D. *Roll, Jordan, Roll*. New York: Random House, 1972.

Gobineau, Joseph Arthur. "Essay on the Inequality of the Races." In *Gobineau, Joseph Arthur, comte de, 1816-1882: Selected Political Writings*, ed. Michael D. Biddiss. New York: Harper and Row, 1917.

Gutman, Herbert G. *The Black Family in Slavery and Freedom, 1750-1925*. New York: Vintage Books, 1976.

Herndon, Dallas T. *Centennial History of Arkansas*. Chicago: S.J. Clark Publishing Co., 1922.

Herskovits, Melville J. *The Myth of the Negro Past*. Boston: Beacon Press, 1958.

Leuizinger, Elsy. *The Art of Africa*. New York: Crown Publishers, 1968.

Littlefield, Daniel. *The Cherokee Freedmen*. Westport, Conn.: Greenwood Press, 1978.

Litwack, Leon. *North of Slavery*. Chicago: Univ. of Chicago Press, 1961.

M'biti, John S. *African Religions and Philosophy*. Garden City, N.Y.: Doubleday, 1970.

Neuman, Robert W. *Geoscience and Man*. Vol. 22 of *Traces of Prehistory: Papers in Honor of William Haag*, ed. Frederick Hadleigh and Robert W. Neuman. Baton Rouge: Louisiana State Univ. Press, 1982.

Oubre, Claude. *Forty Acres and a Mule: The Freedmen's Bureau and Black Land Ownership*. Baton Rouge: Louisiana State Univ. Press, 1978.

Puckett, Newbell Niles. *Folk Beliefs of the Southern Negro*. Chapel Hill, N.C.: Univ. of North Carolina Press, 1926.

Randolph, Vance, ed. *Ozark Folksongs*, vol. 3. Columbia: State Historical Society of Missouri, 1949.

Reuter, Edward Byron. *The American Race Problem*. New York: Thomas G. Crowell Co., 1927.

Schlereth, Thomas J., ed. *Material Culture Studies in America*. Nashville, Tenn.: American Association for State and Local History, 1982.

Taylor, Orville. *Negro Slavery in Arkansas*. Durham, N.C.: Duke Univ. Press, 1958.

Thompson, Robert Farris. "African Influences on the Art of the United States." In *Black Studies in the University*, ed. Amistead L. Robinson et al., p. 127. New Haven: Yale Univ. Press, 1969.

Vern, Ronald, and Teepler, Ronald, eds. *Arkansas Sheriffs Census, 1923 & 1929*. Salt Lake City: Accelerated Indexing Systems, 1976.

Vlach, John Michael. *The Afro-American Tradition in the Decorative Arts*. Cleveland: Cleveland Museum of Art, 1948.

Weatherford, Willis D., and Johnson, Charles S. *Race Relations: Adjustment of Whites and Negroes in the United States*. Boston: D.C. Heath and Co., 1934.

Wiley, Mary Lee, and Wiley, David. *The Third World: Africa*. West Haven, Conn.: Pendulum Press, 1973.

Williamson, Joel. *New People: Miscegenation and Mulattoes in the United States*. New York: Free Press, 1980.

Woodward, C. Vann. *The Strange Career of Jim Crow*. New York: Oxford Univ. Press, 1960.

Periodicals

Angellotti, Mrs. Frank M. "The Polks of North Carolina and Tennessee." *New England Historical and Genealogical Register*, vols. 77, 78 (1923).

Beatty-Brown, Florence R. "Legal Status of Arkansas Negroes before Emancipation." *Arkansas Historical Quarterly* 28 (Spring 1969): 6-12.

"Caddo Cove." *Southern Standard* Aug. 16, 1884, p. 2.

"Eight Negroes Killed." *Nashville News*, Aug. 3, 1919, p. 1.

"Hang Two Negroes." *Nashville News*, Jan. 22, 1910, p. 1.

Howard County Advocate. Fragment dated May 3, 1883.

"Jim Polk Killed." *Nashville News*, July 2, 1910, p. 1.

McCulloch, Lacy Porter. "Alfred Clay Hale, Native Son and Man of Destiny." *Arkansas Historical Quarterly* 35 (Autumn 1976): 251-57.

"Negro Killed." *Nashville News*, May 18, 1910, p. 1.

"Negro Shot." *Nashville News*, Feb. 5, 1910, p. 1.

"Three Killed Resisting Arrest." *Nashville News*, Sept. 27, 1910, p. 1.

Trieber, Jacob. "Legal Status of Negroes in Arkansas before the Civil War." *Arkansas History Commission Publication* 3 (1911): 179.

Documents and Records

Assessment and Extension of Taxes against Real Property in Howard County, Arkansas. 1908, 1909, 1925.

Hot Springs County, Arkansas. Book of Deeds, 1831-1887.

Hot Springs County, Arkansas. Record of Deeds, 1831-1854. Books A and D.
———. Tax Assessment Records, 1830-1860.
Howard County, Arkansas. List of Real Property Assessed for Taxation in Howard County, Arkansas. 1878, 1887, 1900, 1908, 1909, 1925.
———. List of Real Estate Subject to Taxation in Howard County for the Year 1887.
———. Marriage Records. Books B-1, B-2, H, I, K, M, N.
———. Personal Property Tax Books. 1889-1893.
———. Real Estate Tax Book. 1875.
———. Record of Deeds. Book 118.
"Index to the Fifth Census of the United States: 1830 Population Schedules, Territory of Arkansas." Comp. Bobbie Jones McClane. Hot Springs, Ark., 1965.
"Index to the 1840 United States Census of Arkansas. Comp. Bobbie Jones McClane and Inez Halsell Cline." Hot Springs, National Park, Ark., 1967.
Montgomery County, Arkansas. Book of Deeds.
———. Marriage Records.
———. Tax Records. 1840, 1849-1867.
Pike County, Arkansas. Tax Records. 1834-1875.
Santeford, Lawrence Gene, and William A. Martin. "The Conway County Water Supply: Results of Archeological Survey and Testing and a Historical Survey of a Proposed Reservoir Area in Conway County, Arkansas." Fayetteville: Arkansas Archeological Survey, 1980.
Stewart-Abernathy, Leslie. "Statement of Significance: The Polk Site 3H096." Unpublished report. Fayetteville: Arkansas Archeological Survey, 1979.
U.S. Department of Commerce, Bureau of the Census. Census Population Schedules: Arkansas, 1870. Washington, D.C.: G.P.O.
———. Census Population Schedules, 1880. Washington, D.C.: G.P.O.
———. Slave Schedules, 1850. Washington, D.C.: G.P.O.
———. Twelfth Census of Population, 1900: Arkansas. Schedule No. 1, Population. Washington, D.C.: G.P.O.
U.S. Department of Commerce and Labor, Bureau of the Census. Thirteenth Census of the United States, 1910: Population. Washington, D.C.: G.P.O.

Maps

A New Map of Arkansas with Its Canals, Roads and Distances. Philadelphia: S. Augustus Mitchell, 1849.
Colton's Arkansas, 1859. New York: J.H. Colton and Co., 1855 [sic]. Copy at Arkansas History Commission, Little Rock.
Tanner, G.S. A New Map of Arkansas, 1851. Philadelphia: Carey and Hart. Copy at Arkansas History Commission, Little Rock.
Topographical Map of the State of Arkansas, 1900. Copy at Arkansas History Commission, Little Rock.

Index

Africa, cultural survivals from, xv, 89-90; in preparation of food, 90; in handicrafts, 90, 109; in extended family organization, 90-91; in story telling, 95-97; in folk beliefs, 98; in children's games, 102-4; in agriculture, 108-10; in naming practices, 113-15. *See also* cultural traditions

Afro-Americans: oral tradition among, xiii; use of archeology in study of, 142

agriculture, 108-10

Anderson, Carl, 124

Anderson, Jonah, 124

archeological survey: of Polk homestead site, 140-49

archeology: uses of, in Afro-American material culture study, 142; techniques of, in historical research, 142; Afro-American survey sites, 142

Arkansas: blacks in, xi; slavery in, 13-14; education of slaves in, 26; abandoned lands in, 31

Arkansas Archeological Survey, xiv; and Polk Site 3H096, 141-49; Statement of Significance, 147-49

Arkansas Endowment for the Humanities, xiv, xv, 142, 143

artifacts: pulled from archeological survey, 145, 152-53; in family collection, 149-52; significance of, 153

Association for the Study of Afro-American Life and History, xiv

Bastide, Roger, 90

beekeeping: location of gums, 4, 6; source of hives, 112; uses of wax, 112

Benson, Thomas, 44, 68

Benson Nursing Home, 128

Berryman, Mary, 130

Berryman, Oshie, 78

Bethel, Elizabeth Rauh: on naming practices, 113

bird thrashing, 108

bird traps: making of, 106

black codes: restrictions on land ownership, 31

Black Hill, 94

blacks: in Arkansas, xi-xii; acquisition of land by, 31; homestead entries by, 33; treatment of, 85. *See also* free blacks; Muddy Fork, Township; races; racial attitudes; slaves; slavery in Arkansas

Blackwell, J.R., 64, 81

Bland, Charlotte Marie, 133, 138

Bland, Lloyd, 132

Bland, Marjorie Helen (nee Polk), xv, 126, 132

blues: in Polk family music tradition, 100

Blue Vein societies, 52, 54

Boles, Thomas, 125

breakdown (traditional African dance), 27, 101

Bro' Rabbit: adaptation of stories of, 95, 96; African linguistic elements

Bro' Rabbit (continued):
  in, 97; source of stories, 97
Brown, Eva (nee Polk), 136
Browning, Jane, xiv
brush arbor school, 118, 119
brush broom: source of, 92
Bullock, Alfonso, 120
Bullock, Blount, 19; slaves of, 19, 70
Bullock, Dee, 73
Bullock, Dock, 44, 45
Bullock, Edward, 44
Bullock, Hubert 73, 94, 120
Bullock, John 44
Bullock, John Wesley, 95, 101
Bullock, Leander (Mint), 70, 94
Bullock, Mattie Ann. See Polk, Mattie
  Ann
Bullock, Peter Harrison (Bud), 45, 70,
  97
Bullock, Phoebe, 120
Bullock, William (Bill), 44
Bullock, Viney, 74, 123, 130

Cabean, Daisy (nee Turrentine),
  60
Caddo Cove, Ark., 11; location of,
  12; description of, 14
Caddo Gap, Ark., 84
Caddo River, 12
Caddo Township, Ark.; 12
cedar trees, at Polk house site, 5;
  destruction of, 151
cellar: discovery of, 144-45
cemetery, Muddy Fork, 119, 153
Center Point, Ark.: transfer of Muddy
  Fork school to, 121, 124
Chaney, Elbert, 123
Cherokee Indians: in Arkansas, 15;
  slaves of, 15; settlement of, 16;
  cultural influence of, 89
Chesnut, Charles: The Wife of His
  Youth, 52
"Chick-A-My, Chick-A-My, Crainy-
  Crow," 104
Childress, R.C., 121
Childress School District, 121
Choctaw Indians: in Arkansas, 16

City, Maxine (nee Murphy), 134
Clardy, Barney, 153
Clardy, D.C., 136
Clardy, Detroit, 136
Clardy, Hutson, 136
Clardy, Joe Wheeler, xv, 136
Clardy, Leon, 136
Clardy, Nobie (nee Polk), 136
Clardy, Semmie, 135
Clark County, Ark., 12
Clay, Henry: on slavery, 14
Clemens, George, 50, 119
Clemens, Julia (nee Murphy), 50, 119
clothing: making and care of, 92, 121
cockfighting, 107
Coleman, Stephanie, 139
corncrib, 4, 6
Coulter, Mrs. Nealy, 120
Coulter, Ray, 125
Counts, Emily, 44
County Donegal, Ireland, 11
Craft, Annie (nee Polk) 136, 137
Crofton, Bessie, 120
crops: kinds grown on Polk
  homestead, 7, 46, 117
cultural heritage: as determinant of
  Polk family lifestyle, 59
cultural traditions: African influence
  on, in Polk family, 27, 89, 90, 95; in
  music, 98, 99, 101; in games, 101-5;
  in agriculture, 109; in handicrafts,
  109-10; 163 n. 14; 167 n. 12
culture: bonds of, between mulattoes
  and whites, 53-54; use of archeology
  in study of, 142

Dees, Constance (nee Craft)
Deloney, Alice, 135
Deloney, Donald, 138
Depression: impact on Polk family,
  117-18
Dierks Lumber Co., 128
dogtrot: in Polk house, 3; furnishings
  in, 42
Douglass, Frederick, 54
duality of consciousness: in Spencer
  Polk, 21, 51, 54, 62

Dubé, Anthony, xiv
DuBois, W.E.B.: on duality of con-
sciousness, 21
Dunbar High School, Center Point,
Ark., 121, 124

egalitarianism: diminishing of, in
Muddy Fork community, 87, 116
ell room: evidence of, in Polk house,
xiii, xiv, 38; addition of, 39; construction of, 40; disappearance of,
41, 64
epidermicism, 52. See also mulattoes;
skin color
Epperson, Eliza: marriage to Anderson
Polk, 12, 33
Epperson, George: land purchase
from, 33; land owned by, 35; as executor of Taylor Polk estate, 36
Epperson, Sarah (nee Polk): land
transaction with Spencer Polk, 33
Europe: cultural traditions from, 35
extended family, 90, 91

Fallen (Falling) Creek, Muddy Fork of,
1, 23
farm. See Polk, Spencer, homestead
Ferguson, Florence, 78
Ferguson, John L., xv
flaxseeds: use of, 110
Flowers, Martha, 44
Fodder Stack Mountain, 13
folklore: frontier tales, 93; ha'nt tales
(ghost stories), 94-95; purpose of,
95; Bro' Rabbit tales, 95-97; weather
signs, 97-98; beliefs and sayings, 99
folksongs, 99-100
foodstuffs: African tradition in
preparation of, 90; supplements to,
118
free blacks in Arkansas Territory: attitudes toward, 26; difficulty of, in
acquiring land, 33
Freedmen's Bureau: and land distribu-
tion, 31
furnishings in Polk household, 39-42,
127, 145

games: African origin of, 101-2; hull-
gull, 7, 102; "Wild brow limba
lock," 103; "Chick-A-My, Chick-A-
My Crainy-Crow," 103; checker-
boards, 110, 150
Gap Township, Ark., 12
genetic dominance, 20-21
Genovese, Eugene D.: on mulattoes,
53
ghost stories, 94-95
Gilbert, Julia Ann (nee Polk), xv; in-
terview with, 66, 111, 125;
biography, 131
Gilbert, Lorse, 131
Gilbert, Lorse Oliver, 131
Gill, Bess, 126
Gill, Lydia, 126
Glenwood, Ark., 84, 85
Gratten, Rebecca (nee Bland), 132
Graves, Essie (nee Polk), 134
Green, Nona, 120
Griffin, Samuel, 44
Guinn, Mack A.: letter from, 13, 22

Haley, Alex, xii; on oral family
history, 11
handicrafts: African origin of, 90;
basketry, 90, 109; cane and bark
weaving, 90, 109
ha'nt stories, 94-95
Ha'nt Tree: legends of, 94
Hendrix, Anthony Julian, 131
Hendrix, Douglass, 131, 138
Hendrix, Julius Eric, 138
Hendrix, Marquin Anthony, 131, 138
Hendrix, Stanley, 131, 138
Henry, Joan (nee Craft)
herbs: kinds grown in Polk family
garden, 109-10
Herskovits, Melville J.: on African
cultural survivals, 90; on language,
97
home brew: making of, 111-12
homestead. See Polk, Spencer,
homestead
Homestead Acts: of 1862, 31;
Southern, of 1866, 31, 33

homestead entries: by blacks, 33
Hot Spring County, Ark., 12; slave
  population of, 17
house. See Polk, Spencer, homestead
Howard County, Ark., 1, 24, 55
Howard County Advocate, 50
Howell, Charles, 133, 139
Howell, Cindy Lee (nee Polk), xv,
  127; biography, 133
Howell, Ira, Jr., 133
Howell, Linda, 133
Howell, Marsha, 133
Howell, Michael Henry, 133, 138
Howell, Monica, 133
Howell, Nancy, 133
Howell, Rose Marie, 133
Howell, Sandra, 133
hull-gull, 7, 102

"Indian Country," 15; location of, 16
Indian mounds, 94-95
Indians, Cherokees, 15, 16, 89; Choctaws, 16; bark dyeing as cultural element, 110
Ireland: migration of Robert Polk
  from, 11

Jackson, Mary Ellen (nee Murphy),
  134
Jackson-Hinds Treaty, 16
Jim Crowism, 54
Johnson, Annette, xiv
Johnson, Annie. See Polk, Anna
  Mae
Johnson, Beatrice, 135
Johnson, Floyd, 75
Johnson, Glenn, 75, 77, 137
Johnson, Grant, 136
Johnson, John, 136
Jones, Georgia (nee Bullock), 126
Jones, Henry Lee, Jr., 139
Jones, John Arthur, 131, 138
Jones, Karen, 138

Kelley, Calvin P., 126
Kelly, Wiley, 126
kitchens of Polk house: original, 38,

41, 42; addition of second, 38, 42,
  91
Knight, Beatrice, 135
Knott, Fay, xv, 134

land: acreage owned by Spencer Polk,
  10, 31-36; acreage owned by Taylor
  Polk, 25, 34; availability of, to
  former slaves, 31-33
library of Polk home, 64, 92
linguistic elements in stories, 97
"Little Sally Walker," 104
Litwack, Leon: on skin color valuation, 52; on mulattoes, 53
log cabins: in Arkansas, 2
log-pen room, 3, 38
Long, Richard, xv
"Lost My Handkerchief," 104
L'ouverture High School, McAlester,
  Okla., 126
lynching: in Southwest, 86; in death
  of Jimmy Polk, 88

McColloch, Lacy Porter: on Taylor
  Polk homestead, 13, 37
McGraw, Patricia, xiv
McIntosh, Inolia (Mrs. R.C.
  Childress), 121
Mamby, Adele (nee Clardy), xv, 136,
  137
Maple Valley School, Muddy Fork,
  Ark., 120
Masonic Order, 55
Maxwell, Willie Bell (nee Bullock), xv;
  interviews with, 19, 49, 50, 51, 61,
  73
miscegenation: as "big sin," 54
Montgomery County, Ark., 12, 24;
  population of, 23
Moore, Dorothy Jean (Mrs. Raymond
  Clay Polk), 131
Mt. Ida, Ark., 12, 13
Muddy Fork Township, Ark.: location
  of, 1; population of, 36, 44; black
  families in, 44-45; egalitarianism in,
  87; race relations in, 87; church service in, 93; school attendance in,

116-20; cemetery, 119; consolidation
of school district with Center Point,
121, 126
Muddy Fork Creek, 1, 23
mulattoes: Polks described as, 17;
identification on census, 23, 35;
attitudes of blacks toward, 52;
mythology of, 52; invention of term,
52; as class on censuses, 53; relationship with whites, 53; treatment of,
54; reaction of, toward society,
54-55
Murphy, Clay, 73
Murphy, Daniel, 60
Murphy, Henry, 60
Murphy, John Brown, 134, 137
Murphy, Patrick Henry, 134
Murphy, Patrick Henry, Jr., 134, 138
Murphy, Pearl (nee Polk), xv, 134;
letters from, 18, 86; in census listing,
61
Murphy, Reuben, 60
music: in Polk family, 98-101

names: pride in, 92
naming practices: African origin of,
113; in Polk family, 113-14;
necronymic, reverse of, 114
Nashville, Ark., 1; life at, for Arthur
and Mattie Polk, 127
Nashville News: on Jimmy Polk's
death, 84; on racial incidents, 86
New Light C.M.E. Church, 128
Norman, Ark., 22

Old State House Museum, xiv
oral history: uses of, xii; as cultural
tradition, xiii
Ouachita River valley, 11, 22
outlying buildings: of Polk homestead,
2, 7
Oware: similarity to hull-gull, 102

Paine, Thomas, 47
passing for white, 54, 65
Patterson, Kenneth Aaron, 133, 138,
139

Patterson, Kia Kyanna, 133
Patterson, Kuan Kenneth, 133
Patterson, Ruth (nee Polk): reactions
to death, 123; school attendance,
126-27; biography, 133, 137
Patterson, Thomas Edward, 133; on
black school districts, 169 n. 10
Patterson, Thomas Edward, Jr., 133,
139
Patterson, Thomas Edward III, 133
Patterson, Tracey Desmond Dallas,
133
Patterson, Valerie Ellaine, 133, 138
Philander Smith College, 63, 78
Piggee, Nellie (nee Clardy), 136
Piggee, Roland, 137
Pike County, Ark., 23, 24; Polk land
ownership in, 25, 34
Polk, Alfred Sapington (Alf), xiii, 22
Polk, Alice: in census listings, 60, 61;
biography, 67, 134; letter to Jimmy
Polk, 81
Polk, Allen, 35; in census listing, 60;
biography, 63
Polk, Alonzo, 136, 137
Polk, Anderson: marriage of, 12, 29
Polk, Anna Mae (Annie Johnson): in
census listing, 61; biography, 75-77;
letter to author, 76-77; letter from
Jimmy Polk to, 81
Polk, Arthur (Chester Alan Arthur),
xiii; as head of household, 8-9; in
census listing, 61; biography, 68-75;
skills, 69; courtship of Mattie Ann
Bullock, 70-72; marriage, 73; letter
to Jimmy Polk, 82; story telling by,
93-94; making of toys by, 106-7;
handicrafts of, 109; entertainment of
children by, 110; reaction to death
of infant, 122-23; moving of family
to Center Point, 124; abandonment
of homestead, 127-28
Polk, Arthur, Jr., 122-24, 133
Polk, Benjamin Franklin (brother of
Taylor Polk [younger]), 12
Polk, Benjamin Franklin (son of
Taylor Polk [younger]), 67

Polk, Benjamin Franklin (son of
Spencer Polk): in census listings, 60,
61; biography, 67; burial place, 153
Polk, Captain John, 11
Polk, Charlean (nee Davis), 130
Polk, Charles H. (Charlie): biography,
65; in census listings, 60, 61
Polk, Chester. See Polk, Arthur
Polk, Cumberland (brother of Taylor
Polk [younger]), 12
Polk, Cumberland "Cum" (son of
Taylor Polk [younger], xviii, 12, 22;
military exploits, 29
Polk, Dennis, 130
Polk, Douglass, 30, 35; in census
listing, 60; naming of, 62;
biography, 62-63; marriage, 63;
descendants, 63, 125, 134
Polk, Eleanor, 17
Polk, Eliza: birth, 17; description of,
18-20; on census, 25, 135
Polk, Ellen (nee Murphy): marriage to
Spencer Polk, 30; biography, 59-60;
in census listing, 60, 61; description
of, 61; death of, 62; grave site, 153
Polk, Emma Jane, 134, 137; in census
listings, 60, 61; biography, 63-64;
letter to Jimmy Polk, 78
Polk, Frances. See Polk, Mary Frances
Polk, Frank, 17, 29, 135; identified on
census, 25
Polk, Franklin, 60
Polk, Fukue "Terry" (nee Kodama),
132
Polk, Hazel P. See Murphy, Pearl
Polk, Henry (son of Eliza Polk), 135
Polk, Henry Clay (son of Taylor Polk
[younger]), 22, 29
Polk, Herbert Hoover Hadley, 125; in-
terview with, 111; biography, 132
Polk, Ives, 119
Polk, Jack Dempsey, xv; biography,
130
Polk, James (brother of Taylor Polk
[younger]), 12
Polk, James G.B. "Jimmy" (son of
Spencer Polk); in census listing, 61;

letters to and from, 64, 78-83;
biography, 77-88; death, 84; burial,
85
Polk, James Knox, President, 15
Polk, Jane, 60
Polk, Jennie, 136
Polk, Joel, 31
Polk, John Spencer, xii; land ownership of, 10, 30-36; lineage, 11-20,
58, 163 n. 43; birth place of, 12-13;
identification on slave census, 23;
young adulthood, 26; education, 26,
50; relationship to white Polks, 26,
27-29; and slave status, 27-29; personal appearance, 28, 48, 49;
membership of family of, 35, 45, 59,
60, 61, 64, 90, 91; as freedman, 36;
personal property of, 36; death of,
42, 57; uniqueness of, 44; as head of
household, 45, 46, 60, 61; attitudes,
47, 51, 88; characteristics, 46, 47,
48, 54, 154; socioeconomic status,
50; attitudes of neighbors toward,
45, 50-51; and duality of consciousness, 51, 54; leadership of, 55,
56; as legend, 57; in census listings,
60, 61; references to, 140; burial
place, 153. See also Polk, Spencer,
homestead
Polk, Leonidas, Bishop, 15
Polk, Lillian P. See Shelton, Lillian
Polk, Loretta, 138
Polk, Louisa "Lou," 135
Polk, Lucy (nee Murphy), 136
Polk, Marshall, 131
Polk, Mary Frances, 127; in census
listing, 61; biography, 67-68
Polk, Mattie Ann (nee Bullock): love
letters to Arthur Polk, 70-73; mar-
riage to Arthur Polk, 73; stories told
by, 97; and death of infant, 123; life
at Center Point, 124; life at
Nashville, 127-28
Polk, Norman, 137
Polk, Odell, 136, 138
Polk, Pearl. See Murphy, Pearl
Polk, Peter: birth, 17, 20; identified

on slave census, 23; relationship to slave master, 29; in newspaper article, 50; marriages, 135-36; descendants, 135

Polk, Prudence (nee Anderson), 16, 22

Polk, Range Preston, xv, 127; interview with, 111; biography, 134

Polk, Raymond Clay: biography, 130-31

Polk, Robert: immigration of, from Ireland, 11

Polk, Sally (nee Johnson), 136

Polk, Sharon, 130

Polk, Spencer. See Polk, John Spencer

Polk, Spencer, homestead: site of, 1; changes in, 2; outlying buildings, 2, 3, 4, 6, 7, 42, 69; description of, 2-6; diagram of, 4; cedar trees, 5, 151; lands making up, 7, 10, 31, 34, 35; activities on, 8-10, 46; certificate for, 32; growth of, 35; at acme of productivity, 40; crops grown on, 7, 46, 117; importance of, 45; implements used on, 46; abandonment of, 127; purchase by Dierks Lumber Co., 128; appearance of site today, 142; archeological survey of, 143-44; importance as an archeological site, 148; historical significance of, 154
—house: ell room, xiii, xiv, 39, 40, 41, 64; construction of, 3, 30; log-pen room, 3; dogtrot, 3, 42; location of, 4, 37; description of, 37-43; evaluation of, 38; furnishings, 39-42, 127, 145; kitchens, 41-42, 91; occupancy of, 43; disappearance of furnishings, 127; cellar, 144-45; site, 145

Polk, Spencer Herbert, 132

Polk, Susannah, 134

Polk, Taylor (elder), 11, 12; homestead of, 14; death, 15; original log house of, 37

Polk, Taylor (younger), xiii, 11; described, 15; petition signed by, 15; as magistrate in Arkansas Territory, 15; slaves of, 16, 17, 22, 23; and

purchase of Sally, 15-17; relationship to Sally, 17-20; selling of Sally, 18; admission of parentage of Sally's children, 21; land ownership of, 22, 25, 34; and move to Muddy Fork, 23; homestead at Muddy Fork, 25; valuation of property of, 25; prosperity reflected in slaves of, 28; on tax record with former slaves, 31; death, 36; household of, 90; grave site of, 153-54

Polk, Thomas, 31

Polk, Wayne, 131

Polk, William I, 11

Polk, William II, 11

Polk, William Henry: birth of, 73; in school program, 120; biography, 129-30

Polk, Willie, 134

Polk Creek, 13

Polk Meeting House, 55

prehistoric tools, 164

Preston, Cynthia (slave wife of Peter Polk), 135

Promisedland, community of, 113

Puckett, Newbell Niles: on origin of games, 104; on "splitting the cloud," 167 n. 12

race: mythology of, 52

races: opposition to contact between, 55; relationship between, 55

racetrack of Taylor Polk, 22

racial attitudes: as barrier to land ownership by blacks, 33; in Arkansas, 55, 86; conflicts in Southwest, 81, 86; and Jimmy Polk's death, 83; in America, 87; at Muddy Fork, 116

racism, tidal wave of, 55

recreation: cockfighting, 107; fishing, 107; hunting, 107-8; horseshoes, 107 See also games; toys

Reed, Old Man Henry, 9

Reese, John, 48

religious beliefs: of Polk family, 92-93

rice culture, 108

rice fanners, 109

Robinson, Lucy, xiv, 143
rope bed, 39, 41, 127, 145
Royal Ironstone china, 144

Sally: purchase of, by Taylor Polk,
    15-17; description of, 16-18, 20;
    birth of children by Taylor Polk, 17;
    relationship to Taylor Polk, 19;
    descendants of, 129, 135-36
"Sally Good'n": text of, 99; as sung
    by Arthur Polk, 99-100
Sanders, Garland, 136
Sanders, R. Claude, 136
Sanders, Rupert, 136
Sanders, Worthy, 136
"scat": version of, by Arthur Polk, 99
school attendance by Polk children,
    116-20, 122-36; and transportation,
    122, 125
Scoggins, Mattie Sanders (nee Polk),
    136
Scotch-Irish influence on Polk family,
    89, 91
"shadow families": creation of, 53
Sheffield, Cecil E., 125
Shelton, Edward, 134
Shelton, James E., 127, 134
Shelton, Lillian (nee Polk), 93, 127,
    134; in census listing, 61
Sheriff's Census of 1823 & 1829, 29
shuck mops: construction of, 91
skin color: valuation of, 52. See also
    mulattoes
slash-and-burn: use in land prepara-
    tion, 108
slavery in Arkansas: control of by
    magistrates, 15. See also slaves
slaves: population of, in Arkansas, xi,
    xii, 14; absence of on Taylor Polk
    farm, 13; debate over, 13; in Clark
    County, 14; owners of, in Arkansas,
    17; separation of families, 18;
    availability of, in Arkansas, 89;
    parentage of, by white men, 21;
    restrictions on education of, 26
slave seculars, 100-101
Smallden house place, 94

smokehouse: location of, 3, 4, 42; fur-
    nishings in, 42
social Darwinism: and race relations,
    52; ideology of, 55; and separation
    of black families, 59. See also mulat-
    toes; racial attitudes
sorghum: location of mill, 4, 7, 69;
    making of molasses, 7, 69, 122
Southern Homestead Act of 1866, 31,
    33
speechways: in Bro' Rabbit stories, 97;
    characteristics of, among Polk fami-
    ly members, 115
"Spencer Polk: The Man, His Home,
    His Family" (exhibit), xiv, 149
splitting the cloud: African tradition
    of, 97, 167 n. 12
stables: location of, 4, 6
Stephens, Barbara (nee Craft), 137
Stephens, Dwight Gregory, 137
Stephens, Pamela, 139
Stewart-Abernathy, Leslie "Skip," xiv,
    143, 147-49. See also archeological
    survey
storytelling, 93-97
Swanda, Mike, 143
Sypert, John, 124

Taylor, Jacob, 44
Taylor, John W., 14
Taylor, Orville: on slavery in Arkan-
    sas, 15, 21
tools: making and sharpening of, 6;
    sold to Spencer Polk, 36
toys: bull roarer, 104; bean flip, 105;
    cornstalk horses, 105; corncob dolls,
    105; hoop and pad, 105; spinning
    buttons, 106; twine in making of,
    106; trucks, 106; whistles, 106
transportation: types used by family,
    46; and school attendance, 121
trees: kinds of on Polk homestead, 3-5
troughs, 6-7
Turrentine: family name of Spencer
    Polk's first wife, 30
trunk of Jimmy Polk, 78, 83, 84, 85,
    150

vineyard: location of, 7

Walker, Jency, 11
Walton, Ophelia: letters to Jimmy
  Polk, 78-79
Washita Cove, 12
weather signs, 97-98
Weddle, G.W., 126, 169
Wesson, Buster, 125
Wesson, Lenora, 78
West Africa: cultural survivals from,
  89-90; origin of folk tales, 97; and
  naming practices, 114
Westbrook, Lucille, xiv, 143, 144
Westbrook, Parker, xiv, 143, 144
Westbrook, Walter: interviews with,
  40, 46-49, 66, 143
Weyerhaueser Co.: purchase of Polk
  lands, 128
White, Annie (nee Epperson), 100, 118
White, Jack, 118

White, Walter, 54
wild game: use as food, 107-8
Wilds, the: location of, 12; description
  of, 13-15, 17
Williams, LeRoy, xv
Williamson, Joel: on culture, 53; on
  mulattoes, 53-54
Willis, Anderson, 44
will-o-the-wisp, 95
Wilson, Arbella (nee Murphy), 60
Wilson, Taylor, 46
Wilson-Johnson, Eddie Lee (nee Clar-
  dy), xv, 135-37
winnowing: method used by Polk
  family, 109
Wisdom, Lon: sawmill of, 106
Worthen, Bill, xiv, 143

Young, Candice, 132
Young, Cherise Helene (nee Bland),
  132